GENETIC TESTING AND
THE CRIMINAL LAW

Edited by

Don Chalmers

Professor of Law and Dean of Faculty of Law,
University of Tasmania, Australia

UCL
PRESS

First published in Great Britain 2005 by UCL Press,
an imprint of Cavendish Publishing Limited, The Glass House,
Wharton Street, London WC1X 9PX, United Kingdom
Telephone: + 44 (0)20 7278 8000   Facsimile: + 44 (0)20 7278 8080
Email: info@uclpress.com
Website: www.uclpress.com

Published in the United States by Cavendish Publishing
c/o International Specialized Book Services,
5824 NE Hassalo Street, Portland,
Oregon 97213-3644, USA

Published in Australia by Cavendish Publishing (Australia) Pty Ltd
45 Beach Street, Coogee, NSW 2034, Australia
Telephone: + 61 (2)9664 0909   Facsimile: + 61 (2)9664 5420

© UCL Press   2005

Chalmers, Don
Genetic testing and the criminal law
1 DNA fingerprinting 2 Criminal procedure (International law)
I Title
614.1

ISBN 1-84472-016-0

ISBN 978-1-844-72016-3

1 3 5 7 9 10 8 6 4 2

Printed and bound in Great Britain

PREFACE

DNA profiling has been described as the greatest advance in criminal investigations since the advent of finger printing and blood group testing. The effectiveness of genetic testing in securing convictions is widely recognised. There have been many significant cases involving DNA evidence. However, DNA profiling or, more accurately, genetic tests (as a wider range of profiling tests are now used) have proved equally powerful in excluding suspects from an investigation and acquitting the innocent. While the technique is now well-accepted, most countries experienced legitimate civil liberties concerns at the introduction of this powerful investigation weapon. Concerns ranged from the manner of collection of the sample, the scientific accuracy and the reliability of the test, access to the test results by the defence, the statistical probabilities and explanations of the results in the trial process. Civil liberties concerns continue about the circumstances in which it is legitimate for the prosecution authorities to continue to store genetic test results after the conclusion of investigations and court proceedings.

This book draws together a number of chapters, from both common law and civil law jurisdictions, setting out systematically the rules dealing with genetic testing in criminal investigations and prosecutions. Each chapter deals with the entire sequence of events, beginning with the collection of the genetic test sample during an investigation through its testing, use in evidence, reliability, interpretation and ultimate decision about its continued storage or destruction. Interestingly, from a comparative law standpoint, there has been a similar approach to the regulation of genetic tests in the criminal law of both civil and common law jurisdictions. In most countries, specific legislation has been introduced to achieve the critical balance between the public interest in the effective prosecution of offences and individual interests in the protection of civil rights in the criminal investigation and prosecution processes.

The genesis for this book was in a series of national country reports on DNA testing and the criminal law based on replies to a questionnaire. The national reports were consolidated and were presented at the XVth Congress of the International Academy of Comparative Law, *Preuve pénale et test génétique* held in Bristol, England in 1998.

ACKNOWLEDGMENTS

The authors, and especially the editor of this volume, would like to acknowledge their deep appreciation for the outstanding editorial work carried out by Tenille Marsh, Carrie McDougall, Bruce Newey, Emma O'Neill and Elizabeth Sharp, all graduates in law at the University of Tasmania. The publication of this book would have been impossible without the excellent work of these graduates. The authors and editor have been fortunate to have had the outstanding assistance of these students in the editing and organisational management of this project. A special acknowledgment is extended to Gayle McElwee, faculty secretary, who has been involved with this project from 1997 when the original country reports for the International Law Congress of Comparative Law was submitted. She has been involved, at different stages, throughout the project.

We should also like to acknowledge the original contributions of a number of the original country reporters that were not able to be included in this volume. These are:

France: Judge Christain Byk, Université de Poitiers;
Greece: Associate Professor Ilias G Anagnostopoulos, University of Athens;
Netherlands: Professor JF Nijboer (co-ordinator), A Hieronymus, H Janssen and PTC van Kampen, Rijks Universiteit Leiden;
USA: Professor Christopher L Blakesley, JY Sanders Chair and Professor of Law, Louisiana State University Law Centre, Baton Rouge. Published in Volume LXVI American Journal of Comparative Law 605–40.

The editor, on behalf of the other authors, would also like to acknowledge the scientific and practical advice offered by a number of public servants in Australia involved with DNA testing. We would like to thank Andrew Feeney of the QEII Medical Centre, Western Australia, Ron Grice at the Queensland Health Scientific Services, Dr Robinson of the Australian Forensic Testing Laboratory and John West at the Institute of Clinical Pathology and Medical Research for their assistance. The editor particularly acknowledges the considerable assistance given by Lazlo Szabo and thanks him for his considerable patience and valuable assistance, not only in the preparation of the original General Report to the XVth Congress of the International Academy of Comparative Law but also in the completion of this project.

LIST OF CONTRIBUTORS

Argentina
Augusto César Belluscio
Dr Belluscio is currently Vice President of the Corte Suprema de Justicia de la Nación, Argentina. He was formerly Justice of the same court.

Australia
Donald Chalmers
Donald Chalmers is Professor of Law and Dean of the Faculty of Law, University of Tasmania. He has been Chair of the Australian Health Ethics Committee, Law Reform Commissioner for Tasmania. He is currently Chair of the Commonwealth Gene Technology Ethics Committee, a Board member of the Australian Institute of Family Studies and Director of the Centre for Law and Genetics.

Canada
Jean-Louis Baudouin
Mr Justice Baudouin, graduate in law, McGill University 1958; Doctor of Laws, Paris 1962, and postgraduate degrees in comparative law, Madrid and Strasbourg (Mr Justice Baudouin also holds numerous honourary doctorates). He was professor (and still is an associate professor) of law, Université de Montréal 1962–1982. Commissioner and Vice-Chair of the Law Reform Commission of Canada, 1976–1980. Québec Court of Appeal 1989. Member of the Royal Society of Canada.

Denmark
Peter Garde
Peter Garde is a Justice of the Hillerod Criminal Court in Denmark. He has served in the Court for a number of years and is a co-author of *Criminal Law in Denmark* published by Kluwer Press.

Finland
Irma Pahlman
Irmal Pahlman was researcher at the Faculty of Law at the University of Helsinki when she prepared the original country report. A version of her original work appeared as *Penal Proof and Genetic Test* published by Kauppakaari Oyj Lawyers Publishing. She now works with the Finnish Confederation of Salaried Employees (STTK).

Germany
Werner Beulke
Werner Beulke is Professor of Criminal Law, Criminal Procedure and Criminology at the Faculty of Law at the University of Passau (since 1980). He was formerly Professor at the Faculty of Law at the University of Konstanz until 1979. He has published textbooks about the general part of criminal law (at present in its 33rd edition), about criminal law relating to young offenders (at present in its 14th edition) and about the law of criminal procedure (at present in its 6th edition).

Italy
Marcello Stalteri

Marcello Stalteri is currently Ricercatore at the Department of Comparative Law of the University of Florence Law School. He is a specialist in comparative law, law and economics, and law and science. He has recently published a book on the Comparative Law and Economics of Non-profit Organisations.

Japan
Toshihiro Kawaide

Toshihiro Kawaide has been an Associate Professor in Law at the University of Tokyo since 1992 and is a Member of both the Council on Legislation, Ministry of Justice and the Advisory Committee on the Rules of Hearing at the Family Court. His publications include *Research on Pretextual Arrest* 1998 (Bekken Taiho Koryuu no Kennkyu) and *Protection and Care of Crime Victims* 2001 (Yoku wakaru Higaisya Hogo Seido).

New Zealand
Deborah Lawson

Deborah Lawson graduated with a LLB and BA from the University of Otago and was admitted to the Bar. She is currently employed as a Research Asssistant in the Faculty of Law, University of Otago, and is working on her LLM thesis.

PDG Skegg

Peter Skegg is a Professor of Law in the University of Otago and is associated with the Bioethics Centre. He is a former Chair of the Oxford Law Faculty and former Dean of the Otago Law Faculty. He was awarded the Swiney Prize for his book *Law, Ethics and Medicine*.

South Africa
Lirieka Meintjes-Van der Walt

Meintjes-Van der Walt is currently Associate Professor at Rhodes University and is an associate member of the Eastern Cape Society of Advocates. She has worked as a public prosecutor and has been admitted as an advocate of the High Court, practised at the Bar in Grahamstown and sits regularly as an assessor in the High Court. She has published nationally and internationally in the fields of criminal procedure, evidence, labour law and women's rights, and is author of the book *Expert Evidence in the Criminal Justice Process: A Comparative Perspective* (Rozenberg Publishers Amsterdam, 2001). In 2002, she was awarded the Vice Chancellor's Award for Distinguished Research at Rhodes University.

Spain
Carlos M Romeo-Casabona

Carlos M Romeo-Casabona is a Professor of Criminal Law and Director of the Inter-University Chair BBVA Foundation – Provincial Government. He is a Doctor of Laws and a Doctor of Medicine. He has been a judge in the Territorial High Court of Zaragoza. He is editor of the *Law and the Human Genome Review/Revista de Derecho y Genoma Humano*. He is a member of the Advisory Committee on Ethics of Research in Science and Technology to the Spanish Government.

Aitziber Emaldi-Cirión, Amelia Martín-Urango and Pilar Nicolás-Jiménez
Aitziber Emaldi-Cirión, Amelia Martín Uranga and Pilar Nicolás-Jiménez are currently Research Scholarship Holders pursuing postgraduate studies at the Universidad de Deusto and they contributed as assistant authors with Professor Romeo-Casabona in the preparation of the Spanish Chapter.

United Kingdom
Graeme Laurie
Graeme Laurie is Senior Lecturer in Law at the University of Edinburgh and co-director of the Arts and Humanities Research Board Research Centre for Studies in Intellectual Property Law and Technology. His publications include *Genetic Privacy: A Challenge to Medico-Legal Norms*, Cambridge University Press, 2002, and *Law and Medical Ethics*, 6th edn, Butterworths, 2002 (with JK Mason and RA McCall-Smith).

CONTENTS

GLOSSARY OF ABBREVIATIONS

ADN	DNA (the French equivalent acronym)
AJA	Administration of Justice Act (Denmark)
ALRC	Australian Law Reform Commission
BDSG	German Federal Data Protection Act
BGB	German Civil Code
BGH	German Federal Supreme Court
BVerfG	German Federal Constitutional Court
CABI	Committee of Experts in Advances in Biomedical Sciences (Spain)
CCP	Code of Criminal Procedure (Italy and also Spain)
CJPOA	Criminal Justice and Public Order Act 1994 (UK)
DNA	Deoxyribonucleic acid
EDNAP	European DNA Profiling Group
GVG	Judicature Act (Germany)
HLA	Human leucocyte antigen
ISFG	International Society of Forensic Genetics
JGG	German Law of Juvenile Justice
MCCOC	Model Criminal Code Officers Committee (Australia)
NCIDD	National Criminal Investigation DNA Database (Australia)
NCIS	National Crime Intelligence Service (UK)
OWiG	Administrative Offences Act (Germany)
PACE	Police and Criminal Evidence Act (UK)
PCR	Polymerase Chain Reaction
PDS	German Socialist Party
PED	Police Elimination Database (UK)
PITO	Police Information Technology Organisation (UK)
RFLP	Restriction Fragment Length Polymorphism
RiStBV	German Guidelines for Penal Proceedings
SPD	Social-Democrats of Germany
StGB	German Criminal Code
StPO	Code of Criminal Procedure (Germany)
STR	Short Tandem Repeats
StVÄG	Amended Code of Criminal Procedure (Germany)
VNTR	Variable Number of Tandem Repeats

CHAPTER 1

GENERAL THEMES

Professor Donald Chalmers
Dean, Faculty of Law, University of Tasmania

Introduction

In the mid-1980s, some of the emerging knowledge on DNA analysis was extended to forensic investigations following the seminal work of Professor Sir Alec Jeffreys[1] in the UK. The value of DNA testing[2] is great and has been described as 'the single greatest advance in the "search for truth", and the goal of convicting the guilty and acquitting the innocent, since the advent of cross-examination'.[3] The effectiveness of genetic testing in securing convictions has been both powerful and dramatic. However, the technique is equally powerful in excluding suspects from an investigation and acquitting the innocent.[4] The post-conviction use of DNA test results has been significant. For example, in the famous 'Gladsaxe' case in Denmark,[5] the Forensic Genetics Section carried out a DNA analysis of the hairs of a person previously convicted of attempted rape, as a scientific experiment. A match was found with the DNA profile of a person other than the accused convicted of the rape. This led to the retrial of the first case, and the accused was acquitted. The *negative match* was decisive proof of innocence.[6]

---

1   See Jeffreys, Wilson and Thein (1985) at 67–73 and Jeffreys, Wilson and Thein (1985), at 76–79. See also Jeffreys *et al* (1991).
2   The term DNA testing or fingerprinting has often been used but in this chapter *genetic testing* is preferred. DNA testing has been extended to other tests such as RNA testing. *See Chapter 2*. See also Faigman *et al* (2002), Chapter 11 and Lander (1989), at 501. The Danish chapter refers to the exhaustive work by Klumpe (1993).
3   *New York v Wesley*, 140 Misc 2d 306, 533 NYS 2d 643, 644 (1988).
4   See Australian Law Reform Commission (2003); see Innocence Project website www.innocenceproject.org.
5   In Canada, the Supreme Court ordered a new trial for David Milgaard, who had served 23 years after conviction for rape and murder. Milgaard was released, his conviction overturned and a new trial ordered, based on DNA evidence that a serial killer had committed the crime. Milgaard was completely exonerated and police have said that too much time has passed to have a new trial. See Bindman (1997) at 2.
6   See Christian (2001); Urbas (2002); de Foore (2002).

Some general themes can be identified in the chapters that follow, dealing with DNA testing[7] in the various national criminal justice systems considered in this book. First, civil liberties concerns are recurrent themes in all the chapters. The act of taking blood samples may cause bodily harm and generally constitutes an invasion of privacy. Each chapter raises recurrent concerns about consent of the individual to the test, protection of privacy of genetic information,[8] dignity of the individual and the overriding requirement for fairness in the criminal investigation and trial process. For example, the chapter on Spain notes that their Criminal Code is subject to the principle of due process of the law (*principe de legalité*) and the right of privacy, both protected by the European Convention on Human Rights.[9] Argentina only accepts procedures that are compatible with the Constitution, which imposes standards for the respect of human dignity and privacy. In the case of the Constitution of the Republic of South Africa,[10] the rights to dignity,[11] privacy[12] and the right to bodily and psychological integrity[13] are entrenched. Similarly, in New Zealand, courts have held that although compelling someone to give bodily samples against their will, if necessary by force, is *prima facie* an infringement of the fundamental rights implicit in the New Zealand Bill of Rights Act 1999, that Parliament had overcome such barriers to DNA testing through the specific enactment of the Criminal Investigations (Blood Samples) Act 1995.[14] Similarly, in the Netherlands, the Supreme Court (HR 2 juli 1990, NJ 1990, 751) moved in the same direction by deciding that in view of Article 11 Grondwet (the right to bodily integrity) a suspect cannot be forced to give bodily material for DNA comparison without legal consent. Genetic testing has been fully assimilated into the general procedures for the investigation, prosecution and trial of criminal offences.

Secondly, the 1990s saw a general trend towards the introduction of specific legislation dealing with the taking of genetic samples from suspects or accuseds. The specific legislation in each jurisdiction aims to balance the rights of suspects with the wider public interest in gathering satisfactory evidence of serious offences. Generally, the rights of suspects and accuseds are protected by detailed *procedural* safeguards involving consent, authorisation for taking samples by senior police officers or court order, different procedures for intimate and non-intimate samples, prescribed conduct for taking samples, disclosure of results to the person and destruction of samples on discontinuance of proceedings or

---

7   See Faigman *et al* (2002), at 664–761 on the legal issues and scientific status of DNA typing. See also Andrews, Mehlman and Rothstein (2002), Chapter 2.

8   This is a special and critical international public concern with all forms of DNA testing, not only in the criminal investigation arena. This concern has been increased with the expansion of genetic databases. See Laurie (2002); and Australian Law Reform Commission (2003).

9   The chapter on Spain notes that results of genetic tests may affect the essential rights of physical and bodily integrity (Art 15 of the Constitution) and the right to privacy (Art 18).

10 Act 108 of 1996.

11 *Ibid* s 10.

12 *Ibid* s 14.

13 *Ibid* s 12(2).

14 As amended by the Criminal Investigations (Blood Samples) Amendment Act 2003. See, for example, *Down v Van de Wetering and Another* [1999] NZAR 302.

acquittal. Thus, for example, the chapter on Canada[15] noted that DNA evidence was first accepted in criminal proceedings in 1988.[16] Later, in 1995, faced with a number of difficulties surrounding DNA, the Canadian Parliament legislated to establish a body of law dealing with the administration and taking of DNA samples for genetic testing.[17]

Technical scientific standards of testing are generally not included in the specific legislation. In addition, each chapter indicates that legal issues relating to the interpretation of test results, the accuracy and reliability of test results and the admissibility of test results in evidence remain within the general law of evidence.

It is possible to identify some common themes from the details of the specific legislation in the different countries. These are that there are reasons for conducting a forensic procedure; that a person has proper authority to order the conduct of the test (be it a senior police officer or a judge or magistrate); that civil liberties of suspects and accuseds are respected by procedures involving cautions, information or attendance of third parties; that distinctions are recognised between *non-intimate* or *intimate* genetic test samples; and that suitably qualified persons, usually medical practitioners, carry out the test.

Thirdly, the use of genetic testing and evidence in criminal proceedings has been more frequent in cases of serious crimes where there are grounds for serious suspicion. In the Netherlands, more than mere probable cause is required; a serious suspicion needs to be present for the genetic test to be ordered (Code of Criminal Process, Article 195D). Similarly, the UK Police and Criminal Evidence Act 1984 (as amended)[18] provides that a police officer may only give authorisation for the taking of an intimate sample if he or she has *reasonable grounds* (a) for suspecting the involvement of the person from whom the sample is to be taken in a recordable offence,[19] and (b) for believing that the same will tend to confirm or disprove involvement (s 62(1), (1A)). Before any sample is taken, the subject must be informed of the grounds on which the relevant authority has been given

---

15   The relevant sections in Canada are contained in the Criminal Code, ss 487.04–487.09.

16   The first Canadian criminal case involving evidence of a genetic test was *R v Parent* (1988) 46 CCC (3d) 414 (Alberta QB). The technical analysis used was the PCR technique. The first case using the RFLP technique was *R v McNally*, 4 April 1989 (Ont Dist Ct). See the statement made by the then Minister for Justice, l'honorable Allan Rock, reported in *R v Stillman*, [1997] 1 RCS. 607, 687.

17   Le Parlement canadien enacted law C–104 modifying le Code criminel. This law was largely inspired by a report of the Minister for Justice entitled *Collecte et entreposage des prevues medico-légales à caractères génétiques*, 1994 (see also la Loi sur les jeunes contrevenants (analyse génétique à des fins medico-légales) LC 1995, c 27). Law C–104 was brought into force on 13 July 1995 but there have been few decisions on the interpretation of this new legislation.

18   By the Criminal Justice and Public Order Act 1994 and the Criminal Procedure and Investigation Act 1996,the Criminal Evidence (Amendment) Act 1997 and the Criminal Justice and Police Act 2001: see the UK chapter for England and Wales.

19   Defined by the National Police Records (Recordable Offences) Regulations 1985 (SI 1985/1941) which covers any offence punishable by imprisonment.

including, where appropriate, the nature of the suspected offence.[20] In Denmark, under the Administration of Justice Act (Retsplejeloven) (AJA), for any 'viewing of the body' in a criminal investigation of an accused (s 792), there must be *reasonable ground to suspect* that an offence has been committed.

Finally, despite initial grave concerns over DNA testing and some ongoing concerns among civil libertarian groups (especially over longer storage of DNA profiles in some jurisdictions, such as the UK), increasingly strong levels of acceptance of the reliability of DNA evidence have been recorded. For example, the UK Human Genetics Commission commissioned a public opinion survey which found that 94% of people surveyed agreed with DNA testing to identify and eliminate possible offenders from police enquiries, especially for serious offences.[21]

Time in the criminal process when sampling and testing may occur

The national chapters present a broadly common position that genetic testing may occur at any time during the investigative period, subject to prescribed procedures and authorisation by a police officer or, in other cases, by a judicial officer. In France, where a judge conducts the investigation after the criminal charge has been laid, Article 81 of the Code de Procédure Pénal (CCP) (regarding the *juge d'instruction*) and Article 156 of the CPP (jurisdiction) establish the procedural basis for collecting DNA sampling and testing. If the suspect is known, the investigative judge commissions the DNA investigation. Scots law provides that a sheriff can authorise the taking of a sample, even from a person who is not suspected of the crime but is required to assist in the detection of crime.[22] Sampling and testing may occur before arrest, at arrest, after indictment, or after conviction, depending on the circumstances. Arrest is generally not a necessary precondition for a genetic test. For example, in New Zealand, a sample may be taken from a suspect in any criminal investigation in respect of an offence committed or believed to have been committed.[23] There is a general qualification in most jurisdictions that requires that there are reasonable grounds for the ordering of a genetic test. DNA samples may be taken and tested when there is probable cause to believe that a person might be responsible for a crime. However, in Spain, a person must be charged with an offence before a DNA sample can be taken.[24]

---

20 The provisions of the Police and Criminal Evidence Act are supplemented by the Code of Practice for the Identification of Persons by Police Officers (prepared by the Home Secretary operating as a Statutory Instrument), para 5.11B.

21 HGC, 'Human Genetics Commission publishes results of major survey on attitudes to human genetics', HGC Press Notice 2 March 2001/0001.

22 *HMA v Brodie* 1996 SCCR 862, and *Morris v MacNeil* 1991 SLT 607; 1991 SCCR 722.

23 Criminal Investigations (Blood Samples) Act 1995, s 5 (NZ) as amended in 2003.

24 Article 456 of the Criminal Prosecution Law.

Collection of DNA samples

The national chapters show a consistency in the legal requirements for the collection of samples for genetic testing. There are consistent distinctions drawn between samples from 'accuseds' and 'non-accuseds' and samples categorised as 'intimate' or 'non-intimate'.

Reasons for conducting a DNA test: accuseds and non-accuseds

Legislation in the various jurisdictions generally draws distinctions between samples from 'accuseds' and 'non-accuseds.' Thus, the Danish Administration of Justice Act (Retsplejeloven) distinguishes between samples taken for genetic tests from accuseds (s 792c) and other persons (s 792). In the case of an *accused*, the police have authority to take a blood test. The accused has, however a right of challenge to the court (s 746). The court will then by court order decide upon the legality of the measure taken. A *non-accused* person may consent to a genetic test, preferably in writing, although this is not an absolute requirement (s 792d). Similarly, the German Code of Criminal Procedure distinguishes between 'accuseds', suspected persons and other persons (non-suspects). Italian law also allows for samples to be taken from witnesses (Code of Criminal Procedure, Article 392).

In Germany s 81a of the Code of Criminal Procedure Strafprozeßordnung (StPO) allows blood samples to be taken from a suspect without consent by a doctor authorised to do so by a judge. Under s 81a(2) of the StPO, the Department of Public Prosecution and other authorised bodies (police sergeants and higher ranking police officers; see s 152 of the Judicature Act Gerichtsverfassungsgesetz (GVG)) may request that a sample be taken if a delay would hinder the investigation.[25] Where the suspect *consents*, the procedures in s 81a are not mandatory, provided the procedure is not dangerous to health and the accused has knowledge of all-important circumstances and the right of refusal. The legal requirements for taking blood samples from persons other than suspects (including the victim of the crime) are prescribed in s 81c(2) of the StPO. Blood samples may only be taken without consent where there is no danger to health and the measure is absolutely 'indispensable' for the detection of the truth.[26] Measures under s 81c(2) of the StPO take place only at the request of a judge or, where a delay would hinder the investigation under s 81c(4) of the StPO, at the request of the prosecution (and other authorised bodies prescribed in s 15 of the GVG). Where a person refuses, the judge may order that the sample be taken by force.

---

25 The taking of other natural body samples, such as saliva, semen, urine – if at all necessary for DNA analysis – are allowed under the same conditions (on a request by a judge or the prosecution; no damage to health; to be carried out by a doctor).

26 The SPD draft required that blood samples from non-suspects could only be examined if a corresponding sample from a suspect was already available for comparison. It was hoped that through this requirement 'premature' and 'unnecessary' analyses could be avoided on the grounds of protecting the victim.

Whilst the legislation in most countries does not require the placing of formal charges against an individual as a justification for, or precondition to, the carrying out of a DNA test, the legislatures have generally enacted procedures to try to ensure respect for the rights of the individual.[27]

Intimate and non-intimate samples

Most national chapters recognise the further distinction between samples obtained after 'intimate' or 'non-intimate' procedures on a person. The distinction between 'intimate' and 'non-intimate' samples is well defined in the UK's Criminal Justice and Public Order Act 1994 (CJPOA).[28] A 'non-intimate sample'[29] means:

(a) a sample of hair other than pubic hair;

(b) a sample taken from a nail or from under a nail;

(c) a swab taken from any part of a person's body including the mouth but not any other body orifice;

(d) saliva;

(e) a footprint or a similar impression of any part of a person's body other than a part of his hand.

An 'intimate sample' means:

(a) a sample of blood, semen or any other tissue fluid, urine or pubic hair;

(b) a dental impression;

(c) a swab taken from a person's body orifice other than the mouth.[30]

In England and Wales, obtaining intimate samples is dealt with by s 62 of the Police and Criminal Evidence Act 1984 (PACE), as amended. Section 62(1) provides that an intimate sample may be taken from a person in police detention only:

(a) if a police officer of at least the rank of inspector authorises it to be taken; and

(b) if the appropriate consent is given.

---

27   For example, in Canada see Criminal Code Article 487.06(2) and Article 487.07(1); RM Pomerance, 'Bill C–104: a practical guide to the new DNA warrants' (1995) 39 CR (4th) 224, 235.

28   Seabrooke and Sprack (1996) note that this is of considerable importance because a DNA profile can be obtained from some non-intimate samples and the police powers to obtain non-intimate samples are wider than the powers to obtain intimate samples (at 99).

29   The definition of non-intimate sample contained in s 65 of Police and Criminal Evidence Act 1984 (PACE) has been widened by the CJPOA 1994, s 58.

30   These definitions are identical to those found in Art 53 of the Police and Criminal Evidence (Northern Ireland) Order 1989 (as amended by Art 8 of the Police (Amendment) (Northern Ireland) Order 1995). The definition of non-intimate samples is the same under Scots law: Criminal Procedure (Scotland) Act 1995, ss 18(6) and (7).

Section 62(1A) deals with persons not in police detention. For the purposes both of s 62(1) and 62(1A) a police officer may only give authorisation of the taking of an intimate sample if he or she has reasonable grounds (a) for suspecting the involvement of the person from whom the sample is to be taken in a recordable offence, and (b) for believing that the same will tend to confirm or disprove his involvement.

The degree of force that may be used to obtain hair, blood, saliva or other tissue samples

The chapters from the civil law jurisdictions highlight the principle of proportionality requiring a balance between the end to be achieved and the means to be employed in obtaining a sample from an accused or non-accused person. The Danish criminal justice recognises this general principle of proportionality, which also assumes[31] an obligation on both the police and courts to choose the least oppressive means when more than one exists. The principle is dealt with in s 792 of the Administration of Justice Act (AJA). In the Netherlands, the investigative judge may authorise the use of force on the person to obtain the sample. However, the officer is restricted by the principles of proportionality, requiring the officer to do everything within his power to obtain the sample voluntarily. Less specific in its wording, the Italian Code of Criminal Procedure (CCP) prescribes only that 'proper' force may be used in Articles 399 and 132. In Greek criminal procedure,[32] DNA analysis is classified as scientific-expert evidence, which falls within the scope of Articles 181–202 of the CCP.

The common law jurisdictions generally refer to reasonable force. For example, Scotland, England, Wales and Northern Ireland prescribe that reasonable force may be used to take a non-intimate sample, and consent is not necessary (s 19B of the Criminal Procedure (Scotland) Act 1995; s 63 of PACE).

Authority to carry out the test: senior police officers and judges

Most of the chapters indicate a general regime for the taking of DNA samples which requires consent of the person and, in the absence of consent, an order of a senior police officer to carry out a test (usually non-intimate) or a judge or magistrate (usually for intimate tests).[33] Thus, for example, in the UK, s 63 of PACE covers obtaining non-intimate samples which generally may not be taken without written consent but can be taken without consent when the person is in custody and a person of at least the rank of inspector gives authority. In Canada

---

31 Gammeltoft-Hansen: Strafferetspleje (Criminal Justice), I, 1991, p 64ff.

32 For example, in Greece, the principle of proportionality (Arts 181, 253, 256, 257, 282, etc of the CCP); coercive measures may be ordered in cases of serious offences when there is sufficient grounds to believe that they are necessary for investigation's purposes.

33 This distinction may be less significant as it is now possible to take adequate samples from hair roots or saliva without the need for blood samples.

these provisions in Article 487.05 of the Criminal Code require a judge of a provincial court to issue an order to take a sample on reasonable belief about certain conditions. The judge must be convinced that the order will serve the administration of justice:

> The satisfaction of the issuing judge that there are reasonable grounds to believe in the existence of all those criteria does not, however, end the matter as it might with an ordinary search warrant. Additionally, the judge must be satisfied that the issuance of the warrant 'is in the best interests of the administration of justice'. Presumably, the information must contain sufficient material to satisfy the judge on this point no less than the other criteria, since the issuing judge may not look outside the four corners of the sworn information.[34]

Medical or other qualified practitioners required to take samples

The chapters note a consistent requirement that only medical practitioners or other qualified persons may be involved in the actual taking of the sample for testing. For example, in South Africa,[35] only a registered medical practitioner or a registered nurse may take a blood sample. Similarly, in Denmark, a medical practitioner must assist when a 'closer inspection of the body' is conducted. In New Zealand, bodily samples can only be taken by a medical practitioner, or with consent, a registered nurse – s 49 of the Criminal Investigations (Blood Samples) Act 1995, as amended in 2003. Under that legislation, a person is also entitled to have present, when giving a bodily sample, a medical practitioner, a lawyer and one other person (chosen by the person) (s 50(1)(a)). Under the Code of Practice for the Identification of Persons by Police Officers, which supplements PACE in England and Wales, intimate samples or dental impressions may be taken only by a registered medical or dental practitioner as appropriate, with the exception of a urine example.[36]

The New Zealand legislation lays down an additional procedural protection, providing that no member of the police connected with the investigation of an offence in respect of which a bodily sample is being collected may be present where the sample is taken. However, this only applies if the sample is being taken from a suspect pursuant to any consent given in response to a suspect request or a suspect compulsion or juvenile compulsion order (s 52(2)). The sample should be taken in circumstances affording reasonable privacy to that person (s 53). Similar provisions are included in the Australian Crimes Amendment (Forensic Procedures) Act 1998.

---

34 See Fontana (1977), p 249.
35 Criminal Procedure Act 1977, s 37 (South Africa).
36 Code of Practice for the Identification of Persons by Police Officers, para 5.3.

Licence required by the technician or laboratory to conduct the test

In all jurisdictions, some official form of grant, authority or licence is required for laboratories or persons conducting genetic tests. Many jurisdictions noted that these tests are conducted by independent or government organisations. The chapter on Argentina notes that a person conducting DNA tests must be granted this right and administratively listed by the Minister for Public Health. In Denmark, there is the Forensic Genetics section, *Retskemisk Afdeling,* in the Medico-Legal Institute. Difficult cases are submitted to the Medico-Legal Council, *Retslægerådet.* The Forensic Genetics section is regarded as independent and neutral, and it enjoys general confidence.[37] In Germany, the technician or laboratory which carries out the tests is named in the written judicial order and the judge selects those experts or laboratories, which are competent and reliable. Spanish DNA analysis can only be done in the legal medicine institutes, such as the Legal Medicine Chair of the Faculty of Medicine of the Zaragoza University.

In France the technician must be licensed.[38] In South Africa, the Police Forensic Science Laboratory applies the standards of the Technical Working Group for DNA Methods and Analysis (TWGDAM) of the USA and the American Society for Crime Laboratory Accreditation Board.

In some countries special institutions have been established. In Argentina and Canada, special Banque Nationale de Données Génétiques have been created to conduct research and undertake storage of results, subject to strict regulations. In Germany, according to s 81f of the StPO, only expert witnesses who are public servants or who are officially appointed can be chosen by a judge to carry out molecular-genetic examinations. They must not be independent from the investigating body.[39]

Special requirements for specific groups

A number of jurisdictions have special rules for specific groups; the powers to obtain samples for genetic testing vary according to categories of persons from whom samples are taken. In the UK, special rules apply to military personnel,[40]

---

37 The North American controversy in court proceedings on the admissibility of DNA evidence may possibly be explained in part by the different cultural respect for DNA tests in some of the European jurisdictions. The chapter on Denmark noted that the 'battle of experts', sometimes seen in Anglo-Saxon trials, is 'unknown in Danish practice'.

38 A decree of 6 February 1997 (No 97–109) has set up the conditions for licensing persons or laboratories.

39 In this way the 'functional' separation of the institutions was ensured – and at the same time the Federal Criminal Bureau (Bunderskriminalamt: BKA) and the State Criminal Bureaux (Landeskriminalamter: LKA), which already operated on this field, were enabled to continue the carrying out of DNA examinations under this section.

40 Police and Criminal Evidence Act 1984 (Application to the Armed Forces) Order 1997 (SI 1997/15) and PACE, ss 62–65.

prisoners and mentally abnormal offenders,[41] minors and suspected terrorists.[42] Similarly, the US has specific legislation dealing with testing convicts, minors and military personnel. Many states and the federal government have promulgated laws mandating DNA testing of persons convicted of various offences and storage of the specimens.[43]

A number of countries reported that no special rules apply and the general law applies to these categories of persons. For example, in Germany, no special rules apply to these groups. If such persons are juvenile delinquents between 14 and 18 years of age and young people between the ages of 18 and 21, the Law of Juvenile Justice (Jugendgerichtsgesetz: JGG) applies. Special rules apply to minors under 18 years of age in respect of s 81c of the StPO (measures against non-suspects). Similarly, in Japan there are neither special rules nor requirements applied to specific groups.

Disclosure of test results in the criminal process

DNA test results made available to the lawyer for the accused

With the exception of Japan, there was consistency in relation to the duty of disclosure of the results of tests by the prosecution to the defence. In the Japanese Code of Criminal Procedure, the prosecutor is not obliged to disclose the results of the investigations to the defence lawyer at the pre-trial stage. Disclosure depends on the discretion of the prosecutor. All other jurisdictions require disclosure. In Denmark, defence counsel has the right to disclosure of all relevant evidence (AJA, ss 745–46). The New Zealand[44] and Australian[45] legislation provide that any record of the analysis of the blood sample taken by the police and any record of a comparison between that and analysis of material found at the scene shall be made available to the person from whom the sample was taken, or to that person's lawyer, as soon as practicable. The UK Criminal Procedure and Investigations Act 1996 provides that the prosecutor must (a) disclose to the accused any prosecution material which has not previously been disclosed to the accused and which in the prosecutor's opinion might undermine the case for the prosecution against the accused, or (b) give to the accused a written statement that there is no material of a description mentioned in para (a) (s 3).

---

41 The Criminal Evidence (Amendment) Act 1997 inserts s 63(9A) into PACE and extends the categories of person from whom non-intimate samples can be taken under PACE.

42 The Terrorism Act 2000, Sched 15 provides that ss 62(1A), 62 and 63 of PACE do not apply to a person arrested or detained under the Act.

43 See, for example, the US federal DNA Identification Act, 1994, 42 USC, s 14132 (1995) which authorises the FBI to create a criminal DNA database (CODIS) and authorises funding to states to do the same. For the states, see Cal Pen Code, s 290.2 (1995); Ala Code, s 36–18–24 (1995); Or RS, s 137.076 (1995); Okla Stat tit 22, s 991 (Supp 1996); Maine RS tit 25, s 1574 (1996); RS Mo s 650.055; Ohio RC 2901.07; and see *State v Smith*, 1997 WL 476662 (Ohio App 1997).

44 Criminal Investigations (Bodily Samples) Act 1995, s 59.

45 Crimes Amendment (Forensic Amendment) Act 1997, s 23XW. There is also a procedural safeguard for the police officer to inform the suspect of certain matters prior to consent being given (s 23WJ).

The rules of evidence: admissibility of genetic test results

Some differences, of form rather than substance, may be detected between the civil and common law jurisdictions in their traditionally distinctive rules of evidence dealing with the admission of evidence in relation to the results of genetic tests. The absence of a jury in civil jurisdictions places greater responsibility on the judge.

The civil law jurisdictions are generally less burdened by the complexities imposed on the common law by their rules on the admissibility of evidence. The chapter on Denmark notes that although either party may protest against evidence tendered, this is an extremely rare occurrence, as there are few rules of evidence in Danish law and almost none regarding exclusion of evidence. The basic rule is the principle of *material truth*.[46] In cases of unlawfully obtained evidence, the court will generally find that the police acted *ultra vires* and order that the material be destroyed 'at once' (AJA, s 792f(3)). There are no special rules of evidence for the admissibility of DNA test results in France.[47] In Spain, Articles 659 and 7.91 of the Criminal Procedure Law cover the rules on admissibility.

The common law jurisdictions, on the other hand, have been submerged in issues of admissibility.[48] In some cases, specific legislation has been introduced which reiterates the general common law position. The Australian federal Crimes Amendment (Forensic Procedures) Act 1998 (Division 7)[49] provides that forensic procedures carried out in breach of the provisions of the Act are inadmissible evidence. However, the court has discretion to admit such evidence in certain circumstances. The court may consider whether admission is justified in the circumstances[50] including consideration of the probative value of the evidence. However, the probative value of the evidence does not, by itself, justify the admission of the evidence. This provision ensures that the probative value of the evidence is considered in combination with the other factors which include the reasons for the failure to comply, the gravity of the failure to comply and whether the failure was intentional or reckless. The judge must inform the jury of any breach of the provision and must warn the jury about the evidence as the judge thinks appropriate. However, evidence related to material which should have been destroyed is only admissible by the suspect.[51] Similar provisions apply in

---

46 DNA test results are proffered in writing and are thus *second-hand evidence* or 'hearsay'. Such documents are regarded as made 'in furtherance of a public duty' and are admitted directly (AJA, s 877(2)).

47 The Code of Criminal Procedure, Art 156 allows the court to order expert assistance as necessary.

48 See Kaye and Sensabaugh (2000).

49 See also the Federal Crimes Amendment (Forensic Procedures) Act 2001.

50 Section 23XX: the matters that the court must consider make this provision more onerous to discharge than the normal *Bunning v Cross* (1978) 141 CLR 54 discretion concerning the admission of illegally obtained evidence. By allowing discretionary admission, the provision recognises that some breaches may be quite trivial and that admission of evidence might be justified in the public interest. See also the Uniform Evidence Act (Cth and NSW).

51 Section 23XY: this stricter admissibility provision for this class of evidence is designed to ensure that the destruction requirements are not breached in the hope that the court might exercise its discretion and allow the prosecution to admit the evidence.

New Zealand.[52] In the UK, the cases of *R v Doheny* and *R v Adams*[53] (Court of Appeal) laid down a detailed sequential series of judicial procedures for leading DNA evidence.[54] Summarily, these procedures include rules on: scientific comparisons between the crime stain and the defendant's DNA with calculations of the random occurrence ratio; disclosure to the defence; expert evidence to be identified and, if possible, resolved before trial; the presentation of evidence by the expert to the jury on the nature of the matching, the basis of empirical statistical data; the roles of jury and expert; the summing-up and how the judge should explain to the jury the relevance of the random occurrence ratio including a model direction. In England and Wales, most illegally obtained evidence is not automatically excluded. The court may refuse to allow evidence '... having regard to all the circumstances, including the circumstances in which the evidence was obtained, the admission of the evidence would have such an adverse effect on the fairness of the proceedings'.[55]

There is an overwhelming body of case law in the USA on the admission of DNA evidence in criminal trials. The USA has also established case law on the admissibility of DNA evidence. Both federal and state courts have found DNA profiling reliable and admissible.[56] The *Frye* and *Daubert* cases established special rules of admissibility of DNA evidence. The *Frye* test established that where an expert testifies, and an accurate DNA protocol was followed in collecting and processing the evidence, the trial court should admit the expert's evidence.[57] The US Supreme Court in *Daubert v Merrell Dow Pharmaceuticals Inc*[58] replaced the *Frye* standard with one that requires a trial court to act as a gatekeeper to ensure that any and all scientific testimony or evidence admitted is not only relevant but also reliable. *Daubert* also held that Federal Rule of Evidence 702 had superseded the *Frye* standard.[59] In Canada in 1994, judicial direction was given dealing with the new scientific technique of DNA testing that took into consideration the US decision in *Daubert*.[60]

---

52   Criminal Investigations (Blood Samples) Act 1995, ss 69–71.

53   [1997] 1 Cr App R 369.

54   See Chapter 14.

55   PACE, s 78(1). See also Grevling (1997), at 680–81.

56   See, eg, *US v Hicks*, 103 F 3d 837, 845–46 (1996), citing *US v Chischilly*, 30 F 3d 1114, 1153 (1994); *State v Lyons*, 924 P 2d 802, 813 (1996); *Hayes v State*, 660 So 2d 257 (Fla 1995); *Trimboli v State*, 817 SW 2d 785 (1991), 826 SW 2d 953 (affirmed on appeal, 1992).

57   *US v Frye*, 293 F 1013, 1014 (DC Cir, 1923); see *Litton v Litton*, 624 So 2d 472, 475 (La 2d Cir, 1993); cf *State v Simien*, 677 So 2d 1138 (La 3d Cir, 1996); *State in Interest of Braden v Nash*, 550 So 2d 866 (La 2d Cir, 1989). Some jurisdictions apply the *Frye Plus* test, where every aspect of the testing process must be accepted: (1) the theory; (2) the testing processes and procedures utilised; (3) and that the testing was properly performed; see *New York v Castro*, 545 NYS 2d 985 (1989); *ex p Perry*, 586 So 2d 242 (1991).

58   *Daubert v Merrell Dow Pharmaceuticals Inc* 509 US 579 (1993). See Fenner (1996).

59   *Daubert v Merrill Dow Pharmaceuticals Inc*, 509 US 579, 587–88 (1993); The Federal Rule of Evidence 702: 'If scientific, technical, or other specialized knowledge will assist the trier of fact to understand the evidence or to determine a fact in issue, a witness qualified as an expert by knowledge, skill, experience, training or education may testify thereto in the form of an opinion or otherwise...' See Smith and Gordon (1997).

60   *R v Mohan* [1994] 2 RCS 9; 25, see D Tanovich (1996).

Standard of proof which applies to DNA evidence

The national chapters do not indicate any special standards of proof applying to DNA evidence beyond the usual standards of proof in criminal proceedings. In some cases refusal to undertake a test is treated as an offence. In Denmark, the degree of proof is not codified, but in criminal cases certainty beyond reasonable doubt is settled practice. Assessment of evidence is the responsibility of the judge (s 896 of the AJA). There are no special rules of evidence in New Zealand dealing with DNA evidence: it is the same as any other expert evidence and is subject to the normal evidential principles, including consideration of the prejudicial effect outweighing probative value, unfairly obtaining the sample or breach of a procedure.

Challenges to DNA evidence by the lawyer for the accused

From a period of almost unquestioning acceptance of genetic evidence, courts and legislatures have begun to reflect on this position and have developed rules for the admission, interpretation and acceptance of such evidence.[61] DNA evidence was at one time treated with an aura of virtual certainty. Thus, in Denmark, confidence in such tests is high, owing to the high prestige of the Forensic Genetics Section, both as regards expertise and integrity. As in any form of scientific analysis, the testing procedure has potential for error. DNA evidence is subject to the same challenges as any other evidence, but can use more specific objections – such as contamination of the sample, not following testing techniques, unreliability or statistical inaccuracy:

> Prior to planning a strategy for introducing or challenging DNA evidence, the defence and prosecution should critically evaluate each aspect of the DNA typing procedure, as well as the methods used to interpret the audiograms. Prosecutors should not blindly assume that DNA evidence is irrefutable nor should the defence assume that DNA evidence is inherently flawed ... A critical evaluation of the DNA typing evidence should begin with an assessment of the testing laboratory and its personnel ... Prior to evaluating the actual casework results, the scientific integrity of the DNA typing protocol should be assessed ... Once the scientific validity of the DNA typing protocol has been assessed, the application of the protocol to the individual case becomes the primary focus of the investigation.[62]

Statistical probability: a principal area of controversy remains the statistical analysis of degrees of probability of the DNA sample from the suspect matching that of another person and the crime stain. Statistical analysis is crucial.[63] Once a match

---

61 See Faigman *et al* (2000), at 707–45 for an excellent discussion scientific issues of quality, laboratory performance, interpretation of results and challenges to DNA typing evidence.

62 See Chaydo, Gulliver and MacDougall (1991), aux app 351–63.

63 See Goode (2002); Koehler (2001); and Koehler (1997).

has been declared between the crime sample and that of the suspect, the significance of the match is determined by estimating the frequency with which that profile would occur at random in the population. This requires knowledge of the frequency with which the alleles represented occur within a population. DNA typing does not prove without doubt that the two samples are genetically identical; DNA typing, with the aid of population genetics statistics, merely indicates that the two samples are unlikely to have originated from different persons. Some of the US estimates of statistical probability have been extravagant: 'the probability of selecting an unrelated individual of the population from the same race ... who had a genetic profile matching [the defendant] was one in ten billion'.[64] Justice Gerald Sheindlin has remarked:[65]

> [w]hile fully capable of understanding the scientific process used to generate the evidence, the trial lawyers and judge were confused and in awe of the analysis of complicated concepts such as Hardy-Weinberg equilibrium, linkage equilibrium, Wahlund principle, sub-populations, population drift, the Gaussian Curve and other mind boggling statistical complexities used to explain the significance of a match, and deferred to the population geneticist and statistician.

> Assume that four DNA tests were conducted examining four different sections of chromosomes and a computerized match is observed between the DNA sample left at the crime scene and the defendant's DNA. Then the four separate DNA matches are compared to four separate databases consisting of a large number of randomly chosen people whose DNA was previously profiled.

> Thereafter, for example, if two bands are observed, one at 10KB and another at 5KB (10,000 and 5,000 base pairs long), in both the defendant and the random persons tested in the database, and out of 500 people tested only one other person had the same length DNA at both areas of the chromosome, then the opinion is rendered that the odds of a random person having this band is one in 500. Then the match for the next chromosome is compared to a database for that chromosome.

> Assuming there are 1,000 people in this database, and there are two matches at these different lengths of DNA, then again it can be said that the odds that anyone else having this band is two in 1,000 or one in 500. This process continues until the other two matches are compared and their odds are computed. These figures are then multiplied, one with the other (ie, 500 x 500 x 350 x 400), producing fantastic numbers which is the foundation for the opinion that sets forth the odds of randomly finding anyone else in the relevant population (ie black, caucasian, etc) with the same unique DNA pattern over the four chromosomes tested.

> In the example supplied, assuming a caucasian defendant, the expert would render the opinion that the odds of finding a random person in the caucasian population with the same genetic pattern are one in 35 billion. There are, however, only about five to six billion people on earth.

---

64 *Knight v State*, 435 SE 2d 276, 278 (Ga App 1993); quoted in Koehler, Chia and Lindsey (1995) at 201, 202, n 3.

65 See Sheindlin (1995).

The approach in Denmark is far more conservative. The general practice of the Danish Forensic Genetics Section is to exclude a random match as having a probability of 'less than 1:100,000'. The colossal numbers seen in US cases is not encountered.[66] In England and Wales the decision of *R v Doheny and Adams*[67] ended the so called 'prosecutor's fallacy'[68] which had the following steps:

(1) Only one person in a million will have a DNA profile which matches that of the crime stain.

(2) The defendant has a DNA profile, which matches the crime stain.

(3) Therefore, there is a million to one probability that the defendant left the crime stain and is guilty of the crime.

The courts have stated that: '...[i]f no fact is known about the defendant, other than that he was in the United Kingdom at the time of the crime, the DNA evidence tells us no more than that there is a statistical probability that he was the criminal of one in 26.'[69]

Human error: there are possibilities for human error in both the taking and testing of the genetic material, eg, mixing of samples, contaminating samples, mislabelling, using unsterile tools or repositories, among many others. Laboratory error includes all human and technical errors, including: mislabelling, misreporting, case mix-ups, contaminations and interpretive errors.[70]

'False positives' may be caused by human error: false positives are possible in DNA (RFLP) analysis.[71] There are few published studies of actual error rate in forensic DNA testing; those which have been done seem to suggest an error rate of about 1%.

---

66 This conservative approach has been followed in the US in the 1996 report of the National Research Council (NRC), recommending the *product rule* to be used to provide the 'statistical best estimate' of genotype frequencies. The product rule (or 'multiplication rule') as applied in RFLP typing means that the probability of a genetic profile occurring in the population is the product of the probabilities of each individual allele's occurrence in the population. Validity of the rule depends upon whether the individual alleles are actually statistically independent. Two assumptions underlie use of the product rule when calculating genetic profile frequencies: linkage equilibrium, which means that the alleles at different loci are inherited independent of each other, and Hardy-Weinberg equilibrium, which means that one allele at a locus is not predictive of the other allele at that locus (one allele is inherited from the mother, the other from the father). See *State v Copeland,* 922 P 2d 1304 (1996).

67 *R v Doheny and Adams* [1997] 1 Cr App R 369, CA.

68 See Balding and Donnelly (1994).

69 *R v Doheny and Adams,* at 373.

70 See Koehler, Chia and Lindsey (1995), at 201.

71 See Nakashima (1995), at 464.

Contamination: vigilance is required to prevent contamination or other degradation of DNA. Sunlight, temperature, bacteria, moisture and other environmental conditions can cause DNA to degrade. In addition, soil, detergents, and carpet cleaners can contaminate and degrade DNA. These may cause the restriction enzymes used in RFLP (fragmentation) to cut the DNA in the wrong place. There was one case in Japan where the admissibility of the DNA test result was denied on the ground that the storage and test of the sample had been improper (Fukuoka Appellate Court on 30 June 1995, Hanrei-Jihou No 1543, p 181).

Special directions made by judges concerning DNA evidence

There are no fixed rules covering the form of the summing-up in civil law jurisdictions. In Danish law,[72] for example, juries are very rare. In England and Wales, judicially declared procedures have been laid down in relation to DNA evidence proposing the following direction: 'Members of the jury, if you accept the scientific evidence called by the Crown this indicates that there are probably only four or five white males in the United Kingdom from whom the semen stain would have come. The defendant is one of them. If that is the position, the decision you have to reach, on all of the evidence, is whether you are sure that it was the defendant who left that stain or whether it is possible that it was one of that other small group of men who share the same DNA characteristics' – *R v Doheny and Adams.*[73]

Retention and storage of samples/test results

Differences can be detected in the national chapters in relation to regulations dealing with the storage of samples. Many countries are currently considering the establishment of DNA databanks. Others, such as the UK, Canada and Australia, established genetic databases. On the other hand, in Germany, s 81a of the StPO provides that DNA tests may be made only for the purpose of the particular trial and thus the establishment of gene databanks is ruled out. Similarly, in South Africa, the Biology Unit of the Police Forensic Science Laboratory does not make use of a criminal intelligence database. In the Netherlands, all cell material collected is stored at the Forensic Science Laboratory. The DNA legislation also allows the Science Laboratory to record profiles in the DNA profile registration (Besluit DNA onderzoeken, Article 9).

Most states in the USA, in addition to the Federal Bureau of Investigation's national databank, the Combined DNA Index System (CODIS), have DNA repositories or banks. More significantly, some states have introduced legislation

---

72 'Directions', 'summing-up', are only known in Danish law in the very limited number of *jury trials.* Only cases in which a plea of not guilty is entered in the most serious cases of drug crimes, arson, rape, robbery where the prosecution demands four years' imprisonment are tried before a jury: AJA, s 687. About 100 cases each year are tried before a jury.

73 [1997] 1 Cr App R 369.

allowing some categories of convicts access to DNA and other scientific testing results to enable review of their convictions.[74]

The arguments for and against genetic databanks are tending to favour their creation. Civil libertarians are concerned with their potential to affect individual privacy and liberties; police forces argue strongly in favour of databanks to aid investigations. Italy has struck a delicate balance between private and public concerns, and aims of justice and privacy protection. The Department of Justice is able to set up databases instrumental to legitimate public goals (Article 4(d) CCP). Stricter provisions apply to private bodies setting up databases, requiring the consent of each individual whose personal data has been collected and a licence (Article 22.1 CCP).

The destruction of DNA samples and test results

Most jurisdictions require the destruction of samples or data entries at the conclusion of the criminal proceedings where an accused is acquitted or a suspect exonerated. This aspect of DNA testing was a common civil liberties concern when DNA testing was first introduced. Recommendation 92(1) of the Council of Europe on using DNA testing in criminal justice clearly states that 'the samples collected on the body of individuals for the purpose of DNA testing should not be kept after a final decision has been made in the case for which they were used, except if such storage is imposed by reasons directly related to those for which the samples were collected' (Article 8).

Some jurisdictions, particularly those that have set up genetic databases, have specific legislation setting out the circumstances in which the samples must be disposed of. For example, the Australian legislation[75] sets out requirements for the destruction of forensic material where an urgent interim order is disallowed, when 12 months have elapsed, or after discontinuance of the proceedings, acquittal of the defendant, or after all appeal rights have been exhausted. Similarly, in New Zealand, the blood sample, every record of any analysis of the sample and all information linking the person tested with the sample must be destroyed by the police if 12 months expire and the person is not charged, the charge is withdrawn or the person is acquitted, as well as in a number of other circumstances.

Some civil law jurisdictions have no specific rules beyond the general provisions of their codes of criminal procedure in relation to the retention of storage of items as proofs in the criminal process. In France, the general provisions of the Code de Procedure Penale deal with the retention and storage of items used as proofs in a criminal process according. When the final sentence of the court is entered, items can be requested for restitution. In other cases, if they are regarded

---

74   For example, Pa 90–141, 1 January 1998 amending Pa Codes of Civil & Criminal Procedure.
75   Crimes Amendment (Forensic Procedures) Act 1998, Part 1A; Division 8, ss 23YC–YDAB.

as important for the file of the case, they will be annexed to the file and stored in accordance to the 1979 law on national records. The French National Ethics Committee gave advice on 15 December 1989 on the risks derived from the storage of information obtained through the technique of DNA fingerprints. Similarly, in Germany, s 81a(3) of the StPO stipulates that blood samples and other body cells taken from the accused shall be destroyed immediately – without any avoidable delay – after they are no longer needed for the specific proceeding. The destruction clause applies to samples of suspects as well as non-suspect persons (s 81c(5) of the StPO). Sample material is generally stored until the judgment becomes final – after any appeal – if it has not been destroyed before. In Japan there is a statute dealing with the retention of records of criminal trials. This law sets out the period for which the records of criminal trials must be retained. DNA test results, which usually appear as a written expert opinion, must also be retained under this law if they were presented as evidence at trial. The period of the retention is from three to 50 years, according to the seriousness of the crime in question. The storage of data in Spain is maintained until the conclusion of an investigation or final judicial resolution, particularly the verdict of not guilty (Article 20.4 of the LORTAD).

Uniquely, the UK has recently passed legislation removing the obligation to destroy DNA samples, making England, Wales and Northern Ireland the only jurisdictions within which it is possible to maintain samples indefinitely on the national database, regardless of whether a suspect is found to be innocent, or whether a decision is made not to prosecute after samples have been taken.[76] It has been estimated that 80,000 samples were illegally retained before the adoption of the Criminal Justice and Police Act.

Penalties for using samples or results for unauthorised purposes

Many jurisdictions have general and specific penalties for the unauthorised storage or use of samples of results. The Public Authorities' Registers Act of Denmark contains many limitations on the release of personal registered information. Violations of those rules may be punished by a fine (s 29). The French Code Penale, in Articles 226–28, prohibits the use of genetic identification information other than for purposes of criminal justice (one year's imprisonment term and a €15,000 fine). Although there are no specific penalties in Japan for unauthorised release of stored information, all public officers including investigating authorities have a duty not to disclose secrets. Disclosure without proper reason results in penalties (Article 100 of the National Public Service Law; Article 34 of the Local Public Service Law). Similar general prohibitions apply in Spain, where personal character data cannot be used for purposes other than those for which the data gathered (LORTAD, Article 4.2).

---

76 Section 82 of the Criminal Justice and Police Act 2001 amended the existing s 64 of PACE to this effect.

The New Zealand legislation makes it an offence to attempt to gain access to the database or blood sample; to disclose any information on the databank; and to use a blood sample in contravention of the Act, and is punishable by imprisonment for a term not exceeding three years. Section 23YDAG of the Australian Crimes Act 1914 seeks to protect its forensic database with a series of offences and penalties. For example, a person is guilty of an offence if:

(a) the person's conduct causes any identifying information about a person obtained from forensic material taken from the person under this Part to be recorded or retained in a DNA database system at any time after this Part requires the forensic material to be destroyed; and

(b) the person is reckless as to the recording or retention or whether the forensic material is required to be destroyed.

Release of DNA test information

Finally, there is a common theme of prohibition against the unauthorised release of DNA test information to third parties throughout the flow of DNA information at different stages from collection to testing to the court process. In the Netherlands, the Science Laboratory sends its report to the public prosecutor or the investigating judge. Distribution of data to third parties can take place in accordance with the aim of the registration, or with consent of the registree (Article 9 of the Reglement DNA Profielregistratie).

In New Zealand, the analysis can be released to the person the sample was taken from or his or her lawyer[77] and an equivalent provision applies in Australia.[78] The New Zealand legislation also specifies the only purposes for which DNA profiles stored on the databank will be released are:

• for forensic comparisons in the course of a criminal investigation;

• to make the information available in accordance with the Privacy Act 1993, to the person to whom the information relates (s 27(1)).

Most controversial is the question of the release of information to the person concerned. As a rule, people have, on request, the right to all information contained in a private or public register concerning them, usually in writing. If decisive public or private considerations, including the interests of the individual himself, overweigh his interest to be informed, the information can be withheld or possibly only given orally, in which case the individual can request the inspectorate of registers and/or the authority directly responsible, ie, the National Commissioner of Police, to control whether the relevant information has been stored in accordance with the relevant rules. In Denmark, if a DNA profile is released to the police and prosecutor in connection with criminal proceedings, the defence counsel and normally also the defendant have right of disclosure (s 745, AJA).

---

77   Criminal Investigation (Blood Samples) Act 1995, s 59.
78   Crimes Amendment (Forensic Procedures) Act 1997, s 23XW.

References

Andrews, L, Mehlman, M and Rothstein, M (2002) *Genetics: Ethics, Law and Policy,* West Group

Australian Law Reform Commission (2003) *Essentially Yours: The Protection of Human Genetic Information,* Report No 96, Chapter 45 'Post-Conviction Use of DNA Evidence'

Balding, D and Donnelly, P (1994) 'The prosecutor's fallacy and DNA evidence' Crim LR 711

Bindman, S (1997) 'Murder case reopened: Canada' 19 Nat LJ 1

Chaydo, GM, Gulliver, ED and MacDougall, DV (1991) *Forensic Evidence in Canada,* Canada Law Book Inc

Christian, K (2001) 'And the DNA shall set you free' Ohio St LJ 1195

de Foore D (2002) 'Post-conviction DNA testing: a cry for justice for the wrongly convicted' 13 Texas Technical LR 491

Faigman, D, Kaye, D, Saks, M and Sanders, J (2000) *Science in the Law: Forensic Science Issues,* West Group

Fenner, G (1996) 'The Daubert handbook: the case, its essential dilemma, and its progeny' 29 Creighton L Rev 939

Fontana, JA (1977) *The Law of Search and Seizure in Canada,* Butterworths

Goode, M (2002) 'Some observations on evidence of DNA frequency' 23 Adelaide LR 45

Grevling, K (1997) 'Fairness and the exclusion of evidence under s 78(1) of the Police and Criminal Evidence Act' 113 LQR 667

Jeffreys, A, Wilson, V and Thein, S (1985) 'Hypervariable minisatellite regions in human DNA' 314 Nature 67

Jeffreys, A, Wilson, V and Thein, S (1985) 'Individual-specific fingerprints of human DNA' 316 Nature 76

Jeffreys, A *et al* (eds) (1991) *DNA Fingerprinting: Approaches and Applications,* Springer-Verlag

Kaye, D and Sensabaugh, G (2000) 'Reference guide on DNA evidence', in *Federal Judicial Center, Reference Manual on Scientific Evidence,* Washington DC

Klumpe, B (1993) Der *'Genetische Fingerabdruck' im Strafverfahren,* Rechtsprobleme bei der Anwendung gemetischer Analysen in GroBbritannien und Deutschland. Reihe 'Beiträge und Materialiem der Max-Planck-Instituts für ausländishes und enternationales strafrecht', Bol 542, Freiburg 1993, 3445.

Koehler, J, Chia, A and Lindsey, S (1995) 'The random match probability in DNA evidence: irrelevant and prejudicial?' 35 Jurimetrics Journal 201

Koehler, J (1997) 'Why DNA likelihood ratios should account for error' 37 Jurimetrics Journal 425

Koehler, J (2001) 'The psychology of numbers in the courtroom: how to make DNA-match statistics seem impressive or insufficient' 74 Southern California LR 1275

Lander, E (1989) 'DNA fingerprinting on trial' 339 Nature 501

Laurie, G (2002) *Genetic Privacy: A Challenge to Medico-legal Norms,* Cambridge University Press

Nakashima, R (1995) 'DNA evidence in criminal trials: a defense attorney's primer' 74 Nebraska LR 444

Seabrooke, S and Sprack, J, (1996) *Criminal Evidence and Procedure: The Statutory Framework*, Butterworths

Sheindlin, G (1995) 'DNA: is the presentation of statistical evidence necessary?' 214 NYLJ 1

Smith G and Gordon, J (1997) 'The admission of DNA evidence in state and federal courts' 65 Fordham LR 2465

Tanovich, D (1996) 'The admissibility of novel scientific evidence under Mohan: the case of DNA typing' 1 Can Crim LR 221

Urbas, G (2002) 'DNA evidence in criminal appeals and post-conviction inquiries: are new forms of review required?' 2 Macquarie LJ 141

CHAPTER 2

ARGENTINA

Dr Augusto César Belluscio
Corte Suprema de Justicia de la Nación

Time in the criminal process at which DNA sampling and testing may occur

In Argentina, the collection of DNA in criminal investigation procedures occurs at two stages. First, DNA may be collected at the enquiry stage, during which, under the direction of a judge, evidence is assembled in relation to the charge and the defence. Secondly, DNA may be collected during the criminal prosecution procedure. At this stage there is an opportunity for the parties to challenge, on an equal footing, the DNA evidence already obtained or introduced. In either case, the suspect may be either in custody or at liberty.

Under these conditions, the samples for DNA testing can be collected during any of these two stages, before the end of the court hearing. This will depend on the urgency which is required to obtain the sample. For example, in a case of culpable homicide, if it were necessary to determine if the driver of a car was under the influence of alcohol or not, the sample should be taken as early as possible. However, the suspect has a right to a defence and to the control of the sample.

Collection of DNA samples

The procedures required for obtaining DNA samples must be compatible with the National Constitution, the International Human Rights Treaties incorporated into the Constitution by the reform of 1994 and the specific law dealing with DNA sampling. These laws generally impose standards recognising respect for human dignity, privacy and the right to a defence against criminal charges.

The degree of force used in order to obtain samples of hair, blood, saliva or other tissue

The degree of force which can be used to obtain DNA samples (from hair, blood, saliva or other human tissues) is determined by the principle of *proportionality*. Under the principle of *proportionality* there must be an adequate relationship between taking the sample and the desired results from the sample. The principle of *proportionality* also requires basic criteria of causing the least harm possible. Accordingly, the force used depends on the type of sample that is to be taken.

The High Court of Justice has established that the compulsory taking of blood (whether from minors or adults) for the purpose of obtaining proof in relation to the commission of a crime does not, of itself, violate or infringe the right to refuse to make a statement, including a refusal in relation to collaboration in a matter of proof with prosecution, the right to defence, the right to bodily integrity or privacy (either of the accused or the victim). The High Court of Justice has further decided that these rights are not infringed provided the DNA sample is taken according to the principles of *proportionality* and *reasonableness*.[1] Moreover, the High Court has not permitted the compulsory blood sampling of minors who have not been victims of a crime or who have not been involved in any illegal act because this would invade the minor's privacy, restrain his or her freedom to bodily integrity and would damage his or her physical integrity which is subject to juridical protection.[2]

Rules applicable to specific groups such as military personnel, minors and prisoners

There are special rules for different groups that deal with clinical examinations in general but not specifically dealing with DNA or other genetic studies. These general clinical examinations may not relate specifically to a DNA test but they can relate generally to the taking of urine and blood. Some medical examinations could extend to DNA analysis which are primarily for the purpose of detecting illness amongst prisoners, military personnel or employees but including those who are going to be married, where there are epidemics or skin grafts. These types of examinations are obligatory. The High Court of Justice has confirmed the authority of the Federal Police to conduct examinations and chemical analysis to confirm the good health of their police officers and obligatory testing for AIDS.[3] In addition, Article 5 of Law 23511 dealing with genetic studies for histo-compatibility allows the national DNA bank, on an authorised demand, to check for DNA matches.

Testing

Scientific tests for DNA in the criminal procedure

There is no specific scientific test for DNA matching in criminal procedures in Argentina. Different techniques can be used provided they are explained to and evaluated by the judges giving the court certainty on the actual facts. The DNA test must be carried out by an expert. Each party can propose its own expert and

---

1   Decisions of 4 November 1995 in *Re HG*, and of 27 December 1996 in *Re Guarino, Mirta Liliana.*

2   Decision of 13 November 1990, published in Fallos (collection of the judgments of the High Court of Justice), 313, 1113.

3   Decision of 17 December 1996 in *Re BREC Federal Police Argentina.*

the judges must evaluate the opinions of these experts according to the importance of and the validity of the technique employed.

Licence or authorisation

Laboratories and experts who carry out DNA tests must be licensed. Licences are required administratively and are granted by the Minister for Public Health. According to judicial procedures, the courts nominate experts from professional lists. These lists do not prejudice the possibility of the parties themselves proposing other experts who may appear reliable to them.

Specific rules for DNA testing

In Argentina, there is specific legislation dealing with DNA tests. Article 5 of Law 23511 established the National DNA Bank in 1987. Article 5 provides that:

> Without prejudice to other tests conducted by the National DNA Bank, when requested to act to bank genetic samples or to test or establish a consanguinity, the National DNA Bank may: 1.Research blood groups 2.Research systems of histo-compatibility (HLA, A, B, C, and DR), and 3. Research iso-enzymes for research plasma proteins.

In 1983, Law 22990 regulated activities linked to human blood including its components and derivatives and sub-products, notably on the storage and donation of blood without reference to DNA tests.

Use of DNA test results in the criminal process

The results of a DNA test are available during the criminal trial procedure to the lawyer of the accused.

Generally, admissibility of the DNA test results are under the direction of the judge. During the criminal procedure in Argentina, it is the judge who orders and supervises the acquisition of DNA evidence subject to the intervention of the parties. However, there is no rule preventing a test carried out by the parties outside of the process from being presented in the court proceedings. However, the probative value depends on the judicial definition of this test subject to any challenge by the opposing party. The judges in criminal trials frequently request studies from the National DNA Bank on the basis that it is a state institution. Apart from the general judicial control on the admission of evidence, there are many other specific rules dealing with the presentation of DNA evidence in court proceedings.

Interestingly, in the criminal procedure there are no specific standards of proof applicable to DNA tests. On the other hand, in civil matters a refusal by a defendant to submit to a blood test in an action to establish parentage raises a presumption against him or her.[4]

Because of the strength of DNA evidence, it is practically impossible to challenge the results of a DNA test with regard to scientific accuracy. On the other hand, the DNA evidence may be challenged from the point of view of the form of the procedure, for example, where the sample was not under the control of the opposing party or where there are doubts about the safeguarding of the samples. Accordingly, ordinarily a DNA test carries evidential weight taking into consideration the degree of scientific certainty and the absence of other methods of proof of similar probative value.

Finally, there are no special directions made by judges in relation to DNA evidence beyond the general evaluation of evidence. There are only directions in relation to the taking of the samples and the intervention of the parties, apart from the general concerns about how a particular fact must be proved.

Retention and storage of samples and test results

There are no general rules dealing with the destruction or storage of DNA test results. Generally, the judges order the destruction of samples in each case. This occurs generally when the decision has been finally reached in the case.

The samples and results of DNA tests conducted by the National DNA Bank are stored in the Bank itself.[5] In addition, tests conducted by other private institutions (such as laboratories or hospitals) may be stored also by those institutions themselves. The reliability of such tests depends on the manner in which the samples are stored and the conditions imposed preventing tampering or alteration.

In this respect, there are general and specific sanctions for the use of samples or results for unauthorised uses. The major sanctions are those imposed for traditional offences under the Penal Code and related laws which are committed in relation to the use of samples or test results. The specific sanctions are contained in Laws 23511 and 22990. Article 9 of Law 23511, which was introduced in 1987, imposes penalties for alteration of the register or reports from the register.[6] The offence consists of alteration of the authenticated register or reports. Law 22990 was passed in 1983 and imposes sanctions for any misuse of law of blood, any use

---

4   Article 4 of Law 23511. When it is necessary to determine in a lawsuit the parentage of a person and the claim appears probable or reasonable, a genetic test may be undertaken, which will be evaluated by the judge taking into account the experiments and the scientific results on the subject. A refusal to subject oneself to the tests and the analyses necessary raises a contrary presumption with the position argued by the person who refuses the test.

5   Article 8 of law 23511. The books and the records of the National DNA Bank will be preserved in a manner to ensure their inviolability is ensured, and under conditions to ensure their integrity.

6   Article 9 of Law 23511. Any alteration in the registers or reports are punishable offences of falsification of official records. The author and any other countersignatory will be culpable.

for profit of human blood or its derivatives or for any purpose other than that which is authorised.[7]

Law 22990 also contains sanctions for unauthorised storage of samples or test results.[8]

Release of DNA test information

There are no specific rules dealing with the release of DNA test results. However, there are general rules which prevent the release of stored DNA test results except by authorised government instrumentalities or under approved research projects. Generally, the obligation to preserve the confidentiality of the samples and the test results depend on the general duties of medical doctors to preserve confidentiality and the general law.[9] Similarly, there are no specific rules about the privacy of DNA test results but the release of such information could constitute a number of offences such as the violation of professional confidentiality or the release of secret information by public officials. These circumstances amount to punishable offences under Articles 156 and 157 of the Penal Code.[10] Moreover, Law 23798 dealing with AIDS, which was passed in 1990, prohibits the identification of persons suffering from that disease by reason of the use of samples obtained under those regulations.[11]

---

7 Article 92 of Law 22990. Those punished may be sentenced to a period of six months' to two years' imprisonment including persons in charge of haemotherapy services, blood banks, production laboratories for blood derivatives, reagents, diagnostic or serums markers of hematology, when conducting these functions without authorisation and legal capacity.

8 Article 91 of Law 22990. A person will be punished with a term of six months' to five years' imprisonment and a fine of 10,000 to 500,000 Argentinian pesos, whenever he or she has acted as an intermediary or has obtained a benefit by obtaining, donating, preparing, fractionating, storing, conserving, distributing, supplying, transporting, transfusing, importing or exporting, or deriving any form of profit from human blood, its components and its derivatives, outside of the circumstances authorised by this law.

9 Article 11 of Law 17132 of 1967 on the practice of medicine.

10 Article 156 of the Penal Code. A fine of 1,500 to 90,000 pesos may be imposed, and special forfeiture, if necessary, whenever a person discloses a secret, without proper cause, having knowledge of a secret, disclosure of which may cause damage because it relates to a state, trade, employment, profession or art secret. In addition, Article 157 provides that a public servant may be imprisoned for one month to a maximum imprisonment of two years, and special forfeiture of one to four years, where the public servant discloses facts, files or documents considered secret according to the law.

11 Article 2 of Law 23798. The provisions of this law and its complementary standards will be interpreted, taking into account that, in no case may a person: e) identify a person through cards, registers or stored data, which, for this purpose, have been registered in a codified form.

CHAPTER 3

AUSTRALIA

Professor Donald Chalmers
Head of Faculty and Dean, Faculty of Law, University of Tasmania

Introduction

Criminal investigations have benefited from developments in research in molecular biology. Australia has followed developments in the United Kingdom, where tests to identify human genetic characteristics have been applied in criminal investigations. Improvements in molecular biological analysis of human DNA have had a widespread impact on forensic techniques in criminal investigations. By comparing the DNA in a tissue sample from the scene of a crime with samples taken from a suspect, criminal investigators have a tool that provides high statistical certainty in identifying those accused of a crime or excluding those wrongly suspected of a crime.

Objections to the introduction of DNA profiling

When DNA testing was first used in criminal investigation in the late 1980s, a spate of scholarly writing raised ethical concerns about the new procedure.[1] The criticisms fell into four classifications.[2] Objections were raised in relation to the actual laboratory technical procedures regarding the authenticity of the sample, more generally, in relation to civil liberties and, finally, in relation to the statistical probabilities in DNA testing. First, the practical complexities of a DNA test cannot be underestimated. Although the technique is being constantly improved and computerised, the process remains 'very labour intensive and needs more than meticulous expertise and much experience in the reading and interpretation of the bands'.[3] Some of the more notable cases in the United States concerned attacks on the laboratory testing procedures themselves.

---

1   See, for example, Scutt (1989), (1990) and (1990a); Burk (1998); Justice John Phillips (1988) and (1996).
2   See Freckelton (1989).
3   See Dodd (1985).

Secondly, some cases have raised concerns about the actual sample traces of organic material tested, and whether these were authentic. For example, in the famous Pitchfork case in the UK, all the males in the village between the ages of 13 and 30 (over 5,500 males) were tested to try to identify the man responsible for a rape and two murders. Pitchfork, one of only two men who refused to give a sample, had tried to induce workmates to provide some samples on his behalf.[4] He was unsuccessful and later confessed when confronted with the evidence. This case prompted comments about the possibility of falsification of samples. This is a concern, but not one that is unique in criminal investigations to DNA testing. This case did, however, highlight that the elimination of innocent persons from an investigation (in the Pitchfork case, over 5,000 males) is no less important to suspects and police in successfully investigating a crime.

The third group of objections in relation to civil liberties remains far more substantial. Consent to a DNA test is an issue. If a suspect is asked to provide a sample of blood or saliva for DNA testing, the consent of the suspect would depend upon different circumstances: whether the person is in custody, has been arrested or charged. In addition, there may be circumstances where consent may not be required, where the suspect is brought before a magistrate. Such concerns about protecting the civil liberties of a suspect must be balanced against the public interest in obtaining reliable evidence that is likely to confirm or disprove the commission of an offence by the suspect.[5] The procedures for obtaining the DNA sample from a suspect must also incorporate accepted standards of fairness. If police have used undue pressure or deception, the issue of admissibility of the evidence arises. The evidence is not necessarily excluded, as there is judicial discretion to admit or exclude such evidence.[6] Many of these questions are overlapped and are not generically different to concerns of other forms of forensic testing, particularly blood tests. It is, however, the compelling accuracy of DNA tests and the uniqueness of the information that is uncovered which makes the civil liberty concern so vocal.[7] There are also concerns surrounding the establishment of the national DNA database, such as questions about the accuracy of the testing, the security of the data and privacy of the individuals, as well as concerns about the information entered on the register.[8]

Finally, discussions are ongoing about the statistical probabilities involved in DNA profiling. DNA profiling relies on the probability that there is uniqueness in the DNA of individuals and a very low probability that individuals have the same DNA pattern. It has been estimated that the chances of the DNA in two unrelated individuals being the same could be as rare as one in 16 million. However, there

---

4   See White and Green (1988).
5   See Horton (1992).
6   See *Bunning v Cross* (1978) 141 CLR 54; *R v White* [2005] NSWSC 60 and the Uniform Evidence Act (Commonwealth and New South Wales), s 138.
7   See Scutt (1990), (1989) and (1990a).
8   See McLeod (1991).

are continuing doubts about the accuracy of this estimate of statistical probability. Estimates are based on assumptions of random marriage across ethnic groups and geographic areas. These assumptions determine probabilities about the randomness of inherited characteristics within the general population. On the other hand, some geneticists argue that people, in fact, marry within ethnic groups. This may require a substantial revision downward of the possibility of people having the same genetic traits. This is one of the major reasons for establishing a national register that will assist in calculating more accurate statistical probability patterns.

Towards uniformity of DNA testing in Australia

The use of DNA profiling in criminal investigations, particularly for serious offences against the person, is well-established in Australia. In fact, the first conviction in a State Supreme Court based on DNA evidence occurred in 1989.

Criminal law and investigation are generally governed by state rather than federal law in Australia. There are, however, some criminal matters determined by federal law. In 2000, the Model Criminal Code Officers Committee (MCCOC) finalised a model forensic procedures Bill (Model Bill),[9] which provides: powers to request or require that forensic procedures be carried out on suspects, convicted offenders and volunteers; processes for carrying out forensic procedures; evidentiary rules for improperly obtained evidence from forensic procedures; the establishment of a DNA database system; and an interstate jurisdiction scheme.[10] One of the main aims of the Model Bill is to provide a template for State and Territory forensic procedures legislation, in order to achieve true harmonisation of such law throughout Australia.

The Model Bill and the Crimes Act 1914 (Cth)

The Model Bill provisions are closely replicated in Part 1D of the Crimes Act 1914 (Cth). This Part outlines the processes to be followed in the conduct of forensic procedures, including the prerequisites that must be met, and provides for a DNA database for the storing and matching of DNA profiles.

Consent and authority for forensic procedures

Consent is generally required for a forensic procedure, or the procedure should be authorised by a senior constable or a magistrate.

Suspects (other than children or incapable persons) may be asked by a constable to consent to a forensic procedure; if a suspect who is in custody withholds consent, a senior constable can order the performance of non-intimate

9 Model Criminal Code Officers Committee, *Final Draft: Model Forensic Procedures Bill and the Proposed National DNA Database* (2000).
10 See Australian Law Reform Commission (ALRC) (2002), [34.11].

forensic procedures;[11] and a magistrate may order the performance of a forensic procedure on suspects who are either in or out of police custody, or who are children or incapable persons.[12]

Serious offenders, that is, persons under sentence for a Commonwealth offence punishable by a maximum penalty of imprisonment for life or five or more years,[13] may be asked by a constable to consent to a forensic procedure (other than children and incapable persons); if a serious offender withholds consent, a constable may order the performance of a non-intimate forensic procedure; and a magistrate or judge may order the performance of either an intimate or non-intimate forensic procedure upon children or incapable persons.[14]

Volunteers, that is, persons who volunteer to undergo a forensic procedure, or whose parent or guardian volunteers on their behalf in the case of children or incapable persons, are also provided for: a volunteer who is a child or incapable person may be the subject of an order by a magistrate for the performance of a forensic procedure, if the consent of the parent or guardian cannot be reasonably obtained, the parent or guardian withholds consent, or the parent or guardian initially consented to the performance of the procedure but later withdrew consent.[15]

Suspects

A constable may request that a suspect undergo a forensic procedure, provided the constable is satisfied that:[16]

- on the balance of probabilities,[17] the person on whom the procedure is proposed to be carried out is a suspect, that there are reasonable grounds to believe that the forensic procedure will produce evidence tending to confirm or disprove that the suspect committed a relevant offence, *and* that the request for consent to the forensic procedure is justified in all the circumstances;

- the public interest in obtaining evidence likely to confirm or disprove that the suspect committed the offence is balanced with the public interest in upholding the physical integrity of the suspect.[18]

---

11 A 'non-intimate forensic procedure' includes taking a hand, finger, foot or toe print; taking a hair sample other than pubic hair; and taking a sample from a nail or under a nail: see the Crimes Act 1914 (Cth), s 23WA(1).
12 See ALRC (2002), [34.14]–[34.19].
13 Crimes Act 1914 (Cth), s 23WA(1).
14 See ALRC (2002), [34.21]–[34.24].
15 *Ibid* [34.25]–[34.27].
16 Crimes Act 1914 (Cth), ss 23WH, 23WI.
17 This sub-section will prevent police from requesting consent to unnecessary forensic procedures only marginally related to the offence or designed as a 'fishing expedition'.
18 In balancing these competing public interests, factors to be considered include the seriousness of the circumstances surrounding the commission of the offence, the age, physical and mental health, cultural background and religious beliefs (where appropriate) of the suspect to the extent that they are known or can reasonably be ascertained by the constable (by asking or otherwise), and whether there is a less intrusive and reasonably practicable way of obtaining the evidence. If the suspect is an Aboriginal or Torres Strait Islander, the constable must take the suspect's customary beliefs into account.

There are provisions to protect suspects by ensuring they do not consent or refuse consent to a procedure without understanding the consequences of either consent or refusal.[19] A suspect may have an opportunity to consult with a legal practitioner of the suspect's choice before consenting to undergo a procedure.[20] However, the constable need not allow him or her to communicate or attempt to communicate with a legal practitioner in private if the constable suspects on reasonable grounds that the suspect might attempt to destroy or contaminate any evidence that might be obtained by the performance of a forensic procedure.[21]

A constable must also inform the suspect of certain matters prior to consent being given.[22] These include the purpose for which the forensic procedure is required, the offence in question, and the way in which the procedure is to be carried out. The suspect must also be told that the procedure may produce evidence against the suspect that might be used in a court of law, that the forensic procedure will be carried out by an appropriately qualified person, that the suspect may refuse consent, and the consequences of refusal. The section also requires the constable to inform the suspect of the entitlement to have an interview friend present during a procedure. There is also a right to have a medical practitioner or dentist present during most forensic procedures.[23]

Where a suspect in lawful custody gives informed consent to undergo a forensic procedure, that procedure must be carried out within the prescribed investigation period.[24] These time limits vary according to the classification of the suspect: for example, in relation to Aboriginal and Torres Straight Islander suspects not in custody, the procedure must be performed within two hours after the suspect presents to the investigating constable.

As noted previously, a child cannot consent to a forensic procedure (s 23WE(1)), nor can an incapable person consent to a forensic procedure (s 23WE(2)). In the case of suspects who are Aboriginal persons or Torres Strait Islanders, additional procedures must be followed:[25]

- the suspect cannot consent unless an 'interview friend' is present, or the suspect has expressly and voluntarily waived this right;

- before asking the suspect to consent, the constable must inform him or her that an Aboriginal legal aid organisation representative will be notified that the suspect is being asked to consent to such, and notify this representative, unless the suspect has arranged for a legal practitioner to be present;

---

19   Crimes Act 1914 (Cth), s 23WF
20   *Ibid*, s 23WF(2).
21   *Ibid*, s 23WF(3).
22   *Ibid*, s 23WJ.
23   *Ibid*, s 23WJ(2). The taking of prints is not a medical or dental procedure and the presence of a medical practitioner or dentist is not a useful safeguard in these circumstances.
24   Provided for by the Crimes Act 1914 (Cth), s 23WCA.
25   *Ibid*, s 23WG.

- the suspect who has waived the right to have an interview friend present[26] must be given the opportunity to communicate with a legal practitioner of the suspect's choice and to do so in private;

- the suspect must be allowed to communicate with the interview friend and legal practitioner in private.

Section 23WK details the effects of a withdrawal of consent. From the time a person withdraws consent, the procedure is to be treated as one for which consent has been refused and is only to proceed by magistrate's order or, if allowed, by order of a constable.

Section 23WL(1) requires that the giving of information to a suspect, as well as the giving of the consent (if any), be recorded.[27] Section 23WLA(1) provides that the procedure must be carried out as soon as reasonably possible after the suspect presents for the procedure, within a maximum of two hours in the case of an Aboriginal person, a Torres Strait Islander or a child, or a maximum of four hours in any other case.[28]

Division 4 authorises a *senior constable* to carry out a *non-intimate forensic procedure* on a suspect in lawful custody. It also sets out the circumstances in which a senior constable can order the carrying out of a non-intimate forensic procedure, and the matters that must be considered before making such an order.

A list of matters are prescribed of which a constable must be satisfied on the balance of probabilities before ordering a non-intimate forensic procedure:[29] that the suspect is in the lawful custody of a constable; that there are reasonable grounds to believe that the suspect committed a relevant offence; that there are reasonable grounds to believe that the forensic procedure is likely to confirm or disprove that the suspect committed a relevant offence; and that the request for consent to the forensic procedure is justified in all the circumstances.[30]

The constable must balance the public interest in obtaining evidence likely to confirm or disprove that the suspect committed the offence with the public interest in upholding the physical integrity of the suspect.[31] A constable must take

---

26 Or whom a senior constable believes on reasonable grounds that, having regard to the suspect's level of education and understanding, is not at a disadvantage in relation to the request to consent to the forensic procedure in comparison with members of the Australian community generally.

27 The recording requirements are designed to safeguard the rights of suspects as well as to minimise the potential for later uncertainty and dispute as to whether the required information and consent were given. See also s 23WL(2): if a recording is not practicable, a written record must be made and a copy of the record made available to the suspect.

28 Time only starts to run when the suspect presents him or herself for the procedure, rather than immediately upon consent, because, for example, a suspect may prefer to undergo the procedure at a more convenient time.

29 Crimes Act 1914 (Cth), s 23WO.

30 This provision requires an appropriate standard of satisfaction to ensure that police do not order unnecessary non-intimate forensic procedures only marginally related to the offence or designed as a 'fishing expedition'.

31 Crimes Act 1914 (Cth), s 23WO(2).

numerous factors into account in balancing these competing public interests, including whether there is a less intrusive but reasonably practicable way of obtaining the evidence, the age, health, cultural background and religious beliefs (where appropriate) of the suspect, to the extent that they are known or can reasonably be ascertained by the constable (by asking or otherwise) and any reasons the suspect gives for refusing consent. If the constable reasonably believes that the suspect is an Aboriginal or Torres Strait Islander person, then the suspect's cultural beliefs must also be taken into account.[32]

Division 5 authorises a person to carry out a forensic procedure by *order of a magistrate*. It sets out the prerequisites that must be met and the procedures that must be followed in applying to a magistrate for a final order or urgent interim order that a forensic procedure be carried out, in the hearing of that application and in the making of the order. It also establishes limits on the use of material gathered under an urgent interim order, and creates an offence of publishing any information that could lead to the identification of a suspect prior to the suspect being charged with any offence. Finally, it establishes the time limits on the conduct of forensic procedures ordered by a magistrate.

Section 23WT(1) prescribes a list of matters of which a magistrate must be satisfied, on the balance of probabilities, before ordering a forensic procedure. These are: that the person on whom the procedure is to be carried out is a suspect; that on the evidence before the magistrate there are reasonable grounds to believe that the suspect committed a relevant offence; that there are reasonable grounds to believe that the forensic procedure is likely to tend to confirm or disprove that the suspect committed a relevant offence; and that the carrying out of the forensic procedure is justified in all the circumstances. This provision, by providing that the magistrate has to be satisfied on the balance of probabilities, requires a high standard be reached regarding these matters before the order can be made.[33]

Section 23WT(2) provides that in determining whether the carrying out of the forensic procedure is justified in all the circumstances, as required by s 23WT(1), the magistrate must balance the public interest in obtaining evidence that would tend to confirm or disprove that the suspect committed the offence with the public interest in upholding the physical integrity of the suspect. Sub-section 23WT(3) lists a number of factors a magistrate must take into account in balancing these competing public interests, including: the seriousness of the circumstances surrounding the commission of the offence; whether there is a less intrusive but reasonably practicable way of obtaining the evidence; the age, health, cultural background and religious beliefs (where appropriate) of the suspect, to the extent that they are known or can reasonably be ascertained by the magistrate (by asking

---

32 Crimes Act 1914 (Cth), s 23WO(3). The senior constable making the order must record the order made, including the date and time of the order and the reasons for making it, and sign the record (s 23WP).

33 Again, this will help to ensure that police do not seek unnecessary forensic procedures that may only marginally be related to the offence in question, or procedures designed as a 'fishing expedition'.

or otherwise); any reasons the suspect gives for refusing consent; the length of time for which the suspect has already been detained and reasons for any delay in proposing the carrying out of a forensic procedure; and, if the suspect is a child or an incapable person, the welfare of that person. If the suspect is an Aboriginal or Torres Strait Islander, the magistrate must also take his or her cultural beliefs into account to the extent that they are known or can reasonably be ascertained by the magistrate (by asking or otherwise).

A magistrate, on the application of a constable, may issue a warrant directing a person detaining a suspect to deliver the suspect into the custody of the constable for the period of the hearing of an application for an order.[34] Where a suspect is not in custody, a magistrate may, on the application of a constable, issue a summons for the appearance of the suspect or may issue a warrant for the arrest of the suspect.[35] Section 23WX(1) requires an order to be made in the presence of the suspect concerned, unless the magistrate orders otherwise.[36] Section 23WX(2) requires that a child or an incapable person be represented by an interview friend, and stipulates that he or she may also be represented by a legal practitioner during the hearing of an application for an order. Similarly, sub-section 23WX(3) provides that if the applicant believes on reasonable grounds that the suspect is an Aboriginal or Torres Strait Islander, then the suspect must be represented by an interview friend and may also be represented by a legal practitioner.[37] Section 23WX(6) allows a suspect or his or her representative to call or cross-examine any witnesses and to address the magistrate at the hearing of the application for a forensic procedure order. This gives the suspect full opportunity to test the grounds on which the order is sought and to argue against the order. Section 23WX(7) provides that an interview friend can be excluded from the hearing if he or she unreasonably interferes with or obstructs the making of the application.

Section 23WY(1) requires a magistrate, if making an order: to give reasons for the decision; to ensure that a written record of the decision is kept; to order the suspect to attend for the carrying out of the forensic procedure; and to inform the suspect that reasonable force may be used to ensure that he or she complies with the order.[38] Section 23WY(2) allows a magistrate to give directions as to the time, place and manner in which a forensic procedure is to be carried out if required.

---

34 Crimes Act 1914 (Cth), s 23WV(1).

35 *Ibid*, s 23WW(1). The importance of having a suspect informed of a procedure by a court rather than by a constable and, in some cases, the need to prevent a suspect from destroying evidence or going into hiding, necessitates that the suspect to be compelled to attend.

36 This allows a suspect to raise arguments against the making of an order.

37 This provision does not apply if the applicant believes on reasonable grounds that, having regard to the suspect's level of education and understanding, the suspect is not at a disadvantage in relation to the hearing in comparison with members of the Australian community generally.

38 First, this will help to minimise the risk of later legal challenges arising out of dispute as to the terms of the magistrate's decision and, secondly, will ensure that both the suspect and the police are fully aware of their legal positions.

A magistrate may make an urgent interim order authorising a forensic procedure that must be carried out without delay. Interim orders[39] may only be made if the circumstances listed in s 23WR that are relevant to the particular application are satisfied, and the magistrate is satisfied of two matters: first, that the probative value of evidence obtained as a result of the forensic procedure concerned is likely to be lost or destroyed if there is a delay in carrying out the procedure; and, secondly, that there is sufficient evidence to indicate that a magistrate is reasonably likely to be satisfied of the existence of the matters listed in sub-section 23WT(1) when the application is finally determined.[40]

Where there is an interim application, the magistrate must ensure that the suspect and his or her lawyer or interview friend (if relevant) be given an opportunity to speak to the magistrate if possible, or to make a written submission. This gives the suspect an opportunity to oppose the making of the interim order and allows the magistrate to consider the arguments of the suspect and his or her representatives.[41] When the interim order is made, the applicant must be informed, either personally or by telephone or transmission, that the order has been made, the terms of the order and any directions given, particularly about the time, place and manner in which a forensic procedure is to occur.[42]

A record must be made at the time of, or as soon as practicable after, making the application for the interim order, and must be signed by the applicant. This is to reduce the potential for dispute as to the grounds on which an order was sought and the terms of the order (s 23XE(1)). The suspect must be given a copy of the interim order made by the magistrate as soon as practicable after it is received by the applicant (s 23XE(5)).

Section 23XF(1) allows a constable, while the application seeking an interim order is being determined, to use reasonable force to prevent the suspect destroying any evidence that might be obtained by the carrying out of the forensic procedure if the order is made. Section 23XG(1) prohibits the analysis of a sample taken under an interim order, unless the sample is likely to perish before a final order is made, or a final order is actually made.[43]

Section 23XH creates an offence of intentionally publishing in a report the name of the suspect or any information likely to enable the identification of the

---

39 Section 23XA(2) provides that an interim order operates until a final hearing is held, at which time the interim order is confirmed or disallowed. If a magistrate does not ultimately make an order, all samples and information derived from the procedure must be destroyed.

40 Section 23XB(3) provides that an application for an interim order may be made in person or, if this course is not practicable, by telephone, radio, facsimile or other electronic means. This provision establishes a number of alternative cases and the availability of magistrates, while maintaining a preference for the application to be made in person if possible.

41 See s 23XC(1) and (2).

42 Crimes Act 1914 (Cth), s 23XD(1) and (2). A magistrate can use this power to take account of both the need of the police to maximise the evidential value of the sample and the need to minimise the inconvenience and distress caused to the suspect by any procedure ordered.

43 This will help to reduce the incentive to use an interim order to avoid the requirements for obtaining a final order, and there is a penalty for disclosure of the results of an analysis of a perishable sample.

suspect, unless he or she has been charged with the relevant offence, or the magistrate has, by order, authorised the publication. This offence is punishable by a maximum penalty of imprisonment of 12 months.

Serious offenders

Briefly, a constable may ask a serious offender to consent to a forensic procedure if he or she is satisfied, on the balance of probabilities, that this request for consent is justified in all the circumstances, and that the person is an 'offender', if the individual is not serving a sentence of imprisonment.[44] Informed consent is provided if the offender consents to the procedure after the constable has asked the offender to consent, informed him or her about the procedure in accordance with s 23XWJ, and given the offender the opportunity to communicate with a lawyer.[45] If consent is withheld, a constable may order the performance of a non-intimate forensic procedure if he or she has taken into account: whether Part 1D would authorise the procedure to be carried out in the absence of an order; the seriousness of the circumstances surrounding the offence; whether performing the procedure could assist law enforcement; and whether the performance of the procedure without consent is justified in all the circumstances.[46] A magistrate or judge may order the carrying out of an intimate forensic procedure, or a non-intimate procedure on a child or incapable person, if satisfied that this is justified in all the circumstances.[47]

In relation to both suspects and serious offenders, the Australian Law Reform Commission (ALRC) argues that the consent provisions should be removed, and only an order by an appropriate Australian Federal Police officer or judicial officer should authorise the performance of a forensic procedure on a suspect or serious offender. It recommends such in light of concerns that the notion of 'informed consent' underlying the current provisions may not be truly attainable given the 'inherently coercive nature of criminal investigations'. Further, the current provisions allowing requests for consent are arguably redundant due to the capacity to order the performance of a forensic procedure where consent has been withheld. The ALRC recommends, however, that the information that must presently be provided to a suspect or serious offender before they consent should, if the consent provisions are removed, be afforded to him or her prior to the performance of a compulsory forensic procedure.[48]

44   Crimes Act 1914 (Cth), ss 23XWH, 23XWI.
45   *Ibid*, s 23XWG(1).
46   *Ibid*, ss 23XWK, 23XWL.
47   *Ibid*, s 23XWO.
48   See ALRC (2002), [36.4]–[36.15], proposals 36–1 and 36–2.

Volunteers

Briefly, a volunteer or his or her parent or guardian provides informed consent if he or she consents to the procedure after being informed by a constable of the matters listed in s 23XWR, and consents in the presence of an independent person.[49] If a magistrate orders the performance of a forensic procedure in the circumstances outlined above, for example, where consent of the parent or guardian cannot be reasonably obtained, he or she must take into account matters such as the best interests of the child or incapable person, any wishes of the child or incapable person as to whether the procedure should be carried out, and whether the performance of the procedure is justified in all the circumstances.[50]

The conduct of forensic procedures

Division 6 of Part 1D of the Crimes Act 1914 (Cth) regulates the performance of forensic procedures on suspects, serious offenders and volunteers. It establishes the individuals who are authorised to conduct these, and the procedures that must be followed and the requirements that must be satisfied when carrying out a forensic procedure.

A series of general principles are laid down in relation to the conduct of forensic procedures on suspects, which are designed, as far as possible, to protect the dignity and privacy of the person undergoing the procedure.[51] The procedure should be conducted in circumstances affording reasonable privacy to the suspect; it must not be carried out in the presence or view of a person who is of the opposite sex to the suspect, and it should involve minimal removal of clothing and visual inspection of the suspect. There are further requirements:

- no questioning can occur during the forensic procedure;[52]

- the suspect must be cautioned before the forensic procedure starts;[53]

- a constable or a person authorised to carry out a forensic procedure may use reasonable force in performing forensic procedures, and all forensic procedures are to be carried out in accordance with appropriate medical or other professional standards;[54]

- forensic procedures are not to be carried out in a cruel, inhuman or degrading manner;[55]

---

49 Crimes Act 1914 (Cth), s 23XWR.

50 *Ibid*, s 23XWU(2).

51 *Ibid*, s 23XI. This will primarily consider the provisions relating to suspects within this context, as an example of the regulation of the conduct of forensic procedures under the Crimes Act 1914 (Cth).

52 *Ibid*, s 23XIA.

53 *Ibid*, s 23XIB.

54 *Ibid*, s 23XJ.

55 *Ibid*, s 23XK. See the International Covenant on Civil and Political Rights, opened for signature 16 December 1966, ATS 23, Art 7 (entered into force 23 March 1976).

- authorisation to take hair samples does not generally permit removing the root of the hair.[56]

Section 23XM contains a table that lists the persons who are authorised to carry out each forensic procedure. These groups have been chosen to ensure that proper medical or dental skill is employed. In addition, an intimate forensic procedure, other than the taking of a blood or saliva sample, a buccal swab or a dental impression, is to be carried out by a person who, where practicable, is of the same sex as the suspect.[57] The same requirement applies if the suspect is required to remove clothing, other than the specific articles of clothing listed, in the conduct of non-intimate forensic procedures.[58] A suspect is entitled to request that a medical practitioner or dentist of his or her choice be present while a forensic procedure, other than a non-intimate forensic procedure, is performed.[59] There are a number of further requirements in relation to the conduct of forensic procedures on suspects:

- a forensic procedure cannot be carried out on a child or incapable person unless an interview friend and/or legal representative is present during the procedure;[60]

- if the suspect is an Aboriginal or Torres Strait Islander, either an interview friend and/or legal representative must be present during the procedure;[61]

- the number of constables that may be present during the carrying out of a forensic procedure is limited to that which is reasonably necessary to ensure the procedure is carried out effectively and in accordance with Part 1D;[62]

- a forensic procedure (other than the taking of a hand, finger, foot or toe print) must be video recorded unless it is not practicable, or the suspect objects – if not video recorded, an independent person must be present.[63]

Division 6 also regulates conduct *after* the forensic procedure has been performed. Firstly, in relation to samples, s 23XU applies where a sample is taken from a suspect that provides enough material to be analysed both in regard to the investigation of the offence, and on behalf of the suspect.[64] This provision is limited in this way because in many cases insufficient material may be available, for example, where a flake of paint has been removed from under a suspect's fingernail or where a small blood stain is all that is found, and these samples are entirely used in the process of analysis. Under s 23XU(2), where a sufficient

---

56 See the Crimes Act 1914 (Cth), s 23XL.
57 *Ibid*, s 23XN(1).
58 *Ibid*, s 23XN(2). Also, s 23XO(1) provides that a person who is authorised to carry out a forensic procedure under the table in s 23XM is authorised to ask another person to help carry out the procedure.
59 *Ibid*, s 23XP. This provision ensures that a procedure is carried out according to professional standards by providing an outside witness.
60 *Ibid*, s 23XQ. Section 23XQ(3) provides that an interview friend may be excluded from the place where the forensic procedure is being carried out if this person unreasonably interferes with or obstructs the carrying out of the procedure.
61 *Ibid*, s 23XR.
62 *Ibid*, s 23XS.
63 *Ibid*, s 23XT.
64 *Ibid*, s 23XU(1).

sample has been obtained to enable separate analysis, the investigating constable must ensure that part of the material sufficient for analysis is given to the suspect as soon as practicable after the procedure has been carried out, and that reasonable assistance is given to ensure that the sample provided by the suspect is protected and preserved until it can be analysed. This provision aims to minimise the potential for dispute as to whether a sample has been tampered with, and to allow the suspect to arrange his or her own independent tests of the sample.

In regard to photographs, where a photograph of part of the suspect's body has been taken, a copy of the photograph must be made available to the suspect.[65] In relation to the results of analysis, s 23XW provides that if material from a sample is analysed by the police in the investigation of the offence, the investigating constable must ensure that a copy of the results of the analysis is made available to the suspect.

As to the question of destruction of forensic material after testing, Division 8 of Part 1D establishes several requirements. It provides for the destruction of forensic material where an urgent interim order is disallowed, when 12 months have elapsed since the forensic material was taken and proceedings in respect of the relevant offence have not been instituted against the suspect, or have been discontinued, or if the suspect is found to have committed a relevant offence but no conviction is recorded, or the suspect is acquitted and appeals are not lodged or dealt with.[66] A magistrate, on application by a constable or the Director of Public Prosecutions, may extend the period before forensic material must be destroyed, on one or more occasions, if satisfied that there are special reasons for doing so.[67]

Importantly, Division 8A of Part 1D establishes a DNA database system in which DNA profiles may be held. Information obtained from analysis of forensic material may be used for compiling this database for statistical purposes. The evidential value of DNA data obtained from forensic sampling depends upon the ability to compare this data to a background sample group. The more DNA records available, the more accurately the probability of two pieces of DNA having a certain number of shared characteristics can be calculated. Hence, a statistical database is necessary in order to use DNA as evidence. Division 8A stipulates rules pertaining to index matching, and establishes criminal offences for unauthorised activity in relation to forensic material and information held on the database. The Commonwealth DNA database established in line with these

---

65 Crimes Act 1914 (Cth), s 23XV.

66 *Ibid*, ss 23YC and 23YD. An exception to the requirement under s 23YD exists if an investigation into, or proceedings in respect of, another relevant offence are pending. These provisions ensure that police do not retain forensic material obtained from a person who is not found guilty of an offence, except in limited circumstances. It also aims to reduce the incentive for police to carry out a procedure on a person who is not genuinely suspected of a specific offence, because if the person is not ultimately found guilty of the offence, forensic material taken in the procedure must be destroyed.

67 *Ibid*, s 23YD(5).

provisions is the National Criminal Investigation DNA Database ('NCIDD'), and is operated by CrimTrac, an executive agency of the Commonwealth government.

Finally, of further relevance to the conduct of forensic procedures are the general provisions applicable to the operation of Part 1D:

- interpreters: when a constable intends to take a specified action[68] and believes on reasonable grounds that the suspect is unable to communicate orally with reasonable fluency in the English language, either because of inadequate knowledge of this language or because of a physical disability, then the constable must arrange for an interpreter and defer taking any action until the interpreter arrives;[69]

- powers of legal representatives and interview friends: any request or objection that may be made by a suspect or offender may be made by the suspect or offender's lawyer, and, if the suspect is a child, an incapable person or an Aboriginal or Torres Strait Islander, by the suspect or offender's interview friend;[70]

- the obligation of investigating constables relating to tape recordings: any copies of the recordings and transcripts are to be made available to the suspect, offender or volunteer;[71]

- the material required to be made available to suspects, offenders or volunteers: where material from a sample, a copy, or any other material must be given to a suspect, offender or volunteer under Part 1D, it may be sent to the suspect, offender or volunteer, or to his or her lawyer;[72]

- proof of belief or suspicion: a constable must have a belief or suspicion on reasonable grounds as to a matter referred to Part 1D, while the prosecution carries the burden to prove such on the balance of probabilities;[73]

- proof of impracticability: the burden lies on the prosecution to prove that it was not practicable to do something required by Part 1D to be done 'if practicable';[74]

- the burden to prove that time should be disregarded is placed on the prosecution[75] and, in addition, the prosecution has to prove that an Aboriginal or Torres Strait Islander voluntarily waived certain rights and did so with the full knowledge and understanding of the consequences of so doing;[76]

---

68 These are listed in s 23YDA(2) and include: asking a suspect to consent to a forensic procedure, ordering the carrying out of a non-intimate forensic procedure on a suspect who is in custody, cautioning a suspect, carrying out or arranging to carry out a forensic procedure on a suspect, and giving the suspect the opportunity to view any video taken during the process.
69 Crimes Act 1914 (Cth), s 23YDA(1).
70 *Ibid*, s 23YE.
71 *Ibid*, s 23YF.
72 *Ibid*, s 23YG.
73 *Ibid*, s 23YI.
74 *Ibid*, s 23YJ.
75 *Ibid*, s 23YJA. See ss 23 WLA(2), 23XGB(2) and 23XGD(2).
76 *Ibid*, s 23YK.

- liability for forensic procedures: persons who are properly authorised to carry out forensic procedures cannot incur criminal or civil liability where they act within the scope of the authority;[77]

- experts (ie, a medical practitioner, nurse, dentist, dental technician or other appropriately qualified person) are not obliged to carry out forensic procedures.[78]

Use of DNA evidence in criminal proceedings

Admissibility of DNA evidence

DNA evidence is admissible in criminal proceedings if it is relevant to a fact in issue and it is not barred under an exclusionary rule or by judicial discretion.[79] One instance in which DNA evidence is inadmissible is if it has been unlawfully obtained. DNA evidence is inadmissible if it has been acquired under the Crimes Act 1914 (Cth) in breach of, or due to a failure to comply with, the provisions of Part 1D with regard to the forensic procedure or the recording or use of information on the DNA database system.[80] The court has a discretion to admit the evidence, however, if satisfied on the balance of probabilities that there are matters justifying admission of the evidence despite non-compliance, or if the subject of the evidence does not object to its admission.[81] A number of matters are listed that the court may consider in determining whether admission is justified in the circumstances, including the probative value of the evidence, the reasons for the failure to comply, the gravity of the failure to comply and whether this failure was intentional or reckless.[82] If the evidence is admitted, the judge must inform the jury of any breach of, or failure to comply with, the Act's provisions, and must warn the jury about the evidence as the judge deems appropriate.[83] Conversely, evidence which must be destroyed under Part 1D of the Crimes Act 1914 (Cth) is inadmissible.[84]

In addition to the issue of DNA evidence itself, evidence of a suspect's refusal to comply with a reasonable direction for the carrying out of a forensic procedure, or evidence that the suspect obstructed, resisted, hindered, used violence against,

---

77 See the Crimes Act 1914 (Cth), s 23YL.
78 Ibid, s 23YM.
79 See ALRC (2002), [37.3].
80 Ibid, [37.73].
81 Crimes Act 1914 (Cth), s 23XX.
82 Ibid, s 23XX(5). The matters that the court must consider make this provision more onerous to discharge than the normal Bunning v Cross (1978) 141 CLR 54 discretion concerning the admission of unlawfully obtained evidence. By allowing discretionary admission, the provision recognises that some breaches may be quite trivial and that admission of evidence might be justified in the public interest. See also R v White [2005] NSWSC 60.
83 Ibid, s 23XX(7).
84 Ibid, s 23XY. This stricter admissibility provision for this class of evidence is designed to ensure that the destruction requirements are not breached in the hope that the court might exercise its discretion and allow the prosecution to admit the evidence.

threatened or intimated a person in the carrying out of the forensic procedure, is admissible. However, for such evidence to be admissible, the suspect must have been advised or otherwise knew that the above-mentioned actions by him or her could be used in evidence against him or her. Such evidence is not admissible if the forensic procedure was conducted satisfactorily.[85]

The Evidence Act 1995 (Cth) also regulates the admissibility of unlawfully obtained DNA evidence. Under this Act, which governs the admissibility of evidence generally, the court is required, for instance, to exclude evidence led by the prosecution if the danger of unfair prejudice to the defendant outweighs its probative value,[86] or if the evidence has been unlawfully or improperly obtained, unless the desirability of admitting this evidence outweighs the undesirability of admitting evidence acquired in such a manner.[87]

The ALRC observes that at present, disputes over DNA evidence in criminal proceedings largely relate to the integrity of DNA evidence, the ability of juries to understand such evidence, and statistical interpretation of DNA evidence. Regarding the issue of the integrity of DNA evidence, a recent Victorian case, *R v Juric*,[88] emphasised the difficulties in making accurate statistical calculations based on poor quality DNA samples, due to factors such as the age of the sample, the mixing of the sample with the bodily fluids of others, and the poverty of the sample. Related to this, the integrity of DNA evidence may be further lessened by contamination of the evidence with other human DNA at the crime scene – for instance, the nature of the crime may have produced a mixture of fluids and tissues from different individuals – or at the stage of laboratory analysis.[89]

In relation to the further issue of statistical interpretation, the ALRC importantly notes that a match between DNA evidence acquired from a crime scene and the defendant's DNA profile does not conclusively prove that the defendant is guilty of the offence. Such a match may, on the contrary, be due to the sample being innocently left at the crime scene; error or tampering with the sample; or the sample originating from a close relative of the defendant.[90] Furthermore, the evidential value of a match must be carefully evaluated, given that there are various ways of calculating the statistical probability of a match: as Evett highlights, there is no 'real' statistical probability to be assigned to a DNA profile, with the match probability in each case 'personal' to the forensic scientist.[91]

---

85 Crimes Act 1914 (Cth), ss 23YB(2), 23YB(4), 23YB(3) respectively.
86 Evidence Act 1995 (Cth), s 137.
87 *Ibid*, s 138. See also ALRC (2002), [37.75]–[37.77].
88 Unreported, Supreme Court of Victoria, Court of Appeal, Winneke P; Charles and Chernov JJA, 29 May 2002. See also ALRC (2002), [37.11]–[37.13].
89 ALRC (2002), [37.14]–[37.16].
90 *Ibid*, [37.22]–[37.28].
91 See Evett (2000).

As to the question of jury understanding of DNA evidence, the ALRC proposes that the Evidence Act 1995 (Cth) should include a standard jury direction for use in cases where DNA evidence is admitted, requiring that trial judges should provide juries with a specific warning regarding the need for caution in evaluating DNA evidence and the statistical calculations arising from this evidence.[92] Moreover, in light of the importance of comprehension of DNA science and technology within the legal profession, including the judiciary, the ALRC proposes that the National Judicial College of Australia, the Law Council of Australia and the National Institute of Forensic Science should continue to provide education to the profession in relation to DNA evidence.[93]

A final issue regarding the admissibility of DNA evidence is the lack of opportunity afforded to defence counsel to access DNA evidence relied on by the prosecution. The ALRC inquiry notes that there is no federal legislative requirement upon the prosecution to provide all or part of a crime scene sample to the defendant.[94] On the contrary, where a DNA sample is taken from an individual under Part 1D of the Crimes Act 1914, the Australian Federal Police must ensure that part of this material is made available to the individual as soon as practicable.[95] In addition, if this material is analysed in the investigation of the offence, the Australian Federal Police must make the results of this analysis available to the individual.[96]

The potential lack of access to crime scene samples by defence counsel could lead to a unfair trial for the defendant, given that, under such circumstances, defence counsel does not have an opportunity to obtain independent analysis of the DNA evidence, or, in turn, effectively evaluate the probative value of this evidence and cross-examine the prosecution's expert witness.[97] Accordingly, the ALRC has proposed that similar legislative requirements to those imposed upon the Australian Federal Police should apply in relation to crime scene samples; that is, the prosecution should have a duty to provide defendants with reasonable pre-trial notice of DNA samples collected at crime scenes to enable independent analysis of such by defendants.[98]

---

92 ALRC (2002), proposal 37–2.
93 *Ibid*, proposals 37–1 and 37–3.
94 *Ibid*, [37.65].
95 Crimes Act 1914 (Cth), s 23XU.
96 *Ibid*, s 23XW.
97 See ALRC (2002), [37.65]–[37.70].
98 *Ibid*, proposal 37–4.

Interaction of Commonwealth, State and Territory legislation

Perhaps the principal issue in relation to DNA testing and the criminal law within Australia at present is the need for harmonisation of forensic procedures legislation. The recent ALRC inquiry into the law and practices pertaining to human genetic information reviewed the use of such information within the context of law enforcement, with its primary proposal in this area being the harmonisation of forensic procedures legislation throughout Australia. The inquiry observes that the Model Bill has been closely followed in New South Wales and the Australian Capital Territory, while the relevant legislation of Victoria, Tasmania, South Australia and Western Australia contains greater variations. The Model Bill has not been followed at all in the Northern Territory and Queensland.[99] Consequently, the ALRC notes that jurisdictional differences exist, for example, in relation to definitions of non-intimate and intimate procedures, and suspects, offenders and volunteers. For instance, a buccal swab is classed as an intimate forensic procedure under the Model Bill, which is followed in the Commonwealth, South Australian and Victorian legislation, yet it is defined as non-intimate in the Australian Capital Territory, Tasmania, the Northern Territory and Western Australia. Under the New South Wales legislation, buccal swabs are defined separately from intimate and non-intimate procedures, while Queensland does not make a distinction between intimate and non-intimate forensic procedures at all.[100] There are also variations regarding the performance of forensic procedures on children. For example, under the Tasmanian Act, children 15 years and over may consent to a forensic procedure, children aged 10 to 14 years can consent to such with their parent, and no provision is made for a lawyer or interview friend to be present when a forensic procedure is carried out on a child.

The ALRC maintains that harmonisation of forensic procedures legislation throughout Australia is necessary given that, in providing for a DNA database, the Crimes Act 1914 (Cth), under Division 11 of Part 1D, permits the sharing of information held on the DNA database between participating jurisdictions, ie, those jurisdictions in which there is forensic procedure and DNA database legislation in force which substantially corresponds to Part 1D of the Crimes Act 1914 (Cth) or is prescribed in regulations under the Crimes Act. Given the current lack of harmonisation, the ALRC argues that inter-jurisdictional matching by CrimTrac will be complex to administer due to legislative variations, while the transferring of samples or profiles from one jurisdiction with solid privacy and

---

99 The respective legislation for the States and Territories is as follows: Crimes (Forensic Procedures) Act 2000 (NSW); Crimes (Forensic Procedures) Act 2000 (ACT); Crimes Act 1958 (Vic), including as amended by the Crimes (DNA Database) Act 2002 (Vic); Forensic Procedures Act 2000 (Tas); Criminal Law (Forensic Procedures) Act 1998 (SA); Criminal Investigation (Identifying People) Act 2002 (WA); Police Administration Act 1978 (NT); Police Powers and Responsibilities Act 2000 (Qld).

100 ALRC (2002), [35.4]–[35.5].

civil liberties requirements to another jurisdiction with lesser protections could undermine the safeguards provided for in the first jurisdiction.[101] Specifically, in this regard, the ALRC proposes that harmonisation is particularly necessary in relation to the collection, use, storage, destruction and index matching of forensic material and DNA profiles.[102]

Finally, in a recent move, Division 11 of Part 1D, providing for inter-jurisdictional enforcement, was amended as a result of the bombings in Bali on 12 October 2003. The new Division 11A extends the operation of Division 8 dealing with the DNA database system, allowing greater access to information stored on the database, disclosure of such information and matching of DNA profiles if for the purpose of identifying a person who died in or as a result of the bombings in Bali, or for conducting criminal investigations in relation to the bombings. This Division also extends to such activities with regard to incidents occurring outside Australia which the minister determines 'to be an incident to which this Division applies'.[103] This recent development highlights the increasing centrality of DNA evidence to criminal investigations and, correspondingly, the pressing need for true uniformity of forensic procedures legislation in Australia.

Law is stated current to May 2005.

References

Australian Law Reform Commission (ALRC) (2002) *Protection of Human Genetic Information*, Discussion Paper 66

Burk, D (1998) 'DNA fingerprinting: possibilities and pitfalls of the new technique' Jurimetrics Journal 455

Dodd, B (1985) 'DNA fingerprinting in matters of family and crime' 318 Nature 506–07

Evett, IW (2000) 'DNA profiling: a discussion of issues relating to the reporting of very small match probabilities' Crim LR 341

Freckelton, I (1989) 'DNA profiling: optimism and realism' 63 Law Institute Journal 360

Horton, G (1992) 'DNA fingerprinting: informed consent and admissibility and the admissibility of evidence' 7 Auckland Law Review 165

---

101 *Ibid*, [35.21]–[35.22].
102 *Ibid*, proposal 35–1.
103 Crimes Act 1914 (Cth), ss 23YUE–23YUI.

McLeod, N (1991) 'Legal impediments to national DNA data bank' 23 Australian Journal of Forensic Sciences 21

Phillips, Justice John (1988) 'Genetic fingerprinting' 62 Australian Law Journal 550

Phillips, Justice John (1996) 'American tragedy – part 2' 70 Australian Law Journal 798

Scutt, J (1989) 'Individual rights "prickly questions"' *Australian Law News,* 24 September

Scutt, J (1990) 'Beware of new technologies' 15 Legal Service Bulletin 9

Scutt, J (1990a) 'DNA fingerprints – black box or black hole?' 140 New Law Journal 203

White, R and Green, J (1988) 'DNA fingerprinting and the law' 51 Modern Law Review 149

CHAPTER 4

CANADA: LES TESTS GÉNÉTIQUES EN DROIT CRIMINEL CANADIEN[1]

L'honorable Jean-Louis Baudouin
Juge à la Cour d'appel du Québec

L'analyse de l'ADN est un procédé scientifique qui a trouvé sa place comme élément de preuve devant les instances judiciaires en matière criminelle depuis 1988.[2] Toutefois, ce n'est qu'en 1995 que le Parlement canadien a légiféré pour définir le cadre légal applicable à l'administration et au prélèvement de substances corporelles à des fins d'analyse génétique.[3] Jusqu'alors, aucune disposition du Code criminel (C. cr.) canadien ne permettait aux agents de la paix de prélever des substances corporelles pour fins d'analyse génétique, sans le consentement de la personne visée. En outre, aucun texte de loi ne spécifiait l'utilisation qui pouvait en être faite. Ces nouveaux ajouts au Code criminel

---

1   Tout récemment, soit le 25 septembre 1997, le Parlement fédéral adoptait en première lecture le projet de loi C-3, intitulé Loi sur l'identification par les empreintes génétiques, qui prévoit l'établissement d'une banque nationale de données ainsi que la création d'ordonnances autorisant le prélèvement de substances corporelles afin d'établir des profils d'identification génétiques destinés à cette banque. Le projet prévoit également le prélèvement sur certaines catégories de contrevenants qui purgent actuellement des peines. Il contient également des dispositions régissant l'utilisation des substances prélevées, des profils d'identification génétique établis à partir de celles-ci et de l'information contenue dans la banque de même que la communication et l'accès qui y est donné.

2   La première cause canadienne en droit criminel où une preuve génétique a été déposée est l'affaire *R c Parent* (1988) 46 CCC (3d) 414 (Alta QB). La technique d'analyse employée dans cette cause était la technique PCR. La première cause où la technique RFLP a été utilisée est l'affaire *R c McNally*, 4 avril 1989 (Ont Dist Ct). Jusqu'à 1996, plus d'un millier de procès ont admis la preuve d'ADN. Voir la déclaration du Ministre de la justice à cet époque, l'honorable Allan Rock, rapportée dans *R c Stillman* [1997] 1 RCS 607, 687.

3   Le Parlement canadien adoptait le 22 juin 1995 le projet de loi C-104, intitulé Loi modifiant le Code criminel et la Loi sur les jeunes contrevenants (analyse génétique à des fins médico-légales) devenu par la suite LC 1995, c 27. Cette loi a été sanctionnée le 13 juillet 1995. Par conséquent, en raison de son caractère très récent, il existe peu de décisions de nos tribunaux sur l'interprétation de ces nouvelles dispositions. Il faut signaler qu'en vertu de l'article 91(27) de la Loi constitutionnelle de 1867, il appartient exclusivement au Parlement fédéral de légiférer en matière criminelle, les différentes provinces canadiennes n'ayant aucune compétence législative en matière criminelle.

étaient donc devenus nécessaires.[4] Confronté aux nombreuses implications et difficultés que soulevait l'analyse génétique, il appartenait au Parlement canadien de définir un cadre légal approprié en matière de prélèvement de substances corporelles pour fins d'analyse génétique lors de procès criminels.[5]

Le Code criminel définit maintenant la procédure que doivent respecter les agents de la paix pour obtenir, en l'absence de consentement de la personne visée, les échantillons nécessaires pour une analyse de l'ADN à des fins médico-légales et de comparaison. En outre, le Parlement a également adopté certaines dispositions touchant l'utilisation qui peut être faite des substances ainsi prélevées, de même que des résultats obtenus à partir de leur analyse. La loi fixe aussi le moment de leur destruction. D'une manière générale, les récents amendements apportés par l'adoption du Projet de loi C-104 constituent la première étape d'une série de mesures destinées à encadrer l'utilisation de la technique scientifique de l'analyse de l'ADN en matière criminelle.[6] Comme le soulignent les tribunaux canadiens, il s'agit de dispositions qui touchent uniquement la procédure et non le droit substantif.[7]

Il est évident que ces nouvelles dispositions feront l'objet de contestations au regard de certaines dispositions de la Charte canadienne des droits et libertés. Il est toujours possible que certaines d'entre elles soient donc modifiées judiciairement pour les rendre conformes aux préceptes de la Charte canadienne. Il n'en demeure pas moins que, pour le moment, ces nouvelles dispositions

---

4 Avant l'adoption de ces dispositions, aucun article du Code criminel ne permettait le prélèvement de substances corporelles à des fins d'analyse génétique sans l'obtention préalable du consentement de la personne visée. La Charte canadienne empêchait clairement le prélèvement d'une substance corporelle sans le consentement de la personne: *R c Borden* [1994] 3 RCS 145. L'intervention du Parlement fédéral était donc nécessaire pour légaliser et autoriser ce pouvoir exceptionnel. Voir l'opinion de la majorité des juges de la Cour suprême dans l'affaire *R c Stillman* [1997] 1 RCS 607, 633. Même le pouvoir de saisie et de perquisition de la common law applicable en matière criminelle ne permettait pas le prélèvement de substances corporelles pour fins d'analyse génétique: *ibid*, p 640. L'absence de pouvoir légaux pour autoriser les prélèvements explique la faible utilisation des preuves d'ADN en matière criminelle: voir Chayko, Gulliver and MacDougall (1991), p 349.

5 Le Parlement s'est largement inspiré d'un rapport du ministère de la justice intitulé, 'Collecte et entreposage des preuves médico-légales à caractères génétiques' de 1994, pour définir le cadre légal approprié.

6 Le 10 avril 1997, le Parlement adoptait en première lecture le Projet de loi C-94 intitulé Loi concernant l'identification par les empreintes génétiques et modifiant le Code criminel et d'autres lois en conséquence qui établissait une banque nationale de données et régissait l'utilisation des substances corporelles prélevées, les profils d'identification génétique et l'information contenue dans la banque, de même que la communication des informations et de son accès. Ce Projet de loi faisait suite aux nouvelles dispositions adoptées en 1995. Cependant, en raison de déclenchement des élections au niveau fédéral dans les semaines suivantes, le Projet de loi ne fut jamais adopté par le Parlement.

7 *R c Tremblay* [1996] RJQ 187 (CQ) et *R c Good* (1996) 29 WCB (2d) 329.

modifient de manière très importante l'état actuel du droit criminel en matière d'analyse génétique et de prélèvement de substances corporelles.[8]

La délivrance du mandat de saisie

L'article 487.05 du C. cr. fixe les conditions que doit respecter un agent de la paix pour obtenir d'un juge de la Cour provinciale un mandat l'autorisant à prélever un échantillon de substance corporelle.[9] La gravité de l'atteinte à l'intégrité de la personne justifie que la loi accorde au juge de la Cour provinciale un large pouvoir d'appréciation sur la délivrance du mandat.[10] La nature envahissante du prélèvement effectué imposait selon le Parlement canadien une telle approche.[11]

Suite à une dénonciation sous serment,[12] un juge de la Cour provinciale peut émettre un mandat aux conditions suivantes. Il doit, en premier lieu, se satisfaire qu'il existe des motifs raisonnables de croire:

(1) qu'une infraction désignée a été perpétrée. Le mandat peut être délivré seulement s'il y a eu commission de certaines infractions définies à l'article 487.04 C. cr. et susceptibles d'engendrer de la violence ou des blessures sérieuses.[13] Dans ce cas, l'intérêt de la société à la découverte de la vérité l'emporte sur le droit à la vie privée ou à l'intégrité de la personne;[14]

---

8   Bassan (1996) conteste la constitutionnalité du Projet de loi adopté par le Parlement. Selon lui, ces nouvelles dispositions porteraient atteinte aux droits garantis par la Charte canadienne et ne seraient pas justifiées par l'article premier de la Charte. Cependant, les tribunaux ne semblent pas partager cette opinion.
    Dans *R c Brighteyes* (1997) 34 WCB (2d) 328, le juge Murray du Banc de la Reine de l'Alberta a jugé que les nouvelles dispositions violaient le droit à la vie, à la liberté et à la sécurité protégé par l'article 7 de la Charte, mais que cette atteinte était justifiée par l'article premier. Par contre, la majorité des juges de la Cour suprême a affirmé, en *obiter dictum*, que ces nouvelles mesures législatives semblent satisfaire à toutes les exigences constitutionnelles, sans besoin de recourir à l'article premier de la Charte canadienne: *R c Stillman* [1997] 1 RCS 607, 660. Il faut noter qu'il ne s'agit que d'une opinion de la Cour et que la constitutionnalité de ces dispositions n'était aucunement contestée dans cette affaire.

9   Suivant l'article 487 C. cr. qui définit le régime général applicable au mandat de perquisition et l'article 256 C. cr. qui autorise la délivrance d'un mandat pour un prélèvement sanguin lorsqu'une personne a conduit avec les facultés affaiblies, un juge de paix a compétence pour délivrer de tels mandats. Cependant, en matière d'analyse génétique, seul un juge d'une Cour provinciale a compétence pour délivrer un mandat autorisant le prélèvement d'un échantillon d'une substance corporelle. Voir l'article 487.05 C. cr.

10 Si un accusé entend contester la partialité du juge lors de cette procédure, le fardeau de la preuve lui incombe: *R c Beamish* (1997) 32 WCB (2d) 200 (Trial Div PEISC).

11 L'article 487.06(1) C. cr. autorise le prélèvement de cheveux ou de poils comportant la gaine épithéliale, de cellules épithéliales par écouvillage des lèvres, de la langue ou de l'intérieur des joues, ainsi qu'un prélèvement sanguin. En raison de sa rédaction, il est permis de croire que le législateur n'autorise qu'un seul prélèvement par mandat de saisie.

12 Le paragraphe (3) de l'article 487.05 C. cr. permet la transmission d'une dénonciation par téléphone ou autre moyen de télécommunication, conformément aux dispositions pertinentes contenues au Code criminel.

13 Voir *R c Jobb* (1997) 34 WCB (2d) 521 (Sask QB) sur la suffisance des motifs.

14 Voir Pomerance (1995), à 226. De plus, comme l'ajoute l'auteur, il s'agit d'infractions qui sont susceptibles, lorsqu'elles sont commises, de permettre aux agents de la paix de prélever des échantillons de substances corporelles sur la scène du crime.

(2) qu'une substance corporelle a été trouvée sur les lieux du crime, sur la victime ou à l'intérieur de celle-ci, sur ce qu'elle portait ou transportait, sur une personne ou à l'intérieur d'une personne, d'une chose ou en des lieux liés à la perpétration de l'infraction. Cette restriction était nécessaire. Il est, en effet, inutile de procéder à une analyse génétique, s'il est impossible de procéder à une comparaison d'ADN;[15]

(3) que la personne a participé à l'infraction. Même si certaines dispositions du Code criminel définissent la notion de participation,[16] il faut interpréter ce texte en relation avec l'alinéa (d) de l'article. La notion de participation ne doit s'entendre ici que dans la mesure où l'alinéa (b) peut s'appliquer. En d'autres termes, une substance corporelle trouvée sur les lieux de l'infraction doit être susceptible d'appartenir à la personne visée par le mandat;

(4) que l'analyse génétique de la substance corporelle prélevée apportera des preuves selon lesquelles la substance corporelle visée à l'alinéa (b) provient ou non de cette personne. Cet alinéa exige un lien potentiel de probabilité et de pertinence entre l'analyse d'ADN de la substance corporelle trouvée selon l;alinéa (b) et l'analyse de l'ADN de l'échantillon prélevé sur la personne visée à l, alinéa (c).

Il doit, en second lieu, être convaincu que la délivrance du mandat serevirait au mieux l'administration de la justice. Le juge doit donc soupeser deux valeurs contradictoires. Il doit déterminer si le respect de la vie privée ou de l'intégrité de la personne doit l'emporter sur la recherche de la vérité que tend à protéger cette nouvelle procédure de perquisition. La délivrance d'un mandat qui aurait comme conséquence évidente la déconsidération de l'administration de la justice justifierait un refus. Le contenu de la dénonciation doit convaincre le juge que l'administration de la justice ne sera pas déconsidérée:

> The satisfaction of the issuing judge that there are reasonable grounds to believe in the existence of all those criteria does not, however, end the matter as it might with an ordinary search warrant. Additionally, the judge must be satisfied that the issuance of the warrant is in the best interests of the administration of justice.
>
> Presumably, the information must contain sufficient material to satisfy the judge on this point no less than the other criteria, since the issuing judge may not look outside the four corners of the sworn information.[17]

---

15 La substance corporelle trouvée doit nécessairement permettre l'analyse de l'ADN.

16 Voir les articles pertinents du Code criminel qui définissent la notion de participation. Il serait étonnant que cette notion s'entende comme, par exemple, le fait d'avoir conseillé une autre personne de commettre une infraction au sens de l'article 22 C. cr.

17 Voir Fontana (1997), p 249.

En troisième lieu, outre ces deux premiers éléments, le législateur a expressément prévu deux autres impératifs. Ceux-ci ne sont pas exhaustifs.[18] Le paragraphe (2) de l'article 487.05 C. cr. prévoit ceux-ci:

(1) la nature de l'infraction et des circonstances de sa perpétration. Cet élément s'apparente beaucoup à l'appréciation que doit faire le juge lorsqu'il examine si la délivrance du mandat déconsidère l'administration de la justice. L'insistance du législateur démontre toute l'importance que doit accorder le juge;

(2) la possibilité d'avoir une personne qui, de par sa formation ou son expérience, peut effectuer le prélèvement. Cette exigence a pour but évident de voir à ce que l'échantillon prélevé soit utilisable et que la méthode utilisée respecte l'intégrité de la personne.[19]

Comme nous pouvons le constater, le juge jouit donc d'un large pouvoir d'appréciation pour la délivrance d'un mandat de saisie. Reconnaissant la démarche très particulière de ce pouvoir, le Parlement a jugé que cette approche était nécessaire pour assurer un plus grand respect de la vie privée. Ce pouvoir d'appréciation assure à la personne visée par le mandat de saisie une atteinte beaucoup moins importante à sa vie privée. Le respect de la vie privée est donc au coeur même de la procédure de délivrance du mandat de saisie.[20]

L'exécution du mandat de saisie

L'exécution du mandat de saisie d'un échantillon d'une substance corporelle peut survenir à différentes périodes. La loi ne précise pas, en effet, le moment où elle doit être effectuée. Le prélèvement peut donc être fait pendant l'enquête policière, lors de la comparution de l'individu ou lors de son procès. La seule précision que fournit la loi sur le moment de la prise d'échantillon découle de l'article 487.05 C. cr. Le prélèvement ne peut avoir lieu avant qu'une enquête sur une infraction désignée ne soit en cours et qu'il soit possible à ce moment là de satisfaire aux

---

18 L'utilisation du terme 'notamment' montre que ces éléments ne sont pas exhaustifs. Dans *R c Brighteyes* (1997) 34 WCB (2d) 328, le juge Murray soulignait que le fait pour la police de détenir déjà un échantillon de substance corporelle provenant de la personne visée, constitue un élément dont le juge de la Cour provinciale peut tenir compte lors de l'émission du mandat de saisie selon l'article 487.05 C. cr.

19 Voir Pomerance (1995), à 231. D'ailleurs, l'article 487.07(3) C. cr impose à la personne qui procède au prélèvement d'exécuter son mandat dans des conditions qui respectent autant que faire se peut la vie privée de la personne visée. La loi lui impose un tel devoir. Dans *R c B (mF)* (1996) 31 WCB (2d) 381, la Cour du Banc de la Reine de la Saskatchewan estime que la dénonciation ne doit pas nécessairement indiquer le nom de la personne qui va exécuter le prélèvement, ni tous les détails de son expérience ou de son entraînement.

20 Dans *R c W (DD)* (1997) 114 CCC (3d) 506, c'est avec raison que la Cour d'appel de la Colombie Britannique a émis l'opinion que la procédure prescrite par les articles 487.04 et suivants ne permettait pas la délivrance d'un mandat de saisie pour prélever un échantillon de substance corporelle sur une personne accusée d'avoir eu une relation avec sa soeur, afin de comparer son ADN avec celui de l'enfant qui serait issu de cette relation incestueuse. La Cour a jugé que les dispositions du Code ne s'appliquaient pas dans ce cas. La Cour semble baser son opinion sur la déconsidération de l'administration de la justice. Pour ma part, en accord avec la majorité de la Cour, je crois également que les conditions d'application de l'alinéa (b) de l'article 487.05 C. cr n'étaient pas remplies.

autres exigences de la loi. Il n'est donc pas nécessaire que des accusations formelles aient été portées contre l'individu pour justifier l'émission et l'exécution du mandat.

Le législateur s'est également assuré que le déroulement de la procédure de saisie puisse se faire dans le plus grand respecet de la vie privée de l'individu. D'une part, le législateur a accordé au juge qui émet le mandat de saisie le pouvoir d'énoncer certaines modalités propres à assurer une exécution qui soit raisonnable dans les circonstances. Il appartient donc au juge, tenant compte des circonstances particulières de l'affaire, de fixer les modalités d'exécution permettant d'assurer une saisie raisonnable dans les.[21] D'autre part, la loi oblige l'agent de la paix ou la personne qui procède au prélèvement à suivre une procédure spécifique. Il ne s'agit plus ici du respect de modalités qui peuvent varier d'un cas à l'autre, mais d'exigences péremptoires qui s'imposent à chaque cas. Ces exigences sont les suivantes:

> En premier lieu, l'agent de la paix doit informer la personne intéressée de la teneur du mandat de saisie, de la nature du prélèvement autorisé par le juge, du but du prélèvement, de la possibilité que les résultats de l'analyse génétique soient présentés en preuve et de son pouvoir ou de celui de la personne agissant sous son autorité d'employer la force nécessaire pour exécuter le mandat.[22] De plus, s'il s'agit d'un adolescent au sens de l'article 2(1) de la Loi sur les jeunes contrevenants, l'agent de paix doit permettre à ce dernier de consulter un avocat, son père, sa mère, un parent adulte ou un adulte idoine. L'adolescent peut de plus exiger que le mandat soit exécuté en présence de la personne choisie.[23]

En second lieu, l'agent de la paix ou la personne agissant sous son autorité qui procède au prélèvement doit veiller à ce que le mandat soit exécuté dans des conditions qui respectent le plus possible la vie privée de l'intéressé.[24]

L'agent de la paix possède cependant les pouvoirs de contrainte nécessaires pour accomplir son travail. Il peut mettre en détention la personne visée par le mandat pour la période justifiée par les circonstances. Il peut aussi contraindre celle-ci à l'accompagner.[25] Dans ce cas, l'agent de la paix doit l'informer de son

---

21 Article 487.06(2) C. cr. Comme le souligne RM Pomerance (1995), à 235, ces modalités peuvent varier de manière considérable d'un cas à l'autre.

22 Article 487.07(1) C. cr. Même si ce paragraphe n'oblige pas l'agent de la paix à informer la personne visée de son droit à l'avocat s'il y a détention conformément au paragraphe (2) de cette même disposition, l'article (10b) de la Charte canadienne pourrait néanmoins obliger l'agent de paix à le faire. Voir *R c Bartle* [1994] 3 RCS 173.

23 Article 487.07(1) C. cr. Selon le paragraphe (5) de cet article, un adolescent peut renoncer au droit que lui accorde le paragraphe (4). Cependant, ce renoncement pour être valable doit satisfaire aux exigences procédurales du paragraphe (5). Le paragraphe (4) de cet article devra être interprété à la lumière de l'arrêt *R c I(LR) et T(E)* [1993] 4 RCS 504, 518, où la Cour suprême a décidé que l'article (10b) de la Charte canadienne qui assure le droit à l'avocat, implique qu'en aucun cas le père ou la mère ne peuvent remplacer l'avocat. Malgré la rédaction du paragraphe (4), la Charte oblige à conclure que l'adolescent peut exiger et la présence d'un avocat et la présence d'un parent, sauf renonciation express. Inversement, la présence d'un avocat ne doit pas empêcher la présence d'un parent: *R c S (JL)* (1995) 97 CCC (3d) 20.

24 Article 487.07(3) C. cr.

25 Article 487.07(2) C. cr.

droit à l'avocat.[26] Finalement, l'agent de la paix peut utiliser la force nécessaire pour exécuter son mandat de saisie.[27]

L'analyse génétique de l'échantillon

Les nouvelles modifications au Code criminel ne précisent pas qui sont les personnes autorisées à effectuer les analyses d'ADN, ni à quels endroits ces examens doivent se faire, ni les techniques qui doivent être utilisées. La loi accorde donc une discrétion absolue sur le choix du laboratoire, de la technique utilisée et du personnel.[28] Les seules restrictions importantes concernent l'utilisation qui peut être faite des échantillons prélevés et des résultats obtenus à partir de ceux-ci.

Selon le paragraphe (1) de l'article 487.08 C. cr., l'échantillon corporel ne peut être prélevé que dans le cadre d'une enquête relative à l'infraction désignée dans le mandat de saisie. Ce paragraphe limite donc l'objet du prélèvement corporel visé.

Selon les termes du paragraphe 487.08(2) C. cr., les résultats de l'analyse ne peuvent être utilisés que pour l'enquête relative à l'infraction désignée ou à une autre infraction désignée dans un autre mandat. Les résultats peuvent également être utilisés lorsqu'une substance corporelle a été trouvée dans les circonstances visées à l'alinéa 487.05(1)(b) ou dans le cadre de toute procédure y afférente. Le texte limite donc fortement l'objet de l'utilisation des résultats génétiques obtenus et semble interdire toute possibilité de comparaison des résultats obtenus avec ceux obtenus lors d'une enquête subséquente ou antérieure, comme c'est, au contraire, le cas en matière d'empreintes de mains, de doigts ou de pieds.[29]

Quiconque contrevient aux paragraphes (1) et (2) de l'article 487.08 C. cr. est coupable d'une infraction punissable sur déclaration de culpabilité par procédure sommaire. Le législateur a donc voulu montrer sa ferme volonté de limiter l'utilisation des échantillons corporels et des résultats découlant des tests génétiques.

---

26 Au-dessus, note 17.

27 Article 487.07(1)e) C. cr.

28 Le rapport du Ministère de la justice recommandait une intervention législative pour baliser, dès maintenant, les conditions d'habilitation ou d'octroi de permis de laboratoire. Le rapport recommandait également de définir le système qui devait être retenu. Voir: collecte et entreposage des preuves médico-légales à caractères génétiques, Ministère de la justice, 1994, p 14. Il existe au Canada cinq laboratoires publics (Laboratoire de la GRC à Ottawa, le Center Forensic Science à Toronto, la Direction des expertises judiciaires à Montréal et une filiale de la GRC à Edmonton et Halifax) et un laboratoire privé (Hélix Biotech) qui peuvent faire ces analyses génétiques.

29 Voir Pomerance (1995), à 237. Il faut remarquer cependant que le Projet de loi C-94 modifiait l'article 487.08 C. cr. afin d'élargir l'utilisation des résultats génétiques obtenus, en créant une banque nationale de données. La comparaison des résultats jusqu'à maintenant prohibée serait devenue légale avec l'adoption du Projet de loi.

La divulgation des tests d'ADN et le droit à une défense pleine et entière

Dans le système canadien, le droit de l'accusé à une défense pleine et entière est un principe constitutionnalisé à l'article 7 de la Charte canadienne.[30] La Couronne doit donc divulguer ou communiquer sa preuve à la défense avant que l'accusé ne soit appelé à choisir son mode de procès ou à présenter son plaidoyer. C'est un droit constitutionnel d'application générale qui ne souffre que de rares exceptions.[31] De plus, la règle de la divulgation de la preuve s'impose peu importe si celle-ci inculpe ou disculpe l'accusé. Comme l'écrivait la Cour suprême dans l'affaire Stinchcombe:

> Doivent être divulgués non seulement les renseignements que le ministère entend produire en preuve, mais aussi ceux qu'il n'a pas l'intention de produire. Aucune distinction ne doit être faite entre preuve inculpatoire et preuve disculpatoire.[32]

En raison donc de l'interprétation donnée à l'article 7 de la Charte, si la Couronne entend déposer au procès les résultats de tests génétiques pour démontrer la culpabilité de l'accusé, elle devra nécessairement transmettre ou communiquer les résultats de l'analyse à la défense. La pertinence et la valeur probante d'une preuve d'ADN lors d'un procès criminel militent fortement pour l'application stricte de cette règle,[33] même si le résultat est disculpatoire.

Ce droit à une défense pleine et entière emporte-t-il également le droit de faire sa propre analyse des échantillons corporels retrouvés? Que se passe-t-il si la quantité de l'échantillon retrouvé sur la scène du crime ne permet pas à la défense de faire une contre-expertise? L'impossibilité d'effectuer sa propre analyse constitue-t-il alors une violation ou une atteinte à l'article 7 de la Charte canadienne? Aucune décision n'a encore véritablement tranché le débat.[34] Cependant, en raison de la position prise par la Cour suprême dans l'affaire *Egger*, il paraît peu probable que la Cour élève le droit à la contre-expertise en matière d'analyse génétique en principe absolu.[35] Si, donc, un droit à la contre-expertise

---

30   Article 7: chacun a droit à la vie, à la liberté et à la sécurité de sa personne; il ne peut être porté atteinte à ce droit qu'en conformité avec les principes de justice fondamentale.

31   *R c Stinchcombe* [1991] 3 RCS 326, 327. Comme le reconnaît la Cour suprême, le principe de divulgation n'est cependant pas absolu. Le procureur de la Couronne possède le pouvoir discrétionnaire de refuser de divulguer certains éléments ou documents lorsque, par exemple, ce dévoilement peut mettre en péril la poursuite de l'enquête ou permettre l'identification des délateurs ou des informateurs: *ibid*, p 339.

32   *Ibid*, p 343.

33   Il est inutile de rappeler l'importance d'une preuve d'analyse génétique pour établir l'innocence ou la culpabilité de l'accusé. Voir, entre autres, *R c Guy Paul Morin* (1995) 37 CR (4th) 395 (CA Ont), où l'appelant a été innocenté à la suite d'un deuxième procès, lorsqu'une preuve d'analyse génétique a été déposée.

34   Lorsque la quantité des échantillons corporels retrouvés permet une seconde analyse génétique, la défense peut, par requête, conformément à l'article 605 C. cr., demander la communication des substances pour effectuer sa propre analyse. Selon la quantité des échantillons disponibles, le tribunal peut alors obliger la communication des échantillons et émettre différentes conditions afin d'assurer la protection de celles-ci. Voir *R c Call* [1996] RJQ 1193 (CS).

35   Dans l'arrêt *R c Egger* [1993] 2 RCS 451, 468, la Cour suprême écrivait que le droit d'obtenir un échantillon est un droit important. Cependant, il faut analyser ce principe en regard de la disposition litigieuse dans cette affaire qui consacrait expressément le droit d'obtenir un échantillon afin de faire sa propre analyse sanguine (Article 258(1)(d)(i) C. cr.).

existe pour la défense lorsque les échantillons retrouvés permettent une seconde analyse,[36] ce droit semble ne pas s'appliquer lorsqu'une analyse indépendante s'avère impossible en raison de la grosseur ou de la quantité de la substance corporelle disponible.[37] Si la Couronne peut expliquer valablement les motifs l'empêchant de transmettre les substances demandées, le droit à la contre-expertise peut ne pas s'appliquer dans ce cas.[38] Il en irait sutrement en cas de destruction délibérée de l'échantillon disponible, afin d'empêcher toute contre-expertise.[39]

L'utilisation des tests d'ADN durant le procès criminel

Comme le soulignait Grimaud, dans une étude datée de 1994 portant sur la recevabilité d'une preuve d'identification par ADN:

> En règle générale, la qualité des résultats des analyses génétiques fait l'objet de peu de questionnement de la part des scientifiques et de la police. Cependant, on remarque que la preuve ainsi obtenue est encore scrutée devant la justice. En effet, la preuve d'identification d'ADN, à cause de sa récente apparition, fait partie de cette catégorie de preuves scientifiques qui, au Canada, n'ont pas encore obtenu de critères d'admissibilité; aussi en l'absence de standards, il importe de nous interroger sur les critères adéquats de sa recevabilité comme preuve devant nos tribunaux.[40]

La situation qui prévalait alors au Canada a changé quelque peu durant cette même année. La Cour suprême est, en effet, venue définir sommairement dans l'affaire *R c Mohan* les critères d'utilisation d'une nouvelle technique scientifique comme élément de preuve devant les tribunaux.[41] Se référant sans toutefois le

---

36   Article 605 C. cr. D'ailleurs, selon l'arrêt *Egger*, il semble que la Couronne a le devoir d'informer la défense qu'elle peut procéder à une telle analyse. *R c Egger* [1993] 2 RCS 451, 466.

37   Dans *R c Ikhlef*, CSM No 500-01-011675-953, l'honorable Pinard de la Cour supérieure a jugé que l'impossibilité d'effectuer une contre-expertise sur des mégots de cigarettes ne portait atteinte au droit de l'accusé à une défense pleine et entière. La Cour supérieure estime que, malgré l'impossibilité d'effectuer ses propres analyses génétiques sur les mégots, l'accusé pourra toujours, en contre-interrogatoire ou autrement, faire ressortir les faiblesses de la méthodologie employée ou de la manutention des spécimens au laboratoire.

38   Voir *Hung Duc Vu c R*, décision rendue le 26 juin 1997; *R c Chaplin* [1995] 1 RCS 727; *R c Stinchcombe* [1995] 1 RCS 754, où la Cour suprême affirme que l'obligation de divulgation ne s'applique pas lorsque la Couronne peut expliquer les raisons qui l'empêchent de communiquer les éléments de la preuve.

39   *ibid*.

40   Voir Grimaud (1994), à 314. L'admissibilité de la preuve génétique au Canada s'examine au cours d'un voir-dire: 'Il est évident que le voir-dire et le procès lui-même jouent deux rôles différents, le premier servant à déterminer l'admissibilité d'un élément de preuve, le second à trancher l'affaire au fond en fonction de la preuve recevable. Le voir-dire a lieu en l'absence du jury qui doit toujours en ignorer l'objet': *R c Erven* [1979] 1 RCS 926, 931.

41   *R c Mohan* [1994] 2 RCS 9, 20 (jugement unanime de la Cour). Comme le signale la Cour, l'admission d'une preuve d'expert repose sur la pertinence, la nécessité d'aider le juge des faits, l'absence de toute règle d'exclusion et la qualification suffisante de l'expert. En matière de preuve génétique, il faut souligner que la notion d'expert prend une importance particulière (*R c Johnston* [1992] 69 CCC (3d) 395, 402 (Ont Ct)).

mentionner expressément à l'arrêt Daubert de la Cour suprême des États-Unis,[42] notre Cour suprême adopta dans ses grandes lignes, un test basé sur la fiabilité et la pertinence de la preuve offerte.[43]

En résumé, il ressort donc de ce qui précède que la preuve d'expert qui avance une nouvelle théorie ou technique est soigneusement examinée pour déterminer si elle satisfait à la norme de fiabilité et si elle est essentielle en ce sens que le juge de faits sera incapable de tirer une conclusion satisfaisante sans l'aide de l'expert. Plus la preuve se rapproche de l'opinion sur une question fondamentale, plus l'application de ce principe est stricte.[44]

Cette décision ne tranche pas définitivement l'ensemble des questions soulevées par l'utilisation d'une nouvelle preuve scientifique et nombre de celles-ci demeurent encore sans réponse.[45] Il faut donc étudier la question en gardant à l'esprit que la Cour suprême n'a réglé que partiellement les questions relatives aux nouvelles preuves scientifiques.[46]

En ce qui concerne la première branche de l'analyse génétique, soit celle de la comparaison des différentes analyses de l'ADN,[47] Tanovich écrit:

> The reliability of the underlying principles of forensic RFLP typing has been challenged and found to be reliable on enough occasions in our courts that its reliability is now generally accepted in the legal community so as to permit the judicial noticing of its reliability ...

> However, the reliability of PCR and other related DNA typing methods, many of which have not yet been used in criminal cases, have not been frequently challenged in our courts as demonstrated by the few cases in which they have been introduced and the lack of legal commentary considering issues relating to their admissibility. A Mohan hearing should therefore be required to establish the reliability of these methods.[48]

Il faut, donc, conclure, selon l'auteur, que les tribunaux canadiens n'auraient tranché réellement qu'une partie du débat touchant l'utilisation des différentes techniques scientifiques applicables à l'analyse de l'ADN. La technique d'analyse

---

42 *Daubert v Merrell Dow Pharmaceuticals Inc* [1993] 113 Ct 2786.

43 *R c Mohan* [1994] 2 RCS 9, 25. Voir aussi Tanovich (1996), à 228: 'By emphasizing the need for special scrutiny of experimental scientific theory or techniques, *Mohan* goes a long way in protecting our criminal justice system from miscarriages of justice.'

44 *R c Mohan* [1994] 2 RCS 25.

45 Voir Healy (1995), à 425.

46 Tout le débat et toutes les questions demeurent donc, pour l'instant, sans véritable fondement jurisprudentiel.

47 'At least, two distinct branches of science are involved. The first is molecular biology and the second is population genetics (as interpreted with the help of mathematical probability of statistics. Henceforth, reference to population genetics should be understood to include the necessary component mathematics)' (*R c Johnston* (1992) 69 CCC (3d) 395, 401 (Ont Ct)).

48 Voir Tanovich (1996), à 234. 'The most common DNA typing method used over the last few years has been restriction fragment length polymorphism analysis (RFLP) ... RFLP analysis is the technique which leads to what is commonly referred to as genetic fingerprinting ... A second method for DNA typing is known as polymerase chain action (PCR)': *ibid* p 232. L'auteur rapporte que seulement deux causes auraient utilisé la méthode PCR.

RFLP semblerait, contrairement à la méthode PCR, avoir déjà franchi le seuil de la fiabilité.

Pour ce qui est de la seconde branche de l'analyse génétique, soit la preuve statistique de la possibilité de retrouver un type d'ADN particulier dans une population spécifique ou la preuve selon le RMP,[49] l'attitude actuelle des tribunaux reflète la controverse que soulève l'utilisation des différentes méthodes employées pour le calcul des statistiques.[50] Dans ce cas, en raison de l'incertitude prévalant dans le domaine, ainsi que l'examen très limité apporté par les tribunaux canadiens sur ce sujet, l'approche définie dans l'arrêt Mohan devrait s'appliquer à cette seconde branche de l'analyse.[51]

Même si la Cour suprême demeure muette sur ce point, une lecture large de l'arrêt Mohan devrait permettre également de conclure que les tribunaux peuvent examiner la fiabilité des instruments et de la méthodologie employés par les différents laboratoires canadiens.[52] L'examen devrait alors porter sur un ensemble de facteurs:

> Prior to planning a strategy for introducing or challenging DNA evidence, the defence and prosecution should critically evaluate each aspect of the DNA typing procedure, as well as the methods used to interpret the audiograms. Prosecutors should not blindly assume that DNA evidence is irrefutable nor should the defence assume that DNA evidence is inherently flawed ...
>
> A critical evaluation of the DNA typing evidence should begin with an assessment of the testing laboratory and its personnel ... Prior to evaluating the actual casework

---

49 L'expression RMP signifie Random Match Probability.

50 Au Canada, la controverse tire son origine notamment de la population ou des groupes de base pouvant servir au calcul des statistiques, ainsi que de la possibilité du dépôt des calculs statistiques par des personnes non qualifiées. Ces deux éléments affectent sans contredit la fiabilité de cette seconde branche de l'analyse. Voir Tanovich (1996), à 236. Voir aussi Grimaud (1994), à 344.

51 Dans R c Mohan [1994] 2 RCS. 9, 21, la Cour suprême souligne qu'une preuve d'expert peut être rejetée lorsque, en examinant le critère de la pertinence, la valeur probante est surpassée par son effet préjudiciable. Une preuve exprimée en termes scientifiques que le jury ne comprend pas peut fausser le processus de recherche de la vérité. La question qui se pose alors est de savoir si la preuve ou la démonstration des probabilités statistiques peut faire obvier le déroulement normal du procès. Il s'agit là, selon certains auteurs, de la plus grande faiblesse de cette preuve génétique: voir Chayko, Gulliver et MacDougall (1991), p 351. En jurisprudence canadienne, les tribunaux ont refusé ou exclu à l'occasion la preuve des statistiques sur la probabilité que l'ADN prélevé sur des échantillons recueillis sur l'accusé concorde avec ceux prélevés sur les lieux du crime (voir R c Bourguignon [1991] OJ No 2670 (QL)). Cette position du juge Flanigan a cependant été fortement critiquée par certains auteurs de doctrine. 'The significance of the DNA evidence provided by the statistical probabilities creates a greater cogency to the evidence ... Excluding relevant evidence for the reasons set out by Flanigan J essentially creates a test that excludes evidence based on cogency – the more cogent the evidence, the more prejudicial it is, and therefore it should be excluded. Prejudice is a legal term of art' (voir McCormack et Foote (1992) à 90). Par contre, dans d'autres décisions, les tribunaux ont admis ce genre de preuve (par exemple, dans la cause R c Lafferty (1993) 80 CCC (3d) 150 (NTSC)). En l'absence d'indication claire de la Cour suprême sur ce sujet, il serait prématuré de dire avec exactitude la situation juridique qui sera retenue.

52 Voir Tavonich (1996), à 238.

results, the scientific integrity of the DNA typing protocol should be assessed ... Once the scientific validity of the DNA typing protocol has been assessed, the application of the protocol to the individual case becomes the primary focus of the investigation.[53]

Même si certaines décisions préconisent cet examen critique, le contrôle de la fiabilité ne semble pas préoccuper outre mesure les tribunaux canadiens:[54]

The issue of the ability of a laboratory to produce reliable results on a consistent basis is an important one. Unfortunately, Canadian courts have not yet adequately grappled with it. Therefore, I submit that the issue of the reliability of the various DNA laboratories across Canada is still an open one with respect to RFLP testing and certainly with respect to PCR testing and other related methods.[55]

On doit donc conclure qu'au Canada, beaucoup de questions touchant la fiabilité des résultats obtenus lors de l'utilisation d'une preuve génétique pendant un procès criminel demeurent sans véritable réponse. Les tribunaux canadiens, et spécialement la Cour suprême, devront donc établir dans un avenir rapproché les standards applicables en pareil cas afin d'éviter que de graves erreurs se produisent.[56]

La destruction des échantillons et des résultats

Contrairement au Projet de loi C-94 qui prévoyait l'établissement d'une banque nationale de données sous la direction du commissaire de la Gendarmerie royale du Canada qui comprenait certains fichiers criminalistiques et un fichier des condamnés, la présente loi ne crée aucune institution particulière.[57] Les dispositions actuelles du Code criminel ne crée, en outre, aucun mécanisme particulier d'entreposage. Seul le moment de la destruction des échantillons corporels et des résultats obtenus fait l'objet de mesures législatives précises. Loin d'être une simple question de protection de la vie privée, le moment de la destruction des échantillons corporels et des résultats acquiert une importance capitale au regard du droit à l'accusé d'avoir une défense pleine et entière:

---

53 Voir Chayko, Gulliver et MacDougall (1991), aux pages 351–63.

54 Voir l'opinion du juge Verte dans *R c Lafferty* (1993) 80 CCC (3d) 150, 160, où il écrit que: 'The testing procedures, in my opinion, are an indicium of reliability. If there are many testing facilities and there is no standardized testing procedure, or mandatory quality assurance methods, then the reliability of the evidence is brought into question.'

55 Voir Tanovich (1996), à 241.

56 De la même façon, bien que la Cour suprême n'ait pas encore tranché cette question, il est permis de croire que le fardeau de preuve nécessaire à la démonstration de la fiabilité des tests génétiques sera celui de la preuve hors de tout doute raisonnable: Voir l'arrêt *R c Egger* [1993] 2 RCS 451, 474, où la Cour écrit que '... lorsque la recevabilité de la preuve peut avoir un effet concluant relativement à la culpabilité, la norme en matière criminelle est appliquée'. La valeur d'une preuve d'analyse génétique pourrait donc exiger ce fardeau: voir Tanovich (1996), à 245.

57 Le Projet de loi C-94 prévoyait également des dispositions sur l'utilisation des substances corporelles prélevées et les profils d'identification génétique établis à partir de celles-ci. Le Projet de loi prévoyait également les modes de communication de cette information ainsi que leur accès.

La conservation des échantillons pour une contre-expertise est une obligation si on veut satisfaire aux droits de la défense, surtout si une décision finale n'a pas été rendue. C'est un fondement à l'administration de la justice. On ne peut donc interdire aux autorités policières de colliger et de stocker les échantillons biologiques uniquement parce qu'ils contiennent de l'ADN: l'efficacité même du système pénal en dépend.[58]

C'est dans cette double perspective que le moment de la destruction des échantillons corporels et des résultats obtenus à partir de ces échantillons doit être défini. La loi en vigueur doit soupeser ou permettre de soupeser ces éléments importants.[59]

Selon l'article 487.09(1) C. cr., la substance corporelle prélevée et les résultats de l'analyse génétique y afférente sont détruits dès que, selon le cas,[60] les résultats indiquent que la substance visée à l'alinéa 487.05(1)(b) C. cr. ne provient pas de cette personne ou dès que la personne est acquittée définitivement de l'infraction et de toute autre infraction qui découle de la même affaire pour une raison autre qu'un verdict de non-responsabilité criminelle pour cause de troubles mentaux.

Enfin, la destruction doit également avoir lieu à l'expiration d'un délai d'un an suivant sa libération au terme de l'enquête préliminaire, relative à l'infraction désignée ou à toute autre infraction qui découle de la même affaire, ou le rejet de la dénonciation relative à l'infraction désignée ou à toute autre infraction qui découle de la même affaire autrement que par acquittement, ou son retrait, ou enfin, la suspension des procédures engagées contre lle relativement à cette affaire en application des articles 572, 579 ou 795 C. cr.

Toutefois, malgré le paragraphe (1), le paragraphe (2) de l'article 487.09 C. cr., celui-ci permet à un juge de la Cour provinciale de reporter la période de la destruction s'il est convaincu que la substance corporelle et les résultats obtenus pourraient être nécessaires aux fins d'une enquête ou d'une poursuite relative à la personne visée, pour une autre infraction désignée, ou relative à une autre personne, ou pour toute autre infraction qui découle de la même affaire.[61] L'autorisation du juge ne vise pas cependant à permettre une utilisation différente de ce que prescrit l'article 487.08 C. cr., mais simplement de reporter à un moment ultérieur la destruction des échantillons et des résultats. Ce paragraphe ne crée aucune nouvelle forme possible d'utilisation.[62]

Ces dispositions touchant la destruction ont pour but évident de protéger les personnes visées contre d'éventuelles atteintes à la vie privée. C'est un article

---

58 Voir Grimaud (1994), à 332.
59 R c Egger [1993] 2 RCS 451, 472.
60 L'article 487.09 C. cr. ne s'applique qu'à l'égard des échantillons corporels et des résultats génétiques obtenus selon la procédure de saisie définie à l'article 487.05 C. cr. L'obligation de destruction à l'intérieur des délais impartis ne s'applique pas aux autres tests génétiques effectués à partir du consentement des personnes visées.
61 Ce paragraphe accorde un large pouvoir discrétionnaire au juge de la Cour provinciale. La rédaction de ce paragraphe soulève également de nombreuses questions sur son application: S'agit-il d'une demande ex parte? Quelle est la procédure applicable pour faire une telle demande? Pour quelle période le juge peut-il autoriser que la destruction soit reportée? Voir Fontana (1997), p 250.
62 Voir Pomerance (1995), à 240.

d'application stricte qui élève la protection de la vie privée à un niveau pratiquement absolu, peu importe les autres droits en jeu. Également, en raison de la période prescrite, cette disposition respecte l'obligation de garder disponibles les éléments visés, afin de permettre à l'accusé une défense pleine et entière. L'article 489.08 C. cr. concilie donc les objectifs de la protection de la vie privée avec l'obligation d'assurer à l'accusé une défense pleine et entière.

Banque nationale de données génétiques

À la fin de 1998 une banque nationale de données génétiques[63] a été créée au Canada par la Loi concernant l'identification par les empreintes génétiques et modifiant le Code criminel et d'autres lois en conséquence (C-3 décembre 1998 ch 37). Plusieurs lacunes ont par la suite été comblées par l'entrée en vigueur en 2000 de la Loi modifiant la Loi sur la défense nationale, la Loi sur l'identification par les empreintes génétiques et modifiant et le Code criminel (S-10). La Loi concernant l'identification par les empreintes génétiques est entrée en vigueur à la suite d'une vaste consultation.

Le respect de la dignité humaine et des droits fondamentaux a motivé la réaffirmation de trois principes de base qui sont énoncés à l'article 4, soit:

(a) la protection de la société et l'administration de la justice sont bien servies par la découverte, l'arrestation et la condamnation rapides des contrevenants, lesquelles peuvent être facilitées par l'utilisation de profils d'identification génétique;

(b) ces profils, de même que les substances corporelles prélevées en vue de les établir, ne doivent servir qu'à l'application de la présente loi, à l'exclusion de toute autre utilisation qui n'y est pas autorisée;

(c) afin de protéger les renseignements personnels, doivent faire l'objet de protections:

(i) l'utilisation et la communication de l'information contenue dans la banque de données – notamment des profils – de même que son accessibilité,

(ii) l'utilisation des substances corporelles qui sont transmises au commissaire pour l'application de la présente loi, de même que leur accessibilité.

La banque nationale de données génétiques est sous la responsabilité du Commissaire de la Gendarmerie royale du Canada (Loi sur l'identification par les empreintes génétiques: article 5(2)). En vertu des articles 487.04 à 487.09 du Code criminel, les policiers peuvent donc demander à un juge de Cour provinciale un mandat autorisant un prélèvement pour analyse génétique dans le cadre d'une enquête. L'échantillon prélevé est ensuite analysé et les résultats ainsi obtenus peuvent être utilisés en preuve lorsque l'accusation porte sur une infraction

---

63 Voir Marceau (2000) et Duchesnay (2001).

définie par l'article 2. Ces infractions sont celles qui sont les plus graves et perpétrées avec violence et les agressions sexuelles. Les résultats ainsi obtenus peuvent donc servir à établir la culpabilité ou l'innocence de l'accusé.

La banque nationale de données génétiques contient deux fichiers, soit un fichier de criminalistique et un fichier des condamnés. Le fichier de criminalistique contient les profils génétiques établis à partir de substances corporelles trouvées, notamment sur le lieu de l'infraction ou sur la victime (article 5(3)). Le fichier des condamnés pour sa part contient les profils d'identification génétique établis à partir des substances corporelles visées au paragraphe 487.071(1) du Code criminel (ou au paragraphe 196.22(1) de la Loi sur la défense nationale).

Les fonctions de la banque nationale de données génétiques sont définies par l'article 6. Elle permet des comparaisons entre les profils d'identification génétique qui lui sont transmises et aux profils déjà contenus dans la banque. Le commissaire est alors autorisé à en communiquer les résultats, aux fins d'enquête ou de poursuite d'infractions criminelles, à tout laboratoire ou organisme canadien chargé du contrôle et de l'application de la loi (article 6(1)). Le commissaire peut aussi communiquer ces résultats à un gouvernement étranger, à une organisation internationale, si un accord ou une entente a été conclu (article 6(5)) à cet effet.

Examen et rapports: l'article 13 de la loi exige que dans les 5 ans de son entrée en vigueur, un comité du Sénat de la Chambre des communes procède à un nouvel examen des dispositions législatives et de l'application de la loi. Chaque année le commissaire est d'ailleurs tenu de présenter au Solliciteur Général un rapport sur l'activité de la banque, rapport déposé devant chaque chambre du Parlement (13(1)(2)).

Autorisation juridique: tous les renseignements contenus dans le fichier des condamnés sont conservés pour une période indéterminée ainsi que l'autorisation juridique qui y a donné naissance et la condamnation de l'accusé. Le système canadien est donc tout à fait différent de celui de Grande-Bretagne.

L'ordonnance mandatoire ou discrétionnaire: l'article 487.051 du Code criminel prévoit que, lorsque l'infraction a été commise après le 30 juin 2000 et qu'elle est de type primaire, le juge est tenu de rendre une ordonnance de prélèvement. Par ailleurs, lorsque l'infraction a été commise avant le 30 juin 2000 ou est de type secondaire, le juge peut simplement rendre cette ordonnance s'il est convaincu qu'elle servirait l'administration de la justice (487.051(1)(b)).

L'interprétation récente des lois par les tribunaux: les tribunaux ont réaffirmé la validité constitutionnelle des dispositions de cette loi et du Code criminel, ainsi que celle de la procédure *ex parte*. Le juge Cory de la Cour suprême s'exprime ainsi à cet égard: ... les dispositions ... qui autorisent les analyses d'empreintes génétiques peuvent satisfaire à toutes les exigences constitutionnelle (*R c Stillman* [1997] 1 RCS 601 aux pages 660–61). Dans *R c Van Osselaer* (non rapporté, (1999) WL 33203131 BC SC juge Macauley), la Cour a exclu la preuve génétique parce que l'accusé n'avait pas été informé de la possibilité que les résultats servent en preuve contre lui. Dans *R c Feeney* (non rapporté, (1999) 23 CR(5th) 74 BC SC juge Oppal), la Cour a rejeté l'argument de la défense sur la nécessité (selon l'article 7 de la Charte des droits et libertés) d'offrir à l'accusé le choix de substances à prélever pour l'analyse génétique.

Conclusion

L'adoption en 1995 du Projet de loi C-104 a, sans aucun doute, clarifié le pouvoir des agents de la paix de prélever certaines substances corporelles sur une personne visée pour fins d'analyse génétique sans son consentement. Cependant, loin de régler définitivement les nombreux problèmes que soulève l'utilisation de cette technique scientifique lors de procès criminels, ces dispositions, en raison de leur caractère provisoire, suscitent de nombreuses autres questions. Comme l'écrivait Tanovich, elles sont loin de régler tous les problèmes:

> Unfortunately, Parliament did not legislate, along with the DNA warrant provisions, a set of procedures and standards to govern the collection, preservation and ultimate testing of the bodily samples seized ... In addition, Parliament has failed to attempt to level the playing field by legislating defence access to the samples for independent testing and by legislating access to DNA expert for indigent accused in order to assist them in challenging the admissibility of DNA evidence and, if admissible, to assist the triers of facts to the weight they should give to this evidence.[64]

Une intervention future du législateur serait souhaitable afin de clarifier certaines situations découlant de l'utilisation de cette nouvelle preuve scientifique.[65] Comme le démontre le Projet de loi C-94, mort au feuilleton, les mesures actuelles ne sont qu'une première étape dans l'élaboration d'une politique complexe en cette matière. Seule l'adoption d'un prochain Projet de loi permettra de fixer avec exactitude la portée réelle des dispositions relatives à l'analyse génétique effectuée à des fins médico-légales en droit criminel Canadien.

À jour au 1er juin 1998.

References

Bassan, D (1996) 'Bill C-104: Revolutionizing criminal investigation or infringing on charter rights' 54 U of TF of LR 246

Chayko, GM, Gulliver, ED et MacDougall, DV (1991) *Forensic Evidence in Canada*, Canada Law Book Inc

Duchesnay, C (2001) 'Chasseurs d'empreintes' 33 Journal de Barreau 12

Fontana, JA (1997) *The Law of Search and Seizure in Canada*, Butterworths

Grimaud, MA (1994) 'Les enjeux de la recevabilité de la preuve d'identification par ADN dans le système pénal canadien' 24 RDUS 293

Healy, P (1995) 'Developments in the law of evidence: the 1993–94 term', Sup Ct LR 279

---

64   Voir Tanovich (1996), à 223. Comme le soulignait Grimaud (1994), à 327: 'La preuve obtenue par analyse génétique semble être porteuse de bénéfices notables pour la justice dans le domaine de l'identification, mais il ne fait nul doute que l'utilisation de cette preuve sans un contrôle efficace générera de nombreux problèmes ... Les implications sociales sont très graves à cause du caractère intrinsèque de matériel utilisé.'

65   Le Projet de loi C-94 ne réglait pas complètement toutes ces questions.

Marceau, J (2000) 'La mise en oeuvre de la banque d'empreintes données génétiques', Annual Symposium on Forensic DNA Evidence, Toronto, le 14 octobre 2000

McCormack, H and Foote, SM (1992) 'A new type of identification evidence: the admissibility of DNA typing' 7 CR (4th) 76

Pomerance, RM (1995) 'Bill C-104: A practical guide to the new DNA warrants' 39 CR (4th) 224

Tanovich, D (1996) 'The admissibility of novel scientific evidence under *Mohan*: the case of DNA typing' 1 Can Crim LR 221

CHAPTER 5

DENMARK

Judge Peter Garde
Hillerød Criminal Court

Time in the criminal process at which DNA sampling and testing may occur

Inspection of the body as a means of investigation in the criminal process is treated in ss 792ff of the Administration of Justice Act (AJA),[1] a fairly new chapter inserted in 1989 on the basis of an exhaustive report of 1987.

Inspection of the body is subdivided into:

(1) viewing of the body (naked or clothed), photographing, the taking of fingerprints or other impressions of the outer parts of the body, the search of the clothes worn by the person in question, whether accused or not; and

(2) closer inspection of the body, including body cavities, blood tests and other corresponding samples, such as X-raying (s 79(2) of the AJA).

DNA sampling is not mentioned in the Act; indeed, DNA as a means of proof was unknown in Denmark in 1989. However, DNA analysis is undoubtedly legitimate if the taking of samples is authorised, and no further legal requirements are necessary. It is seen that sampling is covered by (2).

The methods under (1) may be applied to an accused (s 792(1) of the AJA), provided there is reasonable ground to suspect that he or she has committed an offence prosecuted by the prosecution service – as opposed to offences privately prosecuted as libel and slander – and the inspection is deemed to be of substantial importance to the investigation. Also, if there are reasonable grounds to believe that the accused has committed an offence which may result in imprisonment for one year and six months or more, which includes most cases in the middle range, (for example, property crimes except for petty larceny, assault except for disturbance of the peace), the accused may be photographed and fingerprinted for later identification, even if this is unnecessary for the prosecution of the offence: s 792(b)(1) of the AJA.

---

1   Administration of Justice Act (Danish Retsplejeloven, Abb Rpl), with its 1,043 sections by far the longest Act in force in Denmark, originally of 1916 and in force from 1919, has been amended hundreds of times, and was recently promulgated with amendments in 2001.

The methods under (2) may be applied to an accused (s 792(a)(2) of the AJA), provided that there is a justified suspicion (ie, more than the degree of suspicion necessary for the application of the lesser means listed under (1) that he or she has committed an offence which may result in imprisonment for one year and six months or more, and provided that the method is deemed to be of decisive importance to the investigation). 'Justified suspicion' corresponds to the condition necessary for pre-trial detention (s 76(2) of the AJA), just as 'reasonable ground to suspect' corresponds to the requirement for mere arrest (s 755 of the AJA).

A recent decision[2] illustrates this point. After the body of a raped and murdered woman had been found, a taxi driver approached the police and told of his being in the neighbourhood. He had stopped his vehicle, urinated, and proceeded on his business almost at once, which was confirmed by a video film. He was first told by the police that he was not suspected. As other leads dried out, he was asked to furnish a blood sample for the purpose of a DNA analysis. He refused, and the police then charged him with the crime and applied for a court order to obtain a blood sample. The accused again refused, alleging his wish not to suffer interference with his body or to be registered by the police. Both the court of first instance and the High Court refused the authorisation of DNA analysis. The High Court expressly stated that there was a 'reasonable suspicion' but not a 'justified suspicion', and referred to the practice of detention and s 762(1) of the AJA. The court of first instance stated that the 'accused's refusal to submit to a blood test did not create a suspicion if none existed before'. The High Court, correctly, did not accept that reasoning, because in a stronger case, the refusal of a suspect to submit to the taking of a sample may tip the scales to the extent that a 'reasonable' suspicion becomes 'justified'. In that respect, the sweeping statement of the court of first instance is untenable.

While the decision is undoubtedly correct as the law stands, a point might be made that the taking of a sample is much less oppressive than detention, so that the conditions for the former should be less circumscribed than for the latter.

In another case,[3] members of a rocker-gang, 'Bandidos', were detained under suspicion of the murder of a 'Hell's Angels' rocker. Blood samples were taken, but had not been analysed for DNA when the suspects were released by court ruling. The High Court ruled, against the court of first instance, that as the conditions for inspection of the body had existed at the time of the taking of the sample, the analysis did not lose its legality because of later developments. The case showed that at least some suspects are painfully aware of the implications of DNA analysis.

---

2   UfR 1997, 972 VLK UfR, Ugeskrift for Retsvæsen (Legal Weekly), the most important collection of decisions; it also contains legal articles. VL, Vestre Landsret, Western High Court. The Eastern and Western High Courts are the intermediate level in the three-tier system of courts in Denmark.

3   VL ruling of 10 February 1997, unpublished, S–0359–97. My thanks to Deputy Chief Constable Elsemette Cassøe for information.

It is immaterial whether an arrest[4] has been made or a criminal charge has been laid. When a means of compulsion has been demanded or imposed, or when the police or prosecution expressly designates a suspect as accused there is no doubt that the formal protection inherent to that status must be applied, especially the right of silence and the right to counsel.

Samples left by an unknown perpetrator (for example, semen in the vagina of a raped woman) can be analysed without any formal requirements.

A non-accused person, whether victim, other witness or outsider, must submit to the methods listed under (1), except that the person in question may always remain clothed, on the same conditions as for applying the methods listed under (2) to an accused, ie, an offence carrying a possible penalty of imprisonment for one year and six months or more and decisive importance to the investigation: s 792(d)(2) of the AJA. The law does not exempt persons who are not compellable witnesses against the accused: s 171 of the AJA.

However, the means under (2) can never be applied to a non-accused except with consent. Perhaps it ought to be possible to order a witness to submit to the taking of a sample in an extreme case (for example, a complainant of rape),[5] but as the law stands, this is not possible.

Collection of DNA samples

Procedures

The procedures to be followed for collection of samples diverge strongly between accused and other persons: s 792(c) of the AJA (accused); s 792(d) (others).

With respect to the *accused*, the police have the competency to decide upon the means listed under (1) *plus* the taking of a blood test, notwithstanding a protest from the accused or defending counsel.

The accused is, however, entitled subsequently to complain to the court, as in all cases of dispute between the parties during the phase of the criminal investigation: s 746, AJA. A court order will then decide upon the legality of the measure taken. A court order must always set out its reasoning. Both parties may appeal against the order to the High Court.

Although the police thus have the formal competency to decide upon the taking of a blood test, the requirement of a 'justified', not merely a 'reasonable', suspicion must have been met.

A court order is necessary for the application of the rest of the means listed under (2), including the taking of other samples than blood tests. If, in a situation in which a court order is necessary, there would be danger in delay, the police may act at once, subject to notification to the court within 24 hours. The court will then hear or possibly read arguments from both sides and decide by court order whether to approve the action of the police, just as in a dispute covered by s 746, AJA.

---

4   AJA, s 792(2) refers to s 758 as an additional authority for taking steps against the body of a person under arrest, but that rule only mentions security and prevention of escape, not investigation of an offence.

5   See Garde (1995), at 15ff.

The *consent* of the accused, which must be given in writing, removes the general competency in all cases from the court to the police. The court must be notified when the police have acted on the spot in a case of (2), but the other legal requirements remain unchanged. The reason for the limited importance of the consent of the accused is that such consent is never completely voluntary – the accused will expect the police to act at once, adducing danger in delay, if the consent is withheld.[6] If counsel is appointed for the accused (rather than privately retained counsel), the counsel's consent is also necessary. This is one of the rare examples of the accused not having full formal competency to waive a right on his or her own.

The consent of the accused does not remove the legal requirements for the inspection of the body; however, it must be assumed that the police are entitled to take a sample upon a demand by an accused seeking to clear him or herself. This may be the case even though the legal requirements for taking the sample have not been met. In the event of a police refusal to take a sample, the accused may be entitled to complain to the court in accordance with s 746, AJA.[7] This question is not settled in the AJA.

Except for the rule of defending counsel's consent, the system described – the requirement of court order, competency of the police in smaller cases or when there is danger of delay, and the limited importance of the accused's consent – is typical of the regulation of means of compulsion in Danish criminal procedure.

If a *non-accused person consents* – preferably in writing, although this is not an absolute requirement: s 792(d), AJA – all means under (1) and (2) may be applied freely without regard to the requirements in the Act. This means that the taking of samples or fingerprints for purposes of elimination not only from witnesses, but also from outsiders (for example, the entire male population of a town from certain age groups), is legal, provided consent is given.

In summary, the methods listed under (1) can be employed against a non-accused without consent, but only by court order, corresponding to the rules relating to accused persons. The methods listed under (2), including the taking of samples, can never be applied to a non-accused except by consent.

In Danish criminal justice a general *principle of proportionality* is assumed,[8] entailing a reasonable proportion between the end to be achieved and the means to be employed. This principle also imposes an obligation on both the police and the courts always to choose the least oppressive means when more than one exists. The principle is expressly stated in s 792(e)(1), AJA, and covers both accused and others.

In addition, sub-section (2) contains a principle of leniency, adding that such means as might violate a sense of decency should only, if feasible, be applied by a person of the same sex as the person whose body is to be inspected, or by medical personnel, especially if undressing is necessary. Of course, only a general sense of decency is protected, not personal idiosyncrasies.

---

6   See the Report of 1987 (1987), at 58ff.
7   See the Report of 1996 (1996), at 19.
8   See Gammeltoft-Hansen (1998), at 61 *et seq.*

Pursuant to sub-section (3), a medical practitioner must assist when a method listed under (2) is to be employed, and must take the inherent pain and medical risk into consideration. The necessity of the means and the proportionality between means and ends is, however, not the medical practitioner's province.

Degree of force

The rules diverge decisively for accused persons and others.

With respect to the *accused*, physical force is not mentioned directly in the AJA, but there is no doubt but that necessary force may be employed.[9] The legislation, by expressly establishing lesser means of compulsion for the non-accused, takes for granted that force may be used against the accused. The police are thus entitled to hold or, if necessary, to strap the accused and carry through the measure in question. The police are, however, bound by the principles of proportionality and maximum leniency, and inspection of the body pursuant to (2), may only be carried through with the assistance of a medical practitioner. Until now, no Danish cases have defined in detail what degree of force is acceptable. The Danish practice of detention in isolation has been challenged unsuccessfully in the European Human Rights Commission: the complainant alleged torture and inhuman or degrading treatment,[10] but not the use of physical force during inspection of the body.

In the comparatively rare cases where methods are applied to a *non-accused* 'instead of direct enforcement' – the very text of the Act – the same means as for recalcitrant witnesses may be applied: s 792(d)(3), AJA (referring to s 178, AJA). Those means include fines, even deprivation of liberty for six months, but not direct coercion.

Special requirements for specific groups

The Report of 1987[11] stressed the question of consent when the victim of an offence is *unconscious or a child* not able to consent to an inspection of the body on its own. When a medical inspection is necessary *per se*, which will often be the case, the police will probably be entitled to utilise the findings gained thereby (for example, to ask for an analysis of a blood sample taken for medical reasons). However, the medical practitioner cannot take steps indicated for purely investigatory reasons.

In cases involving children, the consent of the parents should be obtained before attempting an inspection of the body. The consent of the minor – from about the age of 15 – should also be obtained. If a minor is accused of an offence, the normal rules are followed except for the question of consent, where the parents (or guardian) should accede as well. In the case of a possible clash of interests – for example, a parent accused of molesting his own child – where the

9 See the Report of 1987 (1987), at 60ff.
10 *X v The Kingdom of Denmark* (1978) 27 Eur Comm HR 50. The complaint was dismissed as manifestly unfounded.
11 See the Report of 1987 (1987), at 7ff.

question of consent emerges, a temporary guardian will probably be appointed. The municipal social welfare departments are always involved in cases regarding minors both as victims and as offenders.

The authors of the 1987 Report advised against legislation in this field, probably rightly.

Furthermore, consent from *incompetent adults,* such as the mentally deranged, will probably not be sufficient, but otherwise the normal rules will be followed.

Although not part of criminal justice, a special aspect of the use of DNA analysis involving a specific group of people should be mentioned here: cases involving application for residence permits from dependants, especially children, for *aliens* living in the realm. Consanguinity is an absolute condition for such permits (s 9, Aliens Act) and the applicant must give the necessary information (s 40). Occasionally, suspicions have arisen that the 'child' in question was not really the descendant of the resident alien – originally Turks, and now Somalis have been at the fore – and for some years, the Aliens Department has in doubtful cases asked for blood samples, with a view to ascertaining, through DNA analysis, whether the necessary links exist.[12] Protests have been heard that such tests are in violation of the right to privacy as entrenched in the European Convention of Human Rights,[13] and that no authority existed in law for such demands – as opposed to fingerprinting, which has been mentioned in the Act since 1992. The practice was most probably legal, as in many cases the applicants had themselves begun the process, but in order to ward off all possible suggestions of illegality, the Aliens Act was amended in 1997. A new s 40(c) was inserted by which both the applicant and the resident alien could be obligated to submit to a DNA test, if consanguinity were not satisfactorily established by other evidence. Until now, this is the only statute to mention DNA analysis expressly.

Testing

Scientific tests on DNA samples for use in criminal proceedings

In 1988 and 1989, foreign laboratories carried out DNA analyses in Danish criminal proceedings in, respectively, 1 and 7 cases[14] alongside scientific tests in the Forensic Genetics Section. The Medico-Legal Council (Retslægerådet), a committee of medical doctors of the highest expertise appointed by the state,

---

12　The Forensic Genetics Section, Retsgenetisk Afdeling (part of the Medico-Legal Institute, Retsmedicinsk Institut, at the University of Copenhagen) between 1990 and 96 analysed 76 cases involving 155 children, mainly Turks; in all but one case consanguinity was confirmed. As for Somalis, between 1992 and 97, nine cases involving 36 persons were analysed, including 25 children. In six cases, the analyses negated consanguinity in relation to 17 children (16 with certainty) while in three cases of eight children, the analyses supported consanguinity. In 1997, the Aliens Department asked for analyses of about 500 Somalis (Letter from MD Niels Morling, Head of the Section, to Peter Garde, 26 May 1997).

13　European Convention for the Protection of Human Rights and Fundamental Freedoms, opened for signature 20 March 1950, 213 UNTS 221 (entered into force 3 September 1953).

14　Most statistical and practical information in this section is from the Report of 1996 (1996), at 44ff.

which as late as 1988 had labelled the method 'experimental', in a letter of 1990 to the Ministry of Justice stated that the method was regarded as scientifically reliable. However, the Council added that inherent risks of errors ought not to be disregarded. The Ministry promptly exhorted the police and the prosecution service as to the possibilities of the method and, since then, DNA analysis has been utilised in an ever-growing number of cases. As for *statistics,* analyses have been made in the years 1990–95 in, respectively, 17, 25, 53, 78 (of which 15 reopened), 63 (eight reopened) and 65 (seven reopened) cases. The 206 cases of the three latest years have been broken up into sub-groups, showing that rape is by far the most common scenario in which the method is applied (50, 38, 37), followed by murder.

During the first years, the so-called Restriction Fragment Length Polymorphism (RFLP) method was applied in criminal proceedings, while the probably more promising Polymerase Chain Reaction (PCR) method was applied in paternity cases (469 cases in the years 1990–93). From summer 1996, the PCR method has been routinely applied in criminal proceedings. It is expected that DNA analyses will henceforth be applied in more cases than previously, because of the widening possibilities in cases where only a small or contaminated amount of DNA is available.

Licence requirements

In Denmark, the general practice in cases where questions of forensic medicine arise is for the police to forward the material to a public body: in cases of drunken driving, the Forensic Chemistry Section (Retskemisk Afdeling), in the Medico-Legal Institute; in cases concerning DNA tests, the Forensic Genetics Section; and in cases of criminal insanity, an expert appointed by the court. Both parties invariably accept the findings of the public bodies. Difficult cases are submitted to the Medico-Legal Council, the Retslægerådet. The 'battle of the experts', sometimes seen in Anglo-Saxon trials, is unknown in Danish practice. The Forensic Genetics Section is regarded as independent and neutral, and it enjoys general confidence.

There exists no doubt as to the professional knowledge, skills or integrity of the personnel of the Section, or as to the internal control procedures. Thus, the question of a licence does not arise.

Other rules or regulations

It is inevitable that a mass of information is given by the police to the Forensic Genetics Section, and vice versa. The legal framework regulating the exchange of information between several public authorities, which are mutually independent, is ss 28–32 of the Act on Public Administration (Forvaltningsloven). According to s 28, information regarding an individual's private matters such as race,[15]

---

15 In an important rape case of 1991, described in Garde (1995) at 5, the section mentioned the increased risk of coincidence between the DNA profile of the suspect, who was Ghanaian, and other persons of negroid descent. For the purpose of consanguinity cases, the section must of course know the race and nationality of the individuals concerned.

religion, colour, sexual inclination, former convictions or health can only be given to another authority in the following circumstances: when covered by law; when the individual consents; when private or public interest in the information clearly outweighs the individual's claim for privacy; or when the exchange is necessary for the requesting authority's conduct of its responsibilities. The authority entitled to impart the desired information is also bound to do so on request.

The possessor, private or public, of the relevant blood sample or other sample can be ordered by the court to hand it over by means of an 'order of edition', having prior opportunity to comment on the request: ss 804, 807, AJA. If the possessor is a medical doctor or a hospital, the question of privilege arises: s 170, AJA. Whereas a corresponding privilege of clergymen and defence counsel is absolute, the court may, upon weighing the conflict of interests and taking into consideration the importance of the case and gravity of the alleged crime, order medical doctors and attorneys, other than defence counsel, to divulge the relevant information.

Use of DNA test results in the criminal process

Pre-trial

Availability of test results to defence counsel

Defence counsel has the right of *disclosure*, which normally includes copies of all evidence: s 745, AJA. The hypothetical possibility of limiting his or her right of disclosure – for example, if the safety of the realm is in jeopardy – is of no significance. Of possibly more importance is the implied condition that the right of disclosure only extends to relevant evidence. In a number of recent cases, the police did not consider themselves bound to inform the defence of purely negative investigation, 'nought-reports', but as those reports were later shown to be of interest for the defence, the Attorney-General has stressed the police's duty to disclose everything. If, for example, samples are found at the scene of the crime that are not from the suspect, the police must make those findings available to defence counsel. The problem seems similar to the debate in the US, where the right to discovery covers the entire file.

In most cases, copies of the evidence are handed over to defence counsel when the case is complete, but the defence counsel has a right to running discovery.

The accused does not have the same right to disclosure as does defence counsel. Counsel is allowed to discuss the evidence with the accused and show it to him or her unless the police forbid, but may not hand over the evidence (or copies) unless the police allow. Decisions made by the police contrary to the wishes of the defence may be challenged in court: s 746, AJA.

Whereas the right to disclosure of test results is regulated, there are no rules regarding the possible right of the defence to a portion of the substances available for the purpose of a supplementary analysis. This was indirectly intimated in the recommendation of the Council of Europe of 12 February 1992 under the significant heading 'Equality of Arms'. The question has not arisen in Denmark because defence counsel, until now, has never, in my knowledge, questioned the findings of the Forensic Genetics Section. However, it is by no means unthinkable that the defence will ask the Section to perform supplementary tests. In case of dispute between the parties – the police, for example, may consider such tests irrelevant, unduly time-consuming and/or disproportionately costly – the court adjudges according to s 746, AJA.

Another reason why independent investigation undertaken by the defence is so rare, and in cases of DNA testing, non-existent, is that the defence cannot count on having the *costs* refunded from the public purse. Whereas the defence is not in law barred from investigating independently, the costs incurred will only be refunded if the court (or the prosecution) has given a prior authorisation, or if the court 'as an exception' considers that the defence had reasonable grounds: s 1007, AJA.[16]

During trial

Admissibility of DNA test results

Although either party is entitled to protest against evidence of the opposing party, such protests are extremely rare, as there are very few rules of evidence in Danish law, and almost none regarding exclusion of evidence. The basic rule is the principle of material truth.

DNA test results are submitted in writing, and are thus *second-hand evidence*, 'hearsay'. Such documents are regarded as made 'in furtherance of a public duty' and are admitted directly: s 877(2), AJA. In practice, a representative of the Forensic Genetics Section is commonly called by the prosecution – or was, when this kind of proof was new – to explain the procedure, but this is with a view to enhancing the weight of the evidence, and is not obligatory as a matter of law.

As for *unlawfully obtained evidence*, materials obtained by the police by virtue of the rule of danger in delay, which the court subsequently refuses to approve, must be destroyed (s 792(c)(3), AJA). Furthermore, material obtained by virtue of the police's direct competency, which the court, upon complaint, finds has been obtained through the police acting *ultra vires* (s 746, AJA) must be destroyed 'at once': s 792(f)(3), AJA. The wording 'at once' creates difficult legal questions, which until now have not, to my knowledge, been answered. There is no doubt that such materials and evidence cannot be stored after the case. But can they be used during the case? The categorical wording suggests that they cannot, but the placing of the rule in s 792(f), AJA, the first two sub-sections of which clearly only deal with the (later) storing of materials and evidence, supports the opposite conclusion. The two Reports probably support the view that they can be used during the case.[17] I agree, because of the placing of the rule within the statute, and

---

16 Only once, during my 14 years as a judge, has defence counsel in the earliest stages of a case of serious assault, without prior leave, procured a doctor's report from an eminent retired medico-legal expert, asking the court to refund it. The prosecutor protested. As the report was, in part, relevant to the case and the costs small, I acceded to the request. I rebuked defence counsel, however, as he should have known better.

17 The Report of 1996 (1996), at 29, clearly supports this view. The Report of 1987 (1987), at 91, is less certain. Following p 92 of the 1987 Report, the point could be made that 'at once' is to be read only as 'without awaiting an application'.

also because of the general tendency to admit reliable evidence, even if obtained unlawfully. For example, if the court does not agree that there was danger in delay, but would have decreed the measure at the request of the prosecution applying for a warrant, exclusion of the evidence seems utterly unreasonable. Danish courts are especially reluctant to accede to a request that evidence be physically destroyed.[18] If wilful arbitrariness were to become prevalent in police practice, exclusion might be applied more often, but not in cases of mistakes of form or timing.

More practical is the question of evidence obtained not unlawfully, but *accidentally*, where the evidence could possibly not have been obtained legally (German 'Zufallsfunde'). The most common example is invasion of communication, such as the tapping of telephone lines, which can only be undertaken with the consent of the court and only for the investigation of certain serious cases. For example, it is permitted in drug cases, but not for burglary: s 781, AJA. If lesser offences are disclosed during tapped conversations, the tapping cannot be admitted in evidence during the trial for such offences: s 789, AJA.[19] On the other hand, the police are expressly authorised to use the evidence for the purpose of further investigation and to adduce such derivative evidence: the 'fruits of the poisonous tree' doctrine is thus rejected. In 1997, s 789, AJA was altered, giving the court the power to admit the evidence also in smaller, but not petty, cases on not very strict conditions. The dubious question, never settled in practice – whether s 789, AJA should be applied by analogy to DNA testing – loses all practical relevance.

Other relevant rules of evidence

Independent of the problem of accidentally acquired evidence is the issue of whether a blood sample and possible subsequent DNA testing legally acquired for the purpose of one case can be put to use in *other cases*.[20]

If a sample has been taken from the suspect's body in one case and DNA tested, the police will naturally wish to have the results compared to samples left by unknown perpetrators in unsolved cases. The police have always compared fresh evidence to old materials – for example, unidentified fingerprints at earlier crime scenes – and recent experience in Denmark shows that DNA testing has dazzling possibilities in this respect. No courts have criticised, and no defence counsel has challenged, this practice on the grounds that no 'reasonable' or 'justified' suspicion existed that the accused in the actual case had also committed

---

18   UfR 1992, 318 ØLK. (In the case of a policeman having questioned a detained suspect in the absence of defence counsel, in spite of the expressed wish to the contrary of both suspect and counsel, the court rebuked the police, but refused to order the destruction of the reports. The question of the consequence of the fault was deferred to the trial, in case the prosecution wished to use the reports.) See also UfR 1995, 856 HK.

19   Only lesser offences. In my largest tax fraud case, in the erroneous fear that his own telephone was being tapped, the suspect borrowed his neighbour's telephone, which turned out to be tapped for the purposes of another case. The suspect's revealing conversations were admitted in evidence, because tapping could have been authorised in a case of tax evasion.

20   Garde (1995), at 19ff; Report of 1996 (1996), at 26ff.

the earlier crime, or that there was no connection at all between the cases.[21] Neither in law, nor as a question of policy, have I any misgivings. It must be stressed that this question has nothing to do with the question of establishing a profile register.

If, by consent, samples have been taken from *non-accused persons*, whether witnesses or outsiders, and tested for purposes of DNA identification, the question arises whether such samples may be run against anonymous samples in unsolved cases.[22] After the conclusion of the first case, all samples from such persons much be destroyed (s 792(f)(2), AJA), but until then it is not unthinkable that a policeman with a good memory may become suspicious when an outsider arrives at the police precinct to submit a sample. The police must be entitled to use the sample in another case, as they have lawful possession of it. The person giving up the sample has no claim of immunity in other cases. Perhaps it could be argued that the general willingness to assist the police will be reduced if it is known that samples submitted for elimination are used in other cases, but that is a question of police tactics, not of law.

A *blood sample* taken in a case of drunken driving, for example, is only tested for its amount of alcohol: DNA testing is unnecessary. Such samples are normally stored for one year by the Forensic Chemistry Section to counter a later submission by the accused of irregularities in the course of analysis. If the accused of a drunken driving offence is suspected of, for example, rape during that period, the question arises whether the sample can be analysed for DNA without a new court order. The Norwegian Supreme Court has accepted that a photograph taken for the purpose of proving a road traffic violation may be used in order to prove theft, even though the Ministry of Justice had instructed the road traffic control authority that such photographs could only be used for the directly relevant purpose. The Supreme Court remarked that the evidence was legitimate and the adducing of evidence free when not expressly circumscribed.[23] Nevertheless, a later Norwegian Government Report[24] is inclined to oppose the possibility of a later DNA analysis of a blood sample, as the sample cannot be used as it is – unlike the photograph in the 1990 case – but only after a subsequent analysis. In Danish law the opposite result must be assumed, if one follows the logic of the general rule whereby the only legally contentious question is whether the police have the right to have a sample taken – later analyses are automatically legitimate. The same result must be reached if the sample has been taken in a civil case: for example, a paternity suit.

---

21 German law is restrictive. According to Strafprozessordnung, s 81(a), blood samples or other body cells taken from the suspect can only be used in the actual case or a connected case ('eines anhängigen Strafverfahrens').

22 In the well-known English *Pitchfork* case of 1987, the results from the analyses of 5,509 samples given voluntarily were compared with unsolved cases, and an old case of rape was solved.

23 Rt, Norsk Retstidende, 'Norwegian Legal Gazette' (1990) 1008.

24 NOU, Norges Offentlige Utredninger (1993) 26.

Standard of proof

The assessment of evidence is free: s 896, AJA. The judgment must be based solely upon the evidence adduced in court, directly or indirectly: s 877, AJA. The degree of proof is not codified, but in criminal cases the principle in *dubio pro reo*, or certainty beyond reasonable doubt, is settled practice.[25]

Although there is no special standard of proof applicable to DNA evidence, some tendencies may be discerned. As DNA evidence does not have the same degree of certainty as the classical fingerprint – for which reason I deprecate the popular term 'genetic fingerprint'[26] – a fundamental question remains whether a conviction is safe in cases where there is no other proof but DNA profiling. The general practice of the Danish Forensic Genetics Section is to exclude a random match as having a probability of 'less than 1:100,000'. More specific numbers are added when relatives, other than identical twins or special ethnic groups, are possibly involved. In these cases, the tribunal shall need *additional evidence* in order to establish that the accused, and not one of the other 50 or so possible Danish perpetrators, is the guilty party. For example, in the case mentioned previously, the DNA profile of semen found on the complainant's panties and in her vagina was decisively supported by the complainant's statement that rape had occurred, and partly supported by the accused's admission of having been in the complainant's company earlier on the evening of the alleged crime. Indeed, the Court of Appeal took the complainant's statement as the decisive proof.

If no such evidence is present, an acquittal is not out of the question. Thus, in an early case of murder in 1992 – early for DNA testing to be presented in a Danish court – the '*Lille Skensved* case' (the name of the village where the crime was committed), where the only link between the accused and the crime was a DNA testing, the jury delivered a verdict of not guilty.

Following the increasing number of cases using DNA as evidence, there may perhaps be discerned a tendency to convict even in the absence of significant additional evidence. This occurred in a case which began in 1992 but finished years later.[27] At the scene of an attempted rape against a child of seven were found some hairs, probably from a man's private parts. On the basis of a so-called 'enzyme system test', it was proved that the hairs did not belong to the accused A, a feeble-minded youth. However, he was convicted on other evidence, especially his confession. When later the Forensic Genetics Section carried out a DNA analysis of the hairs as an scientific experiment, and compared the sample with other test results in the possession of the Section, the DNA profile was identical – a random match having a probability of less than 1:100,000 – to that of a man, B, convicted in 1989 of a serious sexual crime. In a retrial of the first case, A was acquitted, the prosecution service assenting. B was then charged; he denied having been near the scene of the crime, but although the DNA profile was the

---

25 See Gammeltoft-Hansen (1998), at 94ff.

26 Garde (1995), at 3. The most exhaustive German work on DNA, to my knowledge, Birgit Klumpe, *Der 'Genetische Finger-abdruck' im Strafverfahren* (1993), retains the term, placing it in inverted commas.

27 Report of 1996 (1996), at 50ff, the 'Gladsaxe' case.

only strong piece of evidence against him, he was convicted. It must be remembered that in Danish law, the criminal past of the accused is known to the court.

The outcome of the retrial in the 'Gladsaxe' case also demonstrates that a *negative match* can be a decisive proof in the accused's favour, even if there is other evidence against him. This was also the case in the classic 'Pitchfork' case, in which an earlier suspect, who had even confessed to one of the two murders under investigation, was released when DNA analyses negated his guilt, even before the real perpetrator was discovered. However, a conviction is not impossible in such a case if the rest of the evidence is particularly strong. Thus, in a lower court case of 1994,[28] the accused's alleged paternity to the child to which his stepdaughter had given birth was the decisive point of contention. The girl consistently denounced the accused. The case was treated by the Forensic Genetics Section as a paternity case: five probes were taken, not four as in ordinary criminal cases. One probe out of the five excluded the accused's paternity. As a mutation was suspected, the Section resumed the investigation, applying five additional systems, all pointing to the accused, who was duly convicted. As in the rape case, the judgment placed the complainant's statement first.

Of course, as the accused need only create a *reasonable doubt* of his guilt, not absolute proof of his innocence, a negative match ordinarily ensures an acquittal, or that the prosecution service will dismiss the case.

Challenges to DNA evidence by the lawyer for the accused

Owing to the high prestige of the Forensic Genetics Section, both as regards expertise and integrity, defence counsel usually do not challenge DNA evidence *per se*, maintaining only that a probability of a random match of 1:100,000 still leaves 50 hypothetical suspects in a population of five million. Also, as in the traditional fingerprint cases, a plant or, more realistically, an innocent explanation of the presence of the sample may be attempted. Thus, in the rape case, the complainant's consent to sexual intercourse would have been a more plausible defence than the statement 'I was never there'. DNA analysis can prove presence, but not coercion.

Judicial interpretation of DNA test results

Danish courts never, or almost never, pronounce on general questions, concentrating always on the case in hand. The laconic character of Danish judgments has been often criticised, in my view rightly so. *Obiter dicta* on the possible weight of DNA evidence are non-existent. No monographs analysing the courts' interpretation of DNA test results have as yet been written. My own article of 1995 and the Report of 1996 have remained, until now, the most extensive treatments of Danish legal practice in the field.

---

28 This case is described by Garde (1995), at 6.

If a *generalised statement* is to be attempted, the courts regard DNA test results as strong evidence, stronger when supporting the accused than otherwise. Perhaps, but only perhaps, there is a discernible tendency to convict even when only scanty additional evidence exists (or no evidence at all). An in-depth study of the cases decided may perhaps result in greater clarity, but this is doubtful.

Judicial directions in relation to DNA evidence

'Directions' and 'summing-up' are only known in Danish law in the very limited number of *jury trials*. Only cases upon a plea of not guilty, where the prosecution demands four years' imprisonment or more, except property crimes without violence – robbery is included, forgery and fraud not – are tried before a jury: s 687, AJA. In practice, only cases of murder, attempted murder, the most serious cases of drug crimes, arson, rape, robbery and political crimes, are jury cases. If the prosecution limits itself to a demand of less than four years, the case is tried before a mixed court of a learned judge with two lay assessors in the first instance, three judges and three assessors on appeal. About 100 cases every year are tried before a jury, as against more than 10,000 in a mixed court, and almost 10,000 before a single judge in shortened trial following a confession: s 922, AJA. There are 50,000 or more smaller cases which are always tried before a single judge, whether the accused confesses or not.

There are no fixed rules covering the form of the summing up in Danish law, only some conventions in practice. For example, there is a warning against convicting solely or mainly on the basis of witnesses whom the defence has had no opportunity to challenge: namely, the *Unterpertinger* judgment of the European Court of Human Rights.[29] No statutory rules, however, regulate the directions to the jury.

In all other cases the court must adduce its reasons and the foundations of the verdict, including possible DNA evidence.

Retention and storage of samples/test results

Time of destruction

Until the legislation of 1989, the two main groups of identification evidence, photographs and fingerprints, were treated divergently by the police. Upon acquittal, photographs of the accused were generally destroyed because of the risk of invasion of privacy where the photographs to be shown to witnesses in later cases. Fingerprints and other samples were only destroyed in cases of proven mistaken identity or clearly wrongful accusation, but not upon acquittal because of insufficiency of evidence.[30]

The Report of 1987[31] proposed the codification of this practice: destruction of photographs upon acquittal, but of fingerprints and all other samples only in the

---

29   *Unterpertinger v Austria* (1986) 13 EHRR 175.
30   See Garde (1995), at 26ff.
31   See the Report of 1987 (1987), at 85ff.

case of non-accused persons and unlawfully obtained evidence. It was argued that the invasion of privacy was minimal, as there was no risk of recognition, and that there were 'not few' cases of the decisive probative value in later cases of fingerprints from accused but not convicted persons. On presenting the Bill in Parliament, the Minister of Justice, who agreed with the Report, added that the fingerprints of the former accused could clear him or her of all suspicion in the new case, with no establishment of alibi or other evidence being necessary. The overwhelming majority of Parliament voted in favour, only the Socialist People's Party dissenting. The relevant rule is s 792(f), AJA.

A couple of years before, a man convicted of rape was granted a retrial on possibly flimsy grounds and was acquitted in the new case. Some time afterwards, two teenage boys were murdered under gruesome circumstances. The fingerprints of the person acquitted of rape, which were still in the police files, clearly pointed to his guilt. He was convicted of the murders and imprisoned for life.

No doubt all members of Parliament remembered the case (the *Kowalski* case) while voting on the Bill: one member directly mentioned it.

While there is no doubt that domestic Danish law upholds the retention of samples without a conviction, the practice has been challenged from the point of view of Article 8 of the European Convention of Human Rights, 'respect for privacy'. After his acquittal for attempted rape, a person brought an action against the prosecution service, demanding the destruction of his fingerprints taken during the criminal case and invoking Article 8 of the Convention. The Western High Court approved the retention of the fingerprints, citing s 792(f), AJA and adding that this rule could not be assumed to be in violation of Article 8 of the Convention.[32]

It has been suggested[33] that the rule is possibly in variance with Article 6((2), 'presumption of innocence', and that the High Court ought at least to have taken that clause into consideration, even though it was not invoked. I disagree: the practice of the Strasbourg Court[34] shows, in my view conclusively, that upon a decision to discontinue criminal proceedings, an act implying that reasons to suspect the person concerned continue to exist, as opposed to an act or statement denouncing the person as guilty, does not in principle violate any provision of the Convention. Article 8 remains the only realistic possibility for challenge.

The Strasbourg interpretation of Article 8 is inconclusive, and the problem has not yet been attacked head-on. The case of *McVeigh v United Kingdom*[35] has, however, come closest to confronting the issue: three men were arrested on suspicion of IRA terrorism and were photographed and fingerprinted. They were released after 45 hours, no suspicion remaining. Their complaint to the European Commission of Human Rights concerning the taking *and retention* of photographs and fingerprints was dismissed, the Commission mentioning the combating of terrorism as the decisive consideration. Whether the reference to terrorism should

---

32 UfR (1992) 948 VLD.

33 *Eva Smith* in UfR (1994) B 99ff, citing the European Commission for Human Rights case 7986/1977, *Krause v Switzerland* 13 DR 73, 3 October 1978.

34 Especially the three cases in vol A 123, *Lutz, Englert,* and *Nölkenbockhoff.*

35 (1977) 25 Eur Comm HR 15.

be regarded as just a clinching argument or as a *conditio sine qua non* implying that retention of such evidence after the discontinuing of criminal proceedings is only allowable in terrorism cases as an exception from other cases, is doubtful. In my opinion, the latter, more far-reaching supposition is untenable, as it is not stated expressly. When or if the complaint of *Williams*, another British case concerning the non-destruction of a DNA profile of a former murder suspect, is adjudged in Strasbourg, the position may be clarified. Currently, however, I maintain that the pragmatic Danish rule is not divergent with human rights.

Retaining, not destroying, DNA samples and test results after the case is one thing; *establishing* a *DNA profile register* is quite another. Without a register, the police are still able to ask the Forensic Genetics Section to analyse samples left at a crime scene and compare them to samples and test results in files in the Section's archives. However, with a DNA profile register, it would be possible to look up all cases and all old test results at once, without the necessity of the veteran detective remembering similar traits from an earlier case.

The Council of Europe's Recommendation No R(92)1 on the use of DNA in the criminal justice system suggests that 'samples ... should not be kept after the rendering of the final decision in the case for which they were used' and that 'the results of DNA analysis and the information so derived [should be] deleted when it is no longer necessary to keep it for the purposes for which it was used'.[36] The Kingdom of Denmark, along with Norway, the Netherlands and Germany, made a reservation to the recommendation.

The Report of 1996[37] strongly recommends a DNA profile register, both electronic and manual, containing profiles of known individuals and of unknown perpetrators on the basis of samples from crime scenes. Draft regulations for a future register are attached to the Report.

Establishing a new public register requires the consent of the minister in question – here, the Minister of Justice – after consultation with the Minister of Research, and regulations for the running of the register must be formulated ensuring compliance with the very detailed precepts of the Public Authorities' Registers Act 1978 (Lov om offentlige myndigheders registre) (several times amended). Legislation is not necessary *per se*, but follow-up legislation is imperative in order to achieve a serviceable registry. The existing rules for the taking of samples mean that the methods employed are of decisive importance to the investigation. For example, if, in a case of rape, the perpetrator is unknown from the beginning and only disclosed by means of DNA samples at the crime scene compared with his own DNA profile, such samples will be included in a register established today. However, if he is caught in the act, DNA analysis is superfluous and thus illegal as a means of investigation in the case at hand. It is obvious that the register must also include the second rapist's DNA profile to be useful in later cases: authority must be established for compelling him to submit to the taking of a sample along the lines of s 792(b)(1), AJA on photographing and fingerprinting for later identification. Also, unless the DNA profiles of the whole

---

36   Council of Europe Recommendation No R(92)1, [8].
37   See the Report of 1996 (1996).

or whole adult population were to be taken – which is not on the books[38] – the persons to be included in the register must be defined, which also necessitates legislation. The Report of 1996 suggests a register comprising the following offences:

- assault or threat against a public servant: s 119 of the Penal Code (PC); assault against witnesses: s 123, PC;
- arson: ss 180–81, PC;
- causing danger to means of transportation, including explosion and highjacking: ss 183, 183(a), 184, PC;
- incest: s 210, PC;
- Sexual crimes, including rape and intercourse with children: ss 216–25, PC;
- obscene behaviour: s 232, PC;
- homicide: s 237, PC;
- dangerous or aggravated assault: ss 245–46, PC (but not simple assault: s 244, PC);
- reckless causation of danger or of a fatal and incurable disease: s 252, PC;
- coercion, deprivation of liberty: ss 260–61, PC;
- aggravated theft: s 276 (cf s 286), PC;
- robbery: s 288, PC;
- crimes against the independence and safety of the state, against the Constitution, and the supreme authorities of the state: chs 12 and 13, PC.

The authors of the Report argue in favour of the same regime as for the fingerprint register, comprising:

(1) persons convicted of the relevant offences, including those convicted of attempt or complicity and those acquitted because of insanity;

(2) persons accused of the same offences, even though not convicted; *but excluding*

(3) persons not accused of the relevant offences (witnesses, victims, outsiders tested for purposes of elimination).

It is suggested that the second group be reduced along the lines of s 792(c)(3), AJA, ie, if the sample has been obtained unlawfully, or in cases of proven mistaken identity or clearly wrongful accusation. Also, normally all profiles shall be destroyed when the relevant person reaches the age of 80, or at least two years after his death. It is expected that about 3,500 people will be included within one year after establishing the register, growing to about 14,500 people within a period of five years.

---

38 The Report of 1996 (1996), at 69, argues that other police registers are limited; that the risks of misuse are increased in proportion to the size of the register; that problems of demarcation would arise especially in relation to aliens residing in the country; and that costs would be daunting: 3,600 DKr per test or at least 14,000 million DKr now and more later. I agree entirely.

The Report adduces traditional arguments for including samples from accused who are not convicted. The Report also acknowledges that in several other Nordic or Western countries such samples are ordered to be destroyed upon acquittal. However, in addition to the well-known commonsense arguments, the Report offers highly significant *statistical data*. Between 1989 and 1993, 15,231 people were convicted of at least one of the offences listed above; of these, 11,732 had neither been accused nor convicted of a relevant offence in 1988. This indicates a risk of conviction within five years of about 0.28% in proportion to the whole population above 15 years or, more realistically, about 0.67% of the male population in the age group of 15–64 years. Moreover, 1,108 had been accused, but not convicted, in 1988, indicating a risk of such conviction of 12.2%. Further, 2,391 were accused in 1988 and later convicted, indicating a risk of 23.2%. Small discrepancies described in the Report did not distort the picture. I consider the findings convincing.

The Report was been submitted to several bodies with a request for an opinion. Each and everyone recommended a register.

The proposal to include non-convicted persons was commented on by many. The Public Inspectorate of Registers (Registertilsynet) concluded in favour of the proposal, as did all representatives of the police and prosecution service. The Medico-Legal Council made no comments, while the Danish Medical Association (Den almindelige danske Lægeforening) and the Law Society (Advokatsamfundet) spoke against the proposal. One academic questioned the interpretation of the statistical data, remarking that formerly accused persons ran a bigger risk of scrutiny in cases of similar unsolved crimes, so that the higher conviction rate mirrored police practice more than a real difference. The chairman of the Commission, after renewed consultation with the Department of Statistics, acknowledged the possibility of minor uncertainties, but maintained that the overall picture was too strong to be disregarded.

Place of storage

All samples and test results are stored in the Forensic Genetics Section. In addition, test results sent by the Section to the police and included in the file of the case remain in the file. Old court files are stored in the archives of the police, judgments and transcripts of records are stored with the courts. Obsolete files are partly deleted, partly deposited in the public archives.

If a register is established a responsible authority must be appointed: s 13 of the Public Authorities' Registers Act 1978. As the register will serve police purposes, it will almost certainly be lodged with the National Commissioner of Police (Rigspolitichefen), along with other police registers.

According to s 12 of the Public Authorities' Registers Act, measures of safety must be taken to ensure that the information stored is not used for unauthorised purposes or divulged to unauthorised persons. The Report proposes that specifically appointed and trained employees with the National Commissioner shall have exclusive access to the register. Every request for information, especially from investigating detective officers from the police districts,[39] must be passed on to one of those employees, each of whom should have his or her own code of access. Also, it must be feasible to trace every attempt of access to a specific person.

Penalties for unauthorised use

The Public Authorities' Registers Act contains many limitations on the releasing of information. Violations of those rules or of specific conditions contained in permissions of release may be punished by a fine: s 29. Furthermore, ch 16 of the Penal Code contains penalties for offences committed by civil servants – police officers are without exception civil servants – and other public officers while exercising their function: for example, the unlawful passing on or exploitation of confidential information obtained in connection with a public office or function (s 15(2); or with a task carried out according to appointment with a public authority (s 152(a)); or with trade or business by virtue of public appointment or authorisation (s 152(b)); as well as later unlawful similar acts committed by persons not having participated in the original offence: s 152(d). Finally, ss 155 and 157 generally cover offences committed by public servants both with intent and 'serious or often repeated breach of duty or carelessness'. Violations of the relevant clauses of the Penal Code are punished by a fine or simple detention (hæfte), or imprisonment for a term not exceeding six months. If committed with the purpose of unlawful gain or under aggravating circumstances, the penalty may be increased to imprisonment for a term not exceeding two years.

Penalties for unauthorised storage

Establishing a private register is only allowed under rather stringent conditions: Private Registers Act (Lov om private registre). In connection with DNA profiles, the relevant rules are ss 3 and 4, whereby information on purely private matters – such as race, religion, colour, sexual orientation, earlier offences, health, social problems, misuse of strong liquors or drugs – must not be stored or revealed unless authorised by other legislation or specifically permitted by the Inspectorate of Registers. However, the consent of the person concerned can legitimise such storage or passing on of information. Violations of the Act are generally penalised by a fine; however, in addition, anyone who unlawfully passes on information or pictures concerning another person's private life is liable to a fine, simple detention or imprisonment for any term not exceeding six months: s 264(d), PC.

---

39 The investigation of crimes is the duty of the local 54 police districts, the Chief Constables enjoying operational independence. Central matters, including registers, are the concern of the National Commissioner.

Release of DNA test information

Special rules

There are no such special rules. As mentioned previously, until now DNA is only specifically mentioned by name in the Aliens Act.

Release of stored test results

The reader is referred to ss 28–32 of the Act on Public Administration.

The question of access is treated at length in the Report of 1996. Most controversial is the question of the release of information to the person concerned. As a rule, persons have on request the right to every information contained in a private or public register concerning themselves, usually in writing. If decisive public or private considerations, including the interests of the individual, outweigh his or her interest to be informed, the information can be withheld or possibly only given orally. In this case, the individual can request the Inspectorate of Registers and/or the authority directly responsible, the National Commissioner of Police, to ensure that the relevant information has been stored in accordance with the relevant rules. The alternatives are named direct and indirect access, respectively. The reason why the interests of the person concerned can militate against openness is that he or she can subsequently freely pass on the information to a third person. This means, for example, that an employer could demand the person to divulge what is contained in the register as a precondition for appointment. As the police must on request give to anyone an extract from police registers showing previous convictions – or confirming the absence thereof – a great number of employers routinely demand such information from every applicant. This means that many youths are effectively barred from employment because of sometimes trivial offences until the expunging of such offences, if not from police records, then from the accessible extract. The Report also notes that the Ministry of Justice has appointed another Commission to consider all legislation on information concerning private matters. Finally, only indirect access is proposed corresponding to the fingerprints register. If a DNA profile is released to the police and prosecutor in connection with criminal proceedings, defence counsel and normally also the defendant have right of disclosure: s 745, AJA.

The lack of access for the person concerned was criticised by the Inspectorate of Registers, the Law Society and the Danish Medical Association. A compromise was suggested, giving a right to complete oral information, thus impeding others from obtaining information indirectly.

Not surprisingly, the Report proposed that private persons be refused information from the DNA register.

Access is proposed to the courts, the police, the prosecution service,[40] the Ministry of Justice and the Parliamentary 'Ombudsman'. Also, the police must be empowered to pass on information to the Forensic Genetics Section, which will

---

40 At local police district level, the police and prosecution service are amalgamated, but on regional and national levels covering prosecution in the higher courts, the prosecution is independent.

also in future be entrusted with DNA testing in criminal proceedings. On a case-by-case basis, the register should also be allowed to consider passing on information to judicial authorities in foreign countries, taking into account the use for which the information is requested, and the need for reciprocity.

The Report proposes that the police shall be allowed to request information in all criminal cases, even if the convicted perpetrator of the offence in hand would not be included in the register. For example, if an as yet unidentified burglar has cut his hand on a windowpane – burglary is normally not regarded as aggravated theft – the police should nevertheless be allowed to ask the register whether the DNA profile from the windowpane be present in the register. I agree. With the brisk wording of the Norwegian Report, a convicted murderer must put up with an increased risk of disclosure when he takes to burglary, but not the other way round.

As is seen, it is not proposed to give defence counsel direct access. The principle of equality of arms could be invoked in favour of such access. On the other hand, defence counsel does not have the right of direct access to other police registers, including the fingerprints register, and I consider it sufficient that defence counsel in case of dispute with the police can appeal to the court: s 746, AJA.

Finally, the Report suggests that the Ministry of Justice, after consultation with the Inspectorate of Registers, shall be empowered to release information for the purpose of scientific or statistical research of considerable importance to society. The terms of such permission ought to take all questions of safety and secrecy into account. The authors add that the purpose of the register is identification, not the gathering of other information about the persons concerned, which must be taken into account when deciding whether to release test results to researchers.

Privacy and DNA test results

There are as yet no such rules but, as seen, the Report of 1996 proposes stringent rules to be introduced with the establishment of a DNA register.

Postscript 2002

Special requirements for specific groups and specific scientific tests on DNA samples for use in criminal proceedings

Since the Report was prepared in 1997–98, analyses have been carried out to a much greater extent than before in criminal cases. Whereas until 1995 less than 100 analyses were made per year, the 200 mark was passed in 1996, and since then numbers have been increasing, as follows: in 1997, 515 analyses; in 1998, 556; in 1999, 702; in 2000, 989; in 2001, 1,930; and in 2002 (until 6 February), 280 analyses. The numbers have not been broken up into sub-groups. However, whereas rape and murder earlier were the most common cases for the application of the method, it is now used in a broad spectrum of cases.

In cases of consanguinity according to the Aliens Act, the tendency is less dramatic. The latest five years show the following number of tests: in 1997, 55; in 1998, 196; in 1999, 134; in 2000, 105; and in 2001, 69.[41]

Standard of proof

The most dramatic single case is the 'Susan' case,[42] where a girl of 10 was strangled, and the perpetrator introduced his penis and/or a blunt instrument in the dead girl's vagina. When the murdered girl was found in a cellar in the big block of flats where she had lived, all men living in the block voluntarily submitted to a test except one man, who refused, citing a conversation with a well-known attorney who had in the press propounded the cause of civil liberties, and whose advice the man had solicited. The man's residence at the spot was, in my view rightly, deemed to distinguish the case from the case of the taxi driver previously discussed.[43] The suspect was arrested, blood-tested by court order, and detained, the refusal being cited as an additional ground for suspicion. DNA testing was very difficult because the material at the scene of the crime was contaminated. However, at the third attempt the analysis was successful and there was a positive identification. At the trial, the most important evidence was the accused's DNA at the scene of the crime and genetic traces from the girl in the accused's flat. The accused was convicted by the jury and sentenced to imprisonment for life, the Supreme Court upholding the sentence. I do not consider it a hazardous supposition that since that case there is a discernible tendency to convict on the strength of a DNA match, even with only a minimal amount of supplementary evidence, and perhaps none at all. Without doubt the courts and the lay judges have grown accustomed to the new kind of evidence; it is used much more often now than in the early 1990s.

Destruction of samples and results

By Act 434/2000, in force since 1 July 2000, a DNA profile register has been established, undoubtedly the most important new development. The Act adheres to the recommendations of the Report of 1996, with minor points of divergence. The register is both manual and electronic and consists of two parts:

(1) profiles of individuals who are or have been accused of one of the offences listed in my main report, if the sample has been taken according to ch 72 and ss 792ff of the AJA;

(2) profiles of unknown perpetrators on the basis of samples from scenes of crime.

Thus, it was decided to include samples from an accused person who is acquitted or against whom the prosecution service has withdrawn the charge. Only a small minority of Parliament voted against. Whereas information pertaining to

---

41 The source of these statistics is a letter from MD Niels Morling, Head of the Forensic Genetics Section, to Justice Peter Garde, 9 February 2002.

42 UfR (2000) 2405 H.

43 UfR (1997) 972 V, above n 2.

convicted persons is retained until the age of 70 (not 80, as originally proposed), information against persons accused, but not convicted, is only retained for 10 years after the acquittal or dropping of charges. That was part of the political compromise; however, both time limits may be extended if it is deemed necessary to retain the information. The other proposed rules – all information purged two years after the relevant person's decease; destruction of samples taken if the suspicion is regarded as 'groundless' (as opposed to 'insufficient evidence', in which case the information is retained); and no registration of samples taken unlawfully or from witnesses – were passed without alteration. I refer to the main text.

As described previously,[44] a Danish court has approved the retention of the fingerprints of an accused following his acquittal for attempted rape. Recently, a new attempt was made. A man was charged of destruction of property, and was fingerprinted and arrested; however, the High Court ordered his release from arrest, as there were no reasonable grounds for suspicion. When the prosecution dropped charges, the accused demanded the destruction of his fingerprints, and upon the refusal of the police to comply with his demand, he brought an action in the High Court, invoking Article 8 of the European Convention of Human Rights, 'respect for privacy' (as in the 1992 case), but also Article 6, 'the presumption of innocence', the principle of equality before the law, and the reasoning of the court ordering his release. He lost on all counts.[45]

Although none of the fingerprint cases reached the Supreme Court, it may be assumed that in a hypothetical case upon a demand that DNA samples be destroyed following acquittal, Danish courts will reach the same result as in those cases. I know of no opposite practice in the European Court of Human Rights.

The register under (2) contains samples from all crime scenes, not only the crimes listed under (1). For example, if a burglar has cut his hand, leaving blood, such blood may be sampled for later storage and may also be compared to other samples in the register, even though burglary is not a listed crime. The information must be purged when the trace has been connected to a person (in which case it could be transferred to the register under (1) when it is no longer of importance to the investigation, or for other, special reasons.

In my view, the most controversial rule is the requirement that the person-based register under (1) can only contain samples taken according to s 792ff, AJA, including the requirement that the taking of the sample be deemed of 'decisive importance to the investigation'. For example, if in a case of rape the perpetrator has escaped, leaving traces of DNA at the scene of the crime, and a suspect is later arrested, the requirements for the taking of a sample will normally be present. As a matter of course, the sample will be compared not only to the traces in the current case, but also traces in the register under (2), thus also investigating the suspect's possible earlier malefactions. However, if the perpetrator is caught in the act – and if, when arrested, the suspect confesses at once – the taking of a sample will be superfluous to the case in hand and will thus not be allowed. A 'serial' rapist will thus only be charged with the crime at hand (but if there is a

---

44 See UfR (1992) 948 VLD.
45 UfR 2000, p 2101 V.

justified suspicion that he has committed an earlier crime, the taking of a sample may be authorised on the basis of that suspicion). Furthermore, whereas photographing and fingerprinting for later identification is allowed, the taking of a sample for such purpose is not allowed. To put it bluntly, speedy confession in the case at hand may protect both the serial offender against discovery of earlier unsolved crimes and the first offender against capture for a later crime. I consider those limitations irrational, and I hope that they will be repealed when the register has proved its efficiency.

As at 12 February 2002, the register contained 2,221 profiles, of which 897 in the register were under (1) and 1,324 under (2), broken up as follows:[46]

(1) Register of persons known:

- convicted: 472;
- sexual crimes, ss 216–25, PC: 95;
- homicide, s 237, PC: 76;
- attempted homicide: 73;
- assault, ss 245–46, PC: 52;
- aggravated theft, s 286, PC: 22;
- robbery, s 288, PC: 114;
- others: 40;
- formerly accused, charges withdrawn: 161;
- formerly accused, acquitted: 24;
- prosecution waived: 3;
- currently accused, case not concluded: 237;
- total: 897.

(2) Register of traces from persons unknown:

- rape: 124;
- homicide, including homicide abroad: 112;
- attempted homicide: 18;
- theft (not only aggravated, see above): 685;
- robbery: 270;
- others: 115;
- total: 1,324.

Since the establishment of the register there have been 166 'hits' or 'matches', as follows:

---

46   Letter from HH Andersen, Head of DNA Section, National Commissioner of Police, to Peter Garde, 12 February 2002.

(a) from trace to trace: 116;

(b) from trace to person: 22;

(c) from person to trace: 28;

Total: 166.

In (a), a profile from one crime scene is matched with a profile from another crime scene, thus proving that the same – as yet unidentified – person has committed more than one crime. In (b), a profile from a new crime scene matches the profile of a person already registered. In (c), a profile from a person now accused matches the profile from a trace already registered.

In almost all cases of drunken driving, a blood sample is taken and routinely retained for one year. If the driver claims mistaken identity or the switching of samples, that hopeless argument may be countered definitively by the taking of a second sample, proving identity with the original sample. As I am informed, in police practice it is regarded as unlawful to match such sample with samples taken at the crime scene ('person to trace'). I am not convinced: since that sample is lawfully in the public domain, following a criminal charge, I consider its use in other cases legitimate.

The data acquired shows that criminals operate not only in one police district, but nationwide. It also shows that criminals do not necessarily stick to one type of crime. For example, in one of the 'person to trace' matches, the profile of a man registered on the basis of an earlier conviction for attempted homicide was later found in a trace at the scene of a burglary. Of considerable interest is a recent case, in which a youth of 19 was registered upon being accused of rape. The charge was later withdrawn because of insufficient evidence. Information of the youth's DNA profile can be retained for 10 years, but one month afterwards, his profile was found on a biological trace at the scene of a burglary. In a criminal justice system where fingerprints and samples are destroyed following an acquittal or the withdrawal of charges, the burglary may have remained unsolved.

Release of stored DNA test results

The rules of access to the DNA profile register were carried through largely as proposed. Access was given to the police, the prosecution service, the Ministry of Justice; foreign courts, police, and prosecution services on a case-by-case basis; the Forensic Genetics Section for use in criminal cases, and to the Parliamentary Ombudsman. The difficult question of release of information to the person concerned was also solved: that information may be given directly and orally, but not in writing.

In conclusion, it can be said that since the composition of my original report for the XV Congress of the Académie Internationale de Droit Comparé in 1998, the genetic test has more than proved itself in the Danish criminal justice system.

References

Gammeltoft-Hansen (1998) *Strafferetspleje (Criminal Justice)*, 2nd edn, I
Garde, P (1995) 'DNA i straffeprocessen' ('DNA in criminal procedure'), NTfK 1
Report of 1987 (1987) *Betænkning nr 1104/1987 om legemsindgreb under efterforskning* (Inspection of the Body During Investigation)
Report of 1996 (1996) *Etablering af et DNA-profilregister – med henblik på behandling af straffesager* (Establishing a DNA Profile Register – With Reference to Criminal Procedure)

CHAPTER 6

FINLAND

Irma Pahlman
Researcher, Faculty of Law, University of Helsinki

Introduction

The history of DNA analysis begins in the 1860s with the publication by the Austrian biologist Gregor Mendel of a study on the heredity of the characteristics of peas in the hybridisation of different varieties. He discovered the principles of heredity in sexual reproduction. The results of his study did not become widely known until the early 20th century; it was then that his ideas about the basic units of inheritance – the genes – met with general acceptance. The chemical structure of the gene was clarified in the 1940s, when the material that carries genes was discovered. That material is nucleic acid. The nucleic acid in the gene is deoxyribonucleic acid. Nucleic acids appear in chains with alternating four bases identified with letters A, C, G and T. The structure of the nucleic acid does not require that the bases take a certain sequence, and the different molecules of nucleic acid and their components, or genes, have different sequences. The sequence of three letters (bases) forms a code which corresponds to a particular amino acid in a protein molecule. In other words, the gene is a chain of base triplets. Each of them directs the corresponding amino acid to take its place in the chain which then forms the protein molecule encoded by the gene. The nucleic acid has the ability to double in such a way as to preserve the sequence. If the structure of a single-stranded DNA is known, the base sequence of the complementary strand can always be inferred. This action of doubling is the basis of the inheritance of the information encoded in the gene. If an error takes place in the doubling, it will be carried to the offspring. Exactly the same genetic inheritance is only possible in identical twins, who develop from one egg.[1]

How can an individual be identified if biological material is available? From that sample, DNA – which may be fragmented – is refined with the use of laboratory techniques. In the analysis of the DNA structure, a genetic fingerprint – a DNA profile which is unique to each person – is found. In Finland, DNA analysis has been used for criminal investigation since 1991.

Within the Council of Europe, Great Britain has the longest tradition of using DNA analysis to investigate crime. The first successful analysis was made there as early as 1987.[2]

---

1   See Mäkelä (1997), pp 11–14.
2   See Himberg et al (1993), p 132.

Before the introduction of DNA analysis, criminal investigation used such methods as fingerprint identification. In Finland, fingerprint analysis has been used since the early 1900s. For more than 20 years DNA analysis has been in use to decide cases before the courts. It was first introduced in paternity disputes, under the Act and Decree concerning examinations relating to hereditary characteristics (702/1975 and 674/1976).[3] In 1976, HLA analysis was introduced which is made from the white blood cells and was used only to determine borderline cases. In 1991 this test was replaced by DNA analysis of the genetic material. Legislation remained unaltered at that stage. Since 1991 DNA analysis has been used in criminal investigation,[4] mostly to investigate violent offences. The Crime Laboratory of the National Bureau of Investigation carries out the analyses. The Laboratory has an independent status in submitting reports. A request for analysis is made by the pre-trial authorities, public prosecutor or judicial authorities (158/1996). The cost of analysis is around 3,000 Finnish marks. (This is part of the cost of the proof process which, as a rule, the accused is required to pay to the state.) The reliability of DNA analysis ranges from one to 100,000 to one million.[5] Before amendments to the Coercive Measures Act, which will be discussed later, the samples taken from suspects were retained and the results of the analyses were recorded in reports. No file was created, although the law permitted a manual file.[6]

Recommendation of the Council of Europe No R(92)1

Finland approved 'Recommendation of the Council of Europe No R(92)1 on the use of analysis of deoxyribonucleic acid (DNA) within the framework of the criminal justice system' on 10 February 1992[7] (Appendix 1). Unlike Denmark, Norway, Germany and the Netherlands, Finland did not make reservations. The nature of the recommendation is to be obligating on domestic law, but does not constitute a legally binding document. The key elements of the recommendation will be discussed later.

After the signature of the Council of Europe Recommendation the next step for Finland was to harmonise its law with the recommendation and the existing scientific data.

In the drafting of the Police Personal Register Bill a need for filing DNA profiles of suspects was recognised; the Government Bill states that characteristics for identification are mainly to be filed on the Personal Description Register and, in future, on the DNA Register to be kept by the National Bureau of Investigation and on the Aliens Identification Register.[8] On 1 July 1997 an amendment to the

---

3   See Aho and Pikkarainen (1997), pp 545 and 548–49.
4   See Aho, Ehnholm and Sajantila (1991), pp 491–98.
5   See Gill *et al* (1996), pp 14–22.
6   HE 20/1997 vp (Government Bill), p 5.
7   See, eg, Rogers and de Bousingen (1995), Appendix, pp 345–50.
8   HE39/1994 vp (Government Bill).

Coercive Measures Act came into force which gives the police the right to take samples and file DNA profiles. Two new paragraphs were added to Chapter six of the Coercive Measures Act. Instead of additions to the old s 4, a whole new s 5 was enacted on the right of the police to file DNA profiles on the Police Personal Register. This approach was taken, first, because the filing of DNA profiles to the same extent that personal descriptions (such as fingerprints) are recorded is not possible. This is in harmony with item 8 of the Council of Europe Recommendation. Secondly, it was considered necessary to permit the recording of certain DNA profiles even in cases involving persons who have committed certain gross offence and where analysis was not made in pre-trial investigation. In such cases, a sample necessary for DNA profiling is taken in a personal search, and the measure requires authorisation specified in the law.[9]

DNA sample and DNA profile

In accordance with Chapter 6, s 5(1) of the Coercive Measures Act the police have in a personal search the right to collect samples from persons suspected of a criminal offence. In order to clarify the offence, a DNA profile may be prepared from these samples. The profile may be retained on the Police Personal Register provided that the requirements specified in the law are fulfilled. A personal search contains a bodily search, a blood sample or other search directed at the body (Chapter 5, s 9 of the Coercive Measures Act). A bodily search may be carried out on the probable suspect of an offence for which the most severe penalty provided is imprisonment of more than six months or if the offence is drunken driving (Chapter 5, s 11).[10]

Item 2 of the Council of Europe Recommendation defines the scope of people who may be subjected to sampling and DNA analysis. In comparison to the scope of the recommendation, the scope of the Coercive Measures Act is, at the outset, more limited. The recommendation states that the collection of samples and even DNA analysis are permitted for the purposes of the identification of a suspect or any other individual in the investigation or prosecution of criminal offence. This means that a DNA analysis may also be made of a victim of an offence. The use of DNA analysis is not restricted to criminal proceedings.[11] The Coercive Measures Act does not limit collection of samples to circumstances where DNA analysis is necessary. Consequently, sampling is permissible even in cases where the pre-trial investigation of a particular offence does not warrant DNA analysis. A further point is that it need not take place in the context of the pre-trial investigation, but can be carried out afterwards. In practice, what this means is a possibility of compiling a file of samples and an equally large or a smaller file of DNA profiles. The law does not in any way define the samples from which a DNA profile may be made. The material which can be used for DNA analysis includes blood, saliva,

---

9   *Ibid.*
10   According to the Government Bill (HE 20/1997 vp), the expression 'an offence for which the most severe penalty provided' means the same as in Chapter 1, s 3(1)(2) of the Coercive Measures Act. See also HE 181/1994 vp (Government Bill).
11   HE 20/1997 vp (Government Bill), p 6.

any type of hair, scale and seminal fluid. A sample may not be taken from pieces of clothing frisked as part of a personal search (see Chapter 5 (ss 9 and 10)).[12]

Section 5(2) defines the scope of persons who have already received a final judgment and who may be subjected to a personal search in order to carry out a DNA analysis and to file the results on the Police Register. The first requirement is that the person's guilt has been established by a final judgment. The second requirement is that the person has committed a gross criminal offence. Thirdly, a person who has been found guilty of such an offence before the entry into force of the Act may be subjected to a personal search if he or she is serving a custodial sentence for that offence or is being treated at a psychiatric hospital. The scope of DNA analysis was extended to persons specified in s 5(2), because experience had proved that recidivism is more common in certain groups of perpetrators. However, the section states that a DNA profile may not be filed if a DNA analysis was already carried out in the pre-trial investigation or if it is otherwise unwarranted. The circumstances where the collection of samples is otherwise unwarranted are not defined in the Act. Item 5 of the Recommendation is more liberal with the permissibility of DNA analysis than is the Coercive Measures Act. The recommendation states that recourse to DNA analysis should be permissible in all appropriate cases irrespective of the seriousness of the offence. Consideration of the appropriateness under s 5(2) is left to practical police work, with no specific limitations in the law.

In practice the police will have a large data bank. In addition to the existing data and samples (see below 'Filing of data'), samples are collected from several groups of people. The first group consists of those from whom a sample has already been taken and of those who are suspected of a criminal offence which carries a maximum penalty of more than six months imprisonment. The second group are convicted persons who are guilty of an offence specified in s 5(2). The third group of samples is of those containing cells which are collected at the scene of the crime or in the general context of the investigation of the crime. Examples are samples taken of blood, hair or saliva in a cigarette.[13] This means that the police will have a large reserve of samples with a potential for DNA profiling and in principle also with a lot of other genetic information part of which can be attributed to a particular person.

The position in the Coercive Measures Act of a person giving a sample can be examined in greater detail. Does the taking of a sample entail only slight interference with personal integrity? To be pricked with a needle can be considered such, but the issue here goes beyond the taking of a blood sample. The sample must be examined in the light of its use; in other words, what specifically is analysed from the sample. Various kinds of data which interfere with personal integrity may be found in the analysis of a blood sample.

The next question that arises is about the meaning of a DNA profile for an individual. A DNA profile is a near certain method to identify a person from the Finnish population. An additional fact to bear in mind is that genetic information has a unique significance for a person. The question here is not unambiguously of

---

12 See HE 20/1997 vp (Government Bill), p 14.
13 Ministry of Justice press release, 21 February 1997 (Government Bill). The police to have a right to record data for DNA profiles: p 1.

slight interference with personal integrity.[14] That is never the case when information of a person's genetic inheritance is analysed. Genetic inheritance lies at the very core of personal integrity. A sample that the police hold contains the person's entire genetic information, although the law permits only the preparation and filing of a profile. This is a border area of which the preamble to the Council of Europe Recommendation urges governments to take account in reminding them of the dignity of the individual and of the respect for the human body, of the rights of the defence and of the proportionality of means in achieving their objectives. Thus, it is not in conformity with the guidance given in the preamble to take samples of everybody only to produce in Finland a DNA file of maximum coverage.

This leads us to the next question. Should the taking of the sample have, in some circumstances, been made subject to the consent of the person and in this way take account of the Council of Europe recommendation? In Great Britain, which was a precursor in the use of DNA analysis,[15] the issue of consent has been emphasised.[16]

In the discussion of interference with personal integrity, the group of sample givers that deserves closer examination is that of persons who are serving their sentence – making up to society for their crime. The mere fact that a person has once committed a particular criminal offence and that statistical probability says something of the risk of recidivism should not justify DNA analysis and thus interference with his or her personal integrity. Perhaps the way to restrict the possibility of DNA analysis would have been to provide for consent as a prerequisite. The *travaux préparatoires* of the Coercive Measures Act draws the line that in practice the blood sample should be taken while the convicted person is serving the sentence and before he or she is released on parole.[17]

Item 4 of the Council of Europe Recommendation states that a sample should not be taken without the consent of the suspect, unless the circumstances warrant this measure. Section 5(1) of the Act does not contravene the Recommendation in this respect. The circumstances that permit personal search are those where there are probable reasons to suspect the person of a crime. The existence of probable reasons is at least on the same level (of justification) as circumstances which warrant DNA analysis.

Filing of data

When a DNA analysis of the sample has been made, the results may be filed on the police record for the performance of the duties specified in s 1(1) of the Police Act (493/1995), if the offence in question carries a maximum penalty of six months or more. The duties listed in the Police Act are: safeguarding of the legal and social order, maintaining of public order and security, and prevention, investigation and prosecution of crime. The Act does not specify what happens to those results of

---

14   Cf HE 20/1997 vp (Government Bill), pp 16–17.
15   See Himberg, Aho, Sajantila and Sippel (1993), p 132.
16   See Rogers and de Bousinger (1995), pp 157–62.
17   HE 20/1997 vp (Government Bill), p 12.

DNA analysis which under the Coercive Measures Act may not be recorded on the Police Personal Register. Item 8 of the Council of Europe Recommendation states that they should be deleted as unnecessary. The same applies to the sample which was analysed. Item 7 reminds governments of the obligation to observe the Council of Europe Data Protection Convention and the recommendations of the Council on data protection, especially Recommendation No R(87)15 on the right of the police to use personal data.

Before the amendment of the Coercive Measures Act, the provisions on personal search permitted the taking of a blood sample from a suspect and did not in any way restrict the choice of techniques to analyse it. Also, s 5(2) of the Police Personal Register Act permitted the setting up of a national manually held file.[18] The present s 5 restricts the information on the file to exclude the results of DNA analysis which contain data on the personal characteristics of the person in question. The techniques of analysis used in criminal investigation are based on producing a DNA analysis from specific points in the non-coding area of the DNA.[19] The DNA profile is retained as a combination of letters and numbers. Thus the profile does not contain sensitive data. The *travaux préparatoires* treat fingerprints and DNA profile equally as part of a personal description which may be recorded whether or not the crime in question is a gross offence.[20] It is probable that this is true for the individual's right to privacy. What may be more problematic is the existence of the samples held by the police and of the possibility of their use for analysis.

The results of analysis made of samples which may be taken under s 5 constitute a personal record. A DNA analysis may be made of blood or other samples found at the scene of the crime without the use of coercive measures under Chapter 5. DNA analysis does not depend on the gross nature or otherwise of the offence. In practice this means that a file is created of the DNA of unidentified persons. In any case, this file is a personal register, because at a later date it is possible to attribute the results of the analysis to a particular individual.[21] This is based on s 2(1) of the Personal Registers Act (471/1987) which defines that personal data refers to a description of a person or his or her living conditions from which a particular individual can be identified. This kind of register of stains or traces is regulated under the Police Personal Register Decree.

Section 6 of the Coercive Means Act provides for time limits for the availability of filed data. The retention of profiles and samples is subject to time limits specified in the section. A DNA sample recorded under s 5(1) of the Act must be erased from the Register one year after the keeper of the register has been notified of the decision of the prosecutor that no criminal offence has been committed or that there is insufficient evidence of offence in the case. The DNA profiles referred to in paragraph 2 must be erased from the register one year after the keeper has been notified of the overturning of the sentence. In any case, the profile must be erased one year after the death of the data subject, if it has not been done earlier. The respective samples must be destroyed at the same time as the profiles are

18   HE 20/1997 vp (Government Bill), p 10.

19   HE 20/1997 vp (Government Bill), p 9.

20   HE 20/1997 vp (Government Bill), p11.

21   HE 20/1997 vp (Government Bill), p 12.

erased. In this way the principles expressed in item 8 of the Council of Europe Recommendation are contained in the domestic law. Item 8 states that samples which have been taken from individuals for DNA analysis should not be kept after a final decision has been rendered in the case for which they were used. However, a sample may be retained in cases where the person so requests and where it cannot be attributed to an individual. When a profile is destroyed, the sample that was recorded for the analysis must also be destroyed.

A justification given for the retention of profiles and samples is that a need of re-analysis may arise. In that context new techniques might give new results, which could be used. Retention might also be justified to safeguard the rights of the suspect. The analysis could be repeated in cases where questions might arise about the possibility of an error in the analysis or about the credibility of the results.[22] The right to new analysis could be invoked on the basis of item 9 of the Recommendation, which contains the equality of arms principle. This principle already exists in s 12 of the Pre-trial Investigation Act (449/1987), which states that the interrogations and other investigation measures requested by the person concerned must be conducted where the person proves that they may influence the case, provided that the measures do not entail unreasonable cost compared with the nature of the case.

Conclusion

DNA sampling and profiling are permissible without the person's consent only on the conditions specified in the Coercive Measures Act. For persons other than those mentioned in the law, sampling and profiling requires the person's consent. As regards legally incompetent persons, their right to speak is exercised by the person having the care and custody of them or other legal representative. An examination of the overall effects of the additions to the Coercive Measures Act and especially of the new opportunities opened by the use of DNA samples and profiles shows that this is a significant advancement. Profiling offers an effective technique for domestic and trans-border criminal investigation while saving police time resources.

Greater attention in the new provisions should have been paid to the group of persons who have already been convicted, especially as regards their personal integrity. In Finland as a whole, the filling of DNA samples is permissible on lesser grounds than is the case in a number of other member states of the Council of Europe. Filing does not even require court decision; the decision is taken by a police officer. Section 5 of the Coercive Measures Act stipulates that a decision on a personal search is made by an officer with the power of arrest.

No sanctions were added to the Act on unauthorised sampling and profiling. Sanctions for such measures can be found through the concepts of public liability under criminal law and general liability under criminal law.

---

22   See HE 20/1997 vp (Government Bill), p 12.

In Finland, the data of an estimated 2,500 to 3,000 persons will be filed each year.[23] It remains to be seen how large the databank of profiles eventually becomes and what proportion of offence can be solved through DNA analysis.

References

Aho K, Ehnholm C and Sajantila A (1991) *Geenitekniikka rikostutkimuksiin* (*Gene Technology in Criminal Investigation*), Defensor Legis

Aho, K and Pikkarainen ,J (1997) *Oikeuslääketieteellisistä tutkimuslausunnoista* (*On Reports of Analyses in Forensic Medicine*), Lakimies

Gill, P *et al* (1996) 'A new method of STR interpretation using inferental logic-development of a criminal intelligence database' Int J Legal Med 109

Himberg K, Aho K, Sajantila A and Sippel H, (1993) 'Rikostekniset laboratoriotutkimukset' ('Laboratory analyses in criminal investigation'), in Penttilä A, Hirvonen J and Saukko P (eds), *Oikeuslääketieteen perusteet* (*The Basics of Forensic Medicine*), Jyväskylä

Mäkelä, PH (1997) 'Geenitutkimus' ('Gene Research'), in Veikko Launis and Juha Räikkä and VL-J (eds), *Geenit ja etiikka* (*Genes and Ethics*), Helsinki

Rogers A and DD de Bousingen (1995) *Bioethics in Europe*, Strasbourg Cedex

---

23   Telephone conversation with Mr Kimmo Himberg, director of the Crime Laboratory of the National Bureau of Investigation, 16 October 1997.

CHAPTER 7

GERMANY

Professor Werner Beulke
Universität Passau

Introduction

It was not until 22 March 1997 that the taking of samples for means of DNA analysis (genetic fingerprinting) was formally recognised in legislation. Nevertheless, genetic fingerprinting had already played a part in penal law as a means of proof. Traces found on suspects and on victims (ie, under fingernails, on clothing) – mainly traces of hair, blood and semen – had always been examined according to current scientific progress, and were introduced into criminal investigations as a means of proof according to the provisions of the Code of Criminal Procedure (Strafprozeßordnung: StPO). This meant that expert opinion on the origin of traces, in particular, on the matching of two separate traces (for example, trace A on the victim's clothing, trace B taken from the hairbrush of the suspect), could be used before the court as evidence. It was not so much the examination of anonymous traces – traces from a (yet) unknown source – that was considered the main problem in this respect, but the taking of comparative samples from the accused.

Blood samples were very suitable for the purpose. The Code of Criminal Procedure generally allowed the taking of blood samples from a suspect for the purpose of criminal proceedings. Originally, the relevant provision (s 81a of the StPO) was mainly used to establish the blood alcohol level of the accused (relevant to certain traffic offences), criminal responsibility at the time of the crime, and sometimes the suspect's competence to stand trial as well. Since s 81a of the StPO did not specify the purpose for which blood could be taken, the taking of blood samples in order to obtain genetic fingerprints was widely regarded as lawful amongst the police.

Although ss 81a and 81c of the StPO had already been acknowledged in the jurisdiction of the highest courts – namely the Federal Supreme Court (Bundesgerichtshof: BGH) and the Federal Constitutional Court (FCC – Bundesverfassungsgericht: BVerfG) – as sufficient legal grounds for the taking of blood samples for DNA analysis in criminal proceedings, doubts were expressed from various sides over issues of constitutional law, as well as criminal law, and with respect to the sensitivity of public opinion as to genetic sciences in general. This concern was alleviated by the draft amendment of the Code of Criminal Procedure, dated 2 March 1995, which has largely become law, and is explicitly founded on 'very general misgivings among many parts of the population about genetic technology'. This draft referred to a discussion paper submitted by the

Federal Ministry of Justice on 20 December 1989, and a later draft by the Federal Ministry of Justice of November 1991, taking into account a commentary by the Federal Data Protection Authority in May 1991 (in particular, on the limitation of DNA analysis to a specific criminal action), which was given in the 13th Annual Report. The Parliamentary Group of the Social-Democrats of Germany (SPD) has proposed its own draft code. On 6 December 1996, the Bundestag passed the StVÄG 1997, which was based on the previous drafts by the Federal Ministry of Justice and the SPD. The Bündnis 90/Green Party and representatives of the Party of German Socialists (PDS) had already rejected the draft code in the Committee on Legal Affairs of the Bundestag, in particular, because it did not expressly prohibit the establishment of gene databanks. The parliamentary Act that changed the StPO and the Administrative Offences Act (Ordnungswidrigkeitengesetz: OWiG) – the StVÄG 1997 – finally came into effect in March 1997.

Due to the relatively short lapse of time since its entry into force, it is not possible to draw on much practical experience in its handling and application. Therefore, the main subject of this paper is based on the legal regulations.

The legal situation according to the StVÄG

Collection of DNA samples

A new s 81e was added to the StPO which now clarifies that material obtained under s 81a, para 1 may also be put to molecular-genetic examination, provided that the examinations are necessary to establish the descent/parentage of a person, or to prove that traces are those of the accused – it is not necessary for a criminal charge to already be laid (at least no formal indictment is necessary). The Code of Criminal Procedure distinguishes between 'accused' – ie, suspected persons – and other persons (ie, non-suspects).

Suspects

According to the regulation of s 81a of the StPO, blood samples may be taken from a suspect *without his or her consent* by a doctor (in accordance with medical standards), on being formally requested and authorised to do so by the judge, in order to detect facts that are relevant to criminal proceedings. However, this applies only insofar as there is no danger of injury to health caused by the act itself, or due to the suspect's general state of health. This restriction rarely proves relevant, because the taking of blood samples, even when taken forcibly, is generally regarded as harmless. Under s 81a, para 2 of the StPO, the Department of Public Prosecution and other authorised bodies – most German police sergeants and higher ranking police officers under s 152 of the Judicature Act (Gerichtsverfassungsgesetz: GVG) – may request that a sample be taken if a delay would hinder the investigation. The taking of other natural body samples, such as saliva, semen, urine – if at all necessary for DNA analysis – is allowed under the same conditions (ie, on a request by a judge or the prosecution; that there be no damage to health; and it is to be carried out by a doctor).

The regulations that came into force through the StVÄG apply only to situations in which there is no consent. Those examinations that the person undergoes voluntarily follow the general rules. Therefore, with the consent of the suspect, the procedure of taking samples does not have to follow the procedure set down in s 81a of the StPO, provided the procedure is not dangerous to health and does not offend decency. Thus, non-doctors can take blood samples from the suspect, for example.

Consent of the accused also renders a formal request under s 81a, para 2 of the StPO unnecessary. For consent, in this sense, it is necessary that a decision be stated explicitly and clearly by the accused, who need not necessarily have legal capacity (ss 104 and 106 of the German Civil Code (Bürgerliches Gesetzbuch: BGB)), but must be sufficiently mentally mature. It is also required that the accused should have knowledge of all important circumstances and should have knowledge of his right of refusal. As a rule, this presupposes the accused is adequately informed and, if necessary, given time to decide. In no case can consent be inferred from pure passivity.

The question of how specific consent must be in the case of taking blood samples for purposes of DNA profiling has hardly ever been dealt with, and it hardly gains relevance since molecular-genetic examination of samples taken from the suspect (accused) is also admissible without his or her consent. In this case, consent is only of relevance if the other requirements under s 81a of the StPO are not fully satisfied. It is obvious that consent cannot be less specific than in the case of injuries by a doctor in the course of medical treatment, punishable under s 223 of the Criminal Code (Strafgesetzbuch: StGB), where consent serves as a general justification. This means, in my view, that the patient has to be placed in the position to make up his own mind and evaluate all possible risks. Therefore, clarification of the use of data would be needed, especially because of the weight of public resentments. In other words, clarification is needed as to the manner and extent of the tests, duration and storage of samples, and the purpose and possible use of data.

Even before the StVÄG it was necessary that the taking of blood samples under the old s 81a of the StPO had to be relevant to criminal proceedings. Through the addition of a third paragraph to s 81a of the StPO, it is now set down that DNA tests may be made from the blood of the accused or any other body cells only for the purpose of the particular trial for which they were taken (or another pending criminal proceeding). By this provision, the establishment of gene databanks, as desired on the part of the police, is ruled out: there will be no gene databanks in German police stations.

Examinations in accordance with s 81e of the StPO are subject to a judicial order (see s 81f, para 1 of the StPO). A subsidiary clause, as provided in other regulations – s 98a, para 1, sentence 2, s 100c, para 1, and s 110a, para 1, sentence 2, for instance – due to which a measure can only be taken if other means of proof are not available, has not been included in s 81e of the StPO, and would have been counter-productive in the opinion of the legislators in order to rule out an accused as a suspect as soon as possible.

No provision is made, in respect of the legality of DNA tests/genetic fingerprinting, for any distinction in the kind or gravity of the offence, which had been an issue in the discussion prior to the StVÄG. Also, the requirement in the SPD draft, that 'strong suspicion' should be a prerequisite for DNA analysis, has not been included in the law. The principle of proportionality, however, which is to be respected in the context of s 81a of the StPO, as well as in any other field of law, makes it necessary to examine whether the measure corresponds with the gravity of the offence in the individual case.

Clearly, it has to be distinguished: the physical act of taking blood samples may cause bodily harm, but DNA analysis is also – as recent discussion on s 81a of the StPO has shown – an invasion of privacy (in that the right of 'informational' self-determination is part of the civil rights guaranteed by the Constitution in the meaning the courts have given to article 2, para 1 of the Federal Constitution (Grundgesetz: GG)). Therefore, genetic examination is not appropriate for all offences (eg, the offence of obtaining transportation without payment under s 265a of the Criminal Code). In the Administrative Offences Act, concerning non-criminal administrative offences, the use of blood samples and other body cells for the purpose of molecular-genetic examination, as prescribed in s 81e of the StPO, is generally not permitted (see s 46, para 4, sentence 2 of the OWiG).

Non-suspects

The legal requirements for taking blood samples from persons other than suspects – this includes, in particular, the victim of the crime – are prescribed in s 81c, para 2 of the StPO. Without the consent of these persons, blood samples may only be taken when no danger to their health can be ensured, and the measure is absolutely necessary ('indispensable') for the detection of the truth. In this respect, no high prerequisites are made, however. The SPD draft required that blood samples from non-suspects could only be examined if a corresponding sample from a suspect was already available for comparison. It was hoped that through this requirement, 'premature' and 'unnecessary' analyses could be avoided on the ground of protecting the victim.

Even when these requirements are satisfied, the measure (taking of a blood sample) can still be inadmissible under s 81c, para 4 of the StPO if the person cannot be burdened with it, taking into consideration all the circumstances of the case. This may rarely become relevant, however.

Measures other than the taking of blood samples (skin, hair, saliva and semen) are not allowed without the consent of the person. An individual may refuse to allow a blood sample to be taken in the same way as to give evidence (see s 81c, para 3, sentence 1 of the StPO). Under German law, fiancées, married partners or close relatives can refuse to testify against the accused (see s 52, para 1, nos 1 to 3 of the StPO).

Measures under s 81c, para 2 of the StPO take place only at the request of a judge or, where a delay would hinder the investigation, under s 81c, para 4 of the StPO, at the request of the prosecution (and other authorised bodies prescribed in s 15 of the Judicature Act: GVG). Where a person unjustly refuses to permit blood sampling ('without legal grounds') under s 81c, para 4 of the StPO, the provisions of s 70 of the StPO apply – this includes powers to impose a fine, and, if this is not recoverable, arrest (see s 70, para 1 of the StPO). If the person still disobeys, the judge may order that the sample be taken by force.

In the StVÄG it is clear that molecular-genetic examination of samples from non-suspects is limited in the same ways as samples from the accused (see s 81e, para 1, sentence 2 of the StPO). By the addition of s 81c, para 5, sentence 2 of the StPO ('s 81a, paragraph 3 applies equally'), it is ensured that samples of blood and other body cells taken from these persons may be used only for the current proceedings (see above) and for no other purposes.

Where, in the course of the investigation, suspicion falls on a person not previously accused, measures under s 81a of the StPO, as an accused person, are permissible against that person.

With the *consent* of the person concerned, substances other than blood may be taken as well. Consent, if not offensive to decency, also overrides all the restrictions established by s 81c of the StPO. Thus, cells other than blood may be taken and put to molecular-genetic examination. Consent also renders a judge's request unnecessary.

Consent is essentially a voluntary, considered and specific agreement, given with full knowledge of the circumstances and the right of refusal. It is under no circumstances a passive submission. The person must be informed of the measures to be taken, and that they cannot be taken without his or her consent, where this is the case. Special rules apply to the consent of minors and people in care who, because of their infirmity, mental or emotional condition, do not have sufficient understanding of their right of refusal (s 81c, para 3, sentence 2 of the StPO). Consent may be withdrawn at any time, but any results obtained up to the time of withdrawal may still be used in court.

Special problems arise in the conduct of 'mass tests' on a voluntary basis. This has recently occurred in Germany. In Munich, for example, over 750 persons driving Porsche cars were invited to give samples of their blood for genetic testing. Another case has been reported where all 138 male participants at a party were asked for a blood test. From 92 persons asked in another case, three refused to give their blood for the purpose of DNA analysis, so that measures under s 81a of the StPO were taken against them as suspects. None of these three persons committed the crime, as it later turned out. The reality of 'consent' in this situation is highly questionable because of the pressure of public opinion upon them, and because of group pressure, especially taking into account the fact that they may be regarded as under suspicion if they refuse to co-operate. One of the legislative intents, as stated in the federal government draft, was to prevent the prosecution from circumventing the lawful requirements by exerting direct or indirect pressures in order to move persons to submit to voluntary molecular-genetic examination.

Minors, prisoners and military personnel

No special rules apply to minors, prisoners or military personnel. If such persons are suspects in criminal proceedings, they can be required to have samples of their blood (or other body cells) taken under s 81a of the StPO. If they are non-suspects in the proceedings, s 81c of the StPO applies, under which their blood may similarly be sampled and examined.

For juvenile delinquents between 14 and 18 years of age, and young people between the ages of 18 and 21 – as prescribed in s 1, para 2 of the Law of Juvenile Justice (Jugendgerichtsgesetz: JGG) – Juvenile Law applies. Juvenile Law refers back to the general law, as far as no special provisions are made (see s 2 of the JGG). As a result, all the conditions regarding DNA sampling already described apply equally to these groups of people. As an accused, they are subject to the regulations of ss 81a, 81e and 81f of the StPO. As far as their consent under s 81a of the StPO is concerned, legal capacity is not required (see above). However, they have to be sufficiently mature to be able to consent.

Special rules apply to minors under 18 years of age in respect of s 81c of the StPO (measures against non-suspects) as far as their right to refuse blood tests and/or testimony is concerned (see s 81c, para 3 of the StPO).

Children under 14 years of age are not criminally responsible. Since no criminal proceedings can be taken against them, s 81a of the StPO cannot be applied to them. They may be required for blood testing under s 81c of the StPO without their consent as non-suspects, however, and for other examinations only with their consent. In respect to their consent, special rules apply under s 81c, para 3 of the StPO: if they do not have sufficient understanding of their rights of refusal, the decision is taken by their legal guardian. If the legal guardian is excluded from the decision – this is always the case under German law when the legal guardian is the accused (see s 52, para 2, sentence 2 of the StPO) – or if the legal guardian is hindered for any other reason from the decision, the measure is only permissible upon the specific request of a judge (s 81c, para 3, sentence 3 of the StPO).

The same regulations apply to persons in care, who on account of physical illness or mental or emotional handicap are unable to fully understand their rights of refusal (see s 81c, para 3, sentence 2 of the StPO).

DNA analysis of unidentified traces

Under s 81e, para 2 of the StPO, molecular-genetic examination may also be carried out on found, secured or confiscated trace material – regardless of its origin – to the same extent as samples taken from the accused under s 81a of the StPO. Again, no distinction is drawn as to whether the traces originate from suspects or non-suspects, adults or children. In addition, traces found on or originating from the victim may be used for molecular-genetic examination under this section. If the victim is alive, however, comparative sample material from the victim can only be obtained under the provisions of s 81c of the StPO in his or her capacity as a witness.

Procedure

According to s 81f, para 1 of the StPO, only the judge and not the prosecution (as in many other provisions) or the police may request the carrying out of molecular-genetic examinations under s 81e of the StPO. An 'emergency' competence for the prosecution, as in other provisions, was not needed, since material taken under s 81a of the StPO (or found, secured or confiscated material within the meaning of s 81e of the StPO) may be examined over a longer period of time – up to two years. The requirement of a judicial order – of a judge – was also meant as additional protection against overzealous investigation on the part of the police, who, in other areas of criminal procedure, have been given many additional powers as a general trend in German criminal procedural law.

A previous hearing of the person is not demanded. However, the technician or laboratory that carries out the tests is to be named in the written judicial order. In this way, the judge who has responsibility for naming the experts can select those experts or laboratories that seem competent and reliable to him or her and, on the other hand, can exclude other individuals or institutions from genetic examinations – which he or she would do if irregularities have occurred in the past.

The judge's responsibility under this section is an exception to the general rule that the power of nominating experts during the investigations lies with the prosecution as long as investigations have not finished (see ss 73 and 161a, para 1, sentence 2 of the StPO and no 70, para 3 of the Guidelines for Penal Proceedings (Richtlinien für das Straf-und Bussgeldverfahren: RiStBV)).

According to s 81f, para 1 of the StPO, only expert witnesses who are public servants or who are officially appointed (and thus have similar duties under the law) can be chosen to carry out molecular-genetic examinations. They must not be employed by the same body conducting the investigation or be a part of that body, unless they are employed by a separate department that is materially and organisationally separate from the investigating body. In this way, the 'functional' separation of the institutions was ensured – and at the same time, the Federal Criminal Bureau (Bunderskriminalamt: BKA) and the State Criminal Bureaux (Landeskriminalamter: LKA), which already operated in this field, were able to continue the carrying out of DNA examinations under this section. During the legislative process the question was raised as to whether foreign laboratories or experts could be nominated as well. It was the view of the federal government that the security precautions provided for in the Act did not allow foreign experts to carry out DNA tests, since there would have been no means of control over them.

The sample is to be passed to the laboratory in an anonymous form – without name, address and day or month of birth (see s 81f, para 1, sentence 3 of the StPO), in order to ensure that the test cannot be associated with a particular person, and to minimise the incentive for unauthorised examinations. It may be doubted, however, whether it would not be possible, in spectacular cases that often attract public attention, for the researcher to associate the sample with a particular suspect, especially if the expert is engaged only with a few samples and if there is only one suspect in the case.

Nature and extent of testing

Section 81e of the StPO, already mentioned several times, simply states: material obtained under s 81A of the StPO may be subjected to molecular-genetic examination. The law deliberately does not specify which genetic tests can be made and how the tests should be carried out, in order not to hinder future development. The legislators did not expect the judge to have the necessary knowledge to decide the best method of examination and specify it in his or her judicial order. It has been considered whether a register of suitable and recognised molecular-genetic tests should be compiled and maintained in accordance with no 70 of the Guidelines for Penal Proceedings (RiStBV), which states in s 3 that a similar register of 'approved' experts on various scientific fields is to be kept for all purposes.

It was considered sufficient to include a clause providing that genetic testing of samples is only permissible if it is *necessary* to determine whether found traces are those of the accused (or to determine a person's parentage or descent). It is thereby laid down that the tests may only extend to the so-called 'non-coding' DNA regions, if this is sufficient for the purpose. If, however, it is not sufficient, the wording of the law does not exclude the other (coding) areas of the DNA from examination. In the previous legal discussion it has repeatedly been stressed that with the new methods only non-coding sequences would be analysed, and information other than the origin of traces (eg, disposition, characteristics of personality) could neither be contained, nor would be profitable for criminal investigations. The majority of legal experts thought that the examination of the coding DNA regions would not be permissible under German constitutional law. If this is correct, the law in its present form extends beyond what is constitutionally acceptable.

This was seen in the legislative process as well: the federal government argued in its draft that the differentiation between coding and non-coding DNA regions did not comply with the latest scientific knowledge, since medical science had shown that even so-called non-coding DNA areas did permit certain conclusions on health dispositions of a person. In addition, it was said that the written reports of the past always contained, in differing degrees, information from coding and non-coding DNA regions. The Bundesrat approved the draft but took the view that a demarcation was possible, and 'for data-protection considerations desirable', and therefore suggested the addition of a clause in s 81e of the StPO, whereby genetic examination should not extend to the area of the human genome, 'which can give information on the hereditary make-up of a person'.

It has to be mentioned that the scientific basis of the court decisions in favour of genetic testing noted at the beginning of this paper has changed. Those decisions were founded upon the general presumption that DNA analysis could not conflict with personal rights of the accused, because only non-coding parts of the DNA irrelevant to a person's personality were being examined.

However, it also has to be taken into consideration that the examination of the human genome remains limited to the purpose of the investigation – to determine the true origin of traces. The gathering of information other than this is not covered by any provisions of the Code of Criminal Procedure. Examinations other than these are not permitted and are illegal – which s 81e, para 1, sentence 3 of the StPO states explicitly. The same also applies to the examination of found, secured or confiscated trace material (see s 81e, para 2, sentence 2 of the StPO). Under these circumstances the decision of the legislators can be accepted. From the narrow limitations of the purpose of the examination (and the compulsory destruction of trace material under s 81a, para 3, sentence 2 of the StPO), it follows that the use for scientific research does not come into consideration.

Storage of samples and test results

Samples

Section 81a, para 3, sentence 1 of the StPO stipulates that blood samples and other body cells taken from the accused shall be destroyed immediately – without any avoidable delay – after they are no longer needed for the specific proceeding (or another pending criminal proceeding). It has been argued that the law does not provide for situations where the samples are not destroyed in time and kept longer than necessary, but this should not be given any importance. The destruction clause applies to samples of suspects, as well as non-suspects, in respect of s 81c, para 5, sentence 2 of the StPO, but does not apply to traces found, secured or confiscated.

There is a similar regulation in s 100b, para 6 of the StPO, concerning the destruction of telephone surveillance, which may have functioned as a model for s 81a, para 3 of the StPO. However, there are no provisions made in s 81a of the StPO for the recording of the destruction, and the law, surprisingly, also refrains from making the prosecution responsible for the proper destruction of sample material. Nevertheless, the view is taken that the prosecution would 'in certain cases' supervise the destruction and keep a written report of the fact. All sample material is to be destroyed under this section without exception, including material not used for the examination (so-called 'surplus material'). Some material may have to be destroyed immediately, while other material that is still needed may be kept. However, nothing may be kept indefinitely.

Sample material is generally stored until the judgment becomes final – and unappealable – unless it has already been destroyed for one reason or another. In the context of s 100b of the StPO mentioned above, which has a similar provision, the question was raised as to whether the clause also requires destruction when a retrial is to be expected in the future. The predominant view on this issue favoured further storage. The same is said to apply to s 81a, para 3 of the StPO. This seems to have been the view of the legislators as well. In the legislative process it was held against the SPD draft that the early destruction of DNA material would limit the chances for the accused to reopen a trial (provided for in ss 359 *et seq* of the StPO).

Some differences can be pointed out, however. The destruction of telephone recordings under s 100b of the StPO does not apply in the same way. Therefore, samples that can be obtained at any time should be destroyed. This does not apply, however, to samples that cannot be reproduced (eg, if the victim has died or is close to death).

For found trace material that is not reproducible (see above) and for the results of the analysis, the destruction rule does not apply according to its clear wording (see below), so that the chances of reopening the proceedings are not narrowed in any way.

Test results

Destruction applies only to the sample material, not to the test results. These become part of the files and form part of the courts' records. As such, they stay with the Department of Public Prosecution after the trial. Storage is subject to special regulation. By contrast, the destruction rules as desired in the SPD draft also applied to the test results. However, these provisions did not become law.

Release of information

Section 101, para 1 of the StPO requires that the persons examined be informed of the measures taken against them as soon as this is possible, without endangering the purpose of the investigation. This clause, originally intended for the interception of postal and telephone surveillance without the knowledge of the accused, has been extended by the StVÄG 1997 to procedures taken under s 81e of the StPO (genetic fingerprints). This means that the person concerned is to be informed that molecular-genetic examinations of samples taken from him or her were carried out, but only insofar as he or she is not already aware. It was the opinion of the members of the legal committee during the legislative process 'that in cases [where] the person concerned is apparently aware of the facts and the extent of measures, a formal notification is not necessary'. The obligation to notify does not extend to the results of the tests, however. The accused may exercise his right of inspection of the files before trial and thus obtain the information, but only through his counsel (see s 147 of the StPO). Persons other than the accused have no means of obtaining further information on the test results (unless if they are possibly read out in court). This is also true for the victim, unless he or she joins the public prosecution as a 'joint claimant', in which case victims have a right of inspection of the files as well (see s 397 in adjunction with s 385, para 3 of the StPO). The release of information to relatives or third parties involved in the proceedings, or to research establishments for the purpose of scientific research, is not allowed.

Regulation and control

Control by the judge

The judge only has the option to exclude an institution or laboratory from carrying out molecular-genetic tests by not nominating it in the judicial order. This power of 'control' must not be underestimated.

Control by the laboratories

The legislators did not rely entirely on the view of the laboratories that they were able to deal responsibly with test results and that there was no difference in this respect to the conventional blood-group analysis they had carried out before: the laboratories, as well as individuals (should they be in a position to carry out DNA tests), have to guarantee 'through technical and organisational measures' that no illegal research or examination is carried out and that no unauthorised persons can obtain test results (see s 81f, para 2, sentence 2 of the StPO). This wording corresponds to s 9 of the Federal Data Protection Act (Bundesdatenschutzgesetz: BDSG). The law does not specify the 'measures' to be taken by the laboratories, and it is also questionable if this could be done. It does, however, impose a duty on these institutions not to misuse samples for illegal purposes, and also to do everything in their power to prevent misuse by third parties.

Control by the supervisory authority

Under s 38, para 1 of the Federal Data Protection Act (BDSG), the authorities determined by state data protection law under s 38, para 6 of the BDSG may 'inspect' institutions in order to ensure the execution of the provisions of the BDSG and other provisions relating to data protection, insofar as these regulate the processing and use of 'personal data'. Under the legal definition in s 3, para 1 of the BDSG, 'personal data' comprises all details of the personal or material circumstances of a person or persons who can be individualised. Section 5 of the BDSG forbids persons engaged with personal data from processing or using personal data without being authorised, and requires them to maintain confidentiality of data. This also applies to DNA fingerprints.

It is normally a prerequisite of the inspection of *non-public* institutions through the supervisory authority that there is sufficient suspicion that regulations of data protection laws are being violated (see s 38, para 1 of the BDSG). Under s 81f, para 2, sentence 4 of the StPO, this requirement does not apply in respect of laboratories concerned with DNA analysis, so that there does not have to be evidence of a violation for the inspection and control exercised by the supervisory authority. Thus, s 81f, para 2 of the StPO extends the scope of control and intervention by the supervisory authorities.

They can demand to be given information (see s 38, para 3 of the BDSG), authorised persons are to be allowed entry to the property and premises during business hours (s 38, para 4 of the BDSG), and under the same requirements are authorised to carry out inspections and examinations on the premises.

Control by the Federal Commissioner for Data Protection

Public institutions – that is, all other federal and state institutions under s 2, paras 2 and 3 of the Federal Data Protection Act – are to ensure themselves the enforcement of the federal data protection law within their area of responsibility (see s 18, para 1, sentence 1 of the BDSG). In addition, they are controlled by the Federal or State Commissioner for Data Protection (see s 24, para 1 of the BDSG for the powers of the Federal Commissioner for Data Protection (Bundesdatenschutzbeauftragter)). For this purpose, he or she is entitled to demand information (see s 24, para 4 of the BDSG) and to be given access to all documentation and entry to all facilities (see also s 24, para 4 of the BDSG). The institutions inspected are informed of the results of the controls and the Federal or State Commissioner for Data Protection can make suggestions to improve data protection in these institutions (see s 24, para 5 of the BDSG). Objections can be made (s 25 of the BDSG) and grave violations are entered into the annual Federal Data Protection Report. The federal government refrained in its draft from the extension of control by the Federal Data Commissioner to the private sector, because such regulations were, in the past, opposed by the Bundesrat, and instead made provisions for control by the supervisory authorities (see above).

Consequences, sanctions and penalties

Results of unlawful obtaining of samples

Statutory offences

Since the taking of blood (or other natural body substances) for the purpose of DNA analysis constitutes a form of physical assault, it is punishable under s 223 of the Criminal Code (Strafgesetzbuch: StGB), unless it is covered by ss 81a–81c of the StPO, or the consent of the person. Both consent and the authority of state compulsion under s 81a of the StPO form recognised justification. Without either of these, the doctor or non-medical person taking the sample may be punished.

However, if the person taking the sample believes that the preconditions apply (in other words, considered circumstances would justify the assault), he or she may not be punished under the law (see s 6 of the StGB).

As a rule, the law is only concerned with the person making the assault, and not with the person who unlawfully ordered the blood to be taken. Since those persons have not committed the assault, they cannot be made legally responsible. Whether such samples may be used as evidence in court is another question.

Consequences for criminal proceedings

Legal opinions are split – the courts have ruled that violations of ss 81a–81c of the StPO do not automatically render the test results invalid in court. Under German law, not every failure to comply with statutory requirements leads to the exclusion of evidence obtained under such conditions. Therefore, certain mistakes in the clarification process before the taking of blood or the taking of blood by a non-medical person, or even the non-observance of the principle of proportionality, do not make the test results invalid. On the other hand, the absence of a formal request (by the prosecution or by the police) or the complete lack of consent (where it is needed) would lead to invalidity of the test results.

Where, however, the prosecution deliberately disregards the provisions of s 81a of the StPO in order to obtain evidence it would otherwise not have been able to obtain in a legal manner, this would be regarded as a violation of the 'fair trial' principle. In this case, the presentation of such evidence in court is not possible.

Results of illegal tests

The dangers that arise with the new method are less concerned with the way sample material is gained than with the possibility of illegal testing and the unauthorised passing on of personal information. Unlawful use of sample material (eg, blood) does not render the taking of it illegal. The person who takes the sample is not criminally liable if another person later conducts illegal tests on the material.

Statutory offences

For experts dealing with samples in laboratories there exist the following, if only fragmentary, statutory offences as counteraction against possible misuse.

Section 203 of the StGB (violation of private secrets)

Under this regulation of the Criminal Code, the unauthorised passing on of confidential information is punishable as an offence. However, this applies only to special groups of persons listed in s 203, para 1 of the StGB (for example, physicians, dentists and lawyers). The draft amendment by the SPD intended to add a new no 7 to the list, which would have included 'specialists engaged in DNA analysis under s 81f of the Code of Criminal Procedure', but this was not adopted. However, under this regulation, attorneys-at-law and counsel for the defence in legal proceedings listed in no 3 can be punished if they pass on information which they have obtained as a result of their right of access to the documents (see s 147 of the StPO).

Section 202a of the StGB (illegal acquisition of data)

Under s 202a, para 1 of the Criminal Code, it is a punishable offence for a person to obtain data that is not intended for him or her and that is protected from unauthorised access. The same applies when the data is passed on to another without authority. Data, in the meaning of this provision, is only that which is stored electronically, magnetically or by other indirect means (see s 202a, para 2 of the StGB). These and further offences, such as the suppression of data (s 274, para 1, no 2 of the StGB) and data alteration (s 303 of the StGB), which apply to the erasure, suppression and alteration of data, and making unusable data, are therefore only concerned with test results that have been processed with the aid of a computer and are in the form of 'data'.

Thus, it is a punishable offence for an expert concerned with DNA analysis to pass on test results that exist in the form of data. However, it is not an offence under this section to extract and pass on samples, for example, blood samples, to a third party for the purpose of non-permitted further examinations.

Similarly, under s 202a, para 1 of the StGB, it is not a punishable offence to conduct illegal tests (for instance, those which reveal facts other than those described in s 81e, para 1, sentence 1 of the StPO) as such, because the information obtained may come under the general definition of data, but the information has not yet been sufficiently protected against access before it was obtained. Before the carrying out of the tests, no data as such exists.

For the same reason, it cannot be said that the data is not 'intended' for the person. Since the data only came into existence as a result of a non-permitted examination procedure, it is, in the sense of the law, 'intended' for that person.

Section 43 of the Federal Data Protection Act (BDSG)

The federal data protection law contains a penal provision in s 43 of the BDSG. The meaning of data in this law includes, as seen, all personal details or material circumstances of a specified or specifiable person (s 3, para 1 of the BDSG). It is thus punishable to store, alter or pass on personal data, but to obtain data is not punishable. However, there is no complete protection in every respect.

Consequences for criminal proceedings

If the misuse is not punishable in every case, let alone prevented, at least for the criminal proceedings, it is presumed that information obtained from illegal tests (contrary to s 81e, para 1 of the StPO) is inadmissible. In contrast with the above, such information about the accused may not be presented as evidence in court, since doing so would be regarded as a new violation of the constitutional rights of the individual (Article 2, para 1 of the Federal Constitution), which the state has to respect and protect. In this respect, it is irrelevant where the information comes from. The incentive for the police to conduct illegal tests under s 81e, para 1 of the StPO is rather small given these preconditions.

Prospects

With the Amendment Order to the Code of Criminal Procedure – StVÄG 1997 – the legislators have succeeded in producing a law that, seen from a democratic standpoint, is an improvement upon previous legal conditions. With the new regulations it is clear that the discussion above on constitutional and legal reservations over DNA analysis for forensic purposes, which will certainly continue in some areas (namely as far as the 'coding' parts of DNA sequences are concerned), will stop. Discussion is already shifting towards questions connected with the evaluation of DNA evidence by the courts. There are some leading cases that have shown that the judge must not rely entirely on DNA evidence. He or she must always be aware that DNA evidence can only lead to a statement of probability, which does not lessen the value of, or free from evaluation, all other evidence that is available.

Postscript 2002

A number of notable developments have occurred in this area since 1998. First, the StPO now includes s 81g, which expressly regulates DNA analysis in criminal proceedings. Section 81g, para 1 states that for the purposes of establishing identity in future criminal proceedings, cell tissue may be collected from an accused suspected of a criminal offence of 'substantial significance' – this includes a serious offence against sexual self-determination, serious bodily injury, and theft in a particularly serious case. The cell tissue may then be subjected to molecular-genetic examination if the nature of the offence, the means of its commission, the accused's personality or other information provide grounds for assuming that new criminal proceedings shall be conducted against the accused for a criminal offence of 'substantial significance'. Under s 81g, para 2, the collected cell tissue is to be destroyed without delay once it is no longer required for the purposes stated in para 1. Section 81g, para 2 also provides that information other than that required to establish the DNA code may not be ascertained during the examination, and the tests to establish such information are inadmissible.

Secondly, the constitutionality of 'genetic fingerprinting' was the subject of a Federal Constitutional Court (FCC) ruling on 18 January 2001. The court ruled on three cases in which the appellants had contested that the ordering of 'genetic fingerprints' by lower courts, under s 2 of the DNA *Identitätsfeststellungsgesetz* (Statute on Identification Through DNA Testing) and s 81g of the Code of Criminal Procedure, was a violation of their constitutional right to privacy, and the right to 'self-determination over personal information' derived from this right to privacy. The FCC held, however, that these statutes allowing the creation of 'genetic fingerprints', and the use of these fingerprints in a database, are constitutional. In so doing, the court held that the facilitation of future investigations of serious crimes is a compelling public interest that justifies interference with the right to self-determination over personal information.

The FCC also accepted the requirement under the above statutes that DNA testing and storage of the results must be based on a finding that probable cause exists to assume the person tested will be involved in a similar crime again. The court emphasised that this must involve a careful prognosis founded upon the complete facts of every individual case, and to ensure that this occurs, the FCC stated that the courts, in deciding whether to order 'genetic fingerprinting', must demonstrate in their reasoning exactly how the prerequisites are met in each case. For example, simply stating that the possibility of a repeat offence cannot be ruled out does not satisfy this standard.

In a commentary on this decision, Hanebeck notes that the court placed heavy emphasis upon the fact that the above statutes prohibit testing that will reveal any 'sensitive' genetic data. He therefore contends that the decision leaves open the issue of gaining more sensitive genetic data that would be a far greater interference with the right to privacy, yet may also prove a greater aid to criminal investigations.[1] Hanebeck also notes that the court did not decide, since the appellants were all convicted criminals, whether it is constitutional under s 81g of the StPO to order 'genetic fingerprinting' of those persons who have only been accused in criminal procedure and not yet convicted.[2] Under s 2 and s 81g of the respective statutes, DNA testing is permitted if the person is convicted of a serious crime and there is probable cause to assume that this person will be involved in similar crimes in the future.

---

1   See Hanebeck (2001).
2   *Ibid.*

Reference

Hanebeck, A (2001) 'DNA analysis and the right to privacy: Federal Constitutional Court clarifies rules on the use of genetic fingerprints' 2(3) German Law Journal [7–8] www.germanlawjournal.com/article.php?id=50 at 3 December 2002

CHAPTER 8

ITALY

Professor Marcello Stalteri*
Research Fellow, University of Florence

Introduction

Italy is said to be the land of saints, navigators and heroes. Although we do not have on record data that could confirm or deny such long-standing traditions, it is not to exaggerate to say that in this country many esoteric events keep occurring, almost on a regular basis. Sometimes lawyers come across 'miracles': this is easily demonstrated by the unique and recent circumstances that have left the country in a sort of limbo in the field of genetic evidence as applied to criminal procedure, at least until specific regulations concerning its use are enacted.

One day, a little marble Madonna, standing in a small private backyard, shows some blood-like signs around the eyes. This is quite a big event for a town located in the middle of Italy; soon a huge crowd of pilgrims gathers near the place where the prodigious event occurs.

Looking at things sceptically, the birthplace of a miracle can attract a flood of pilgrims, boost the local economy and give high visibility and social prestige to the person who allegedly has witnessed the prodigious event.[1] So many materialistic incentives raise a strong suspicion: an allegedly 'holy' event could hide a wilful exploitation of the popular faith. In a paternalistic and probably far-fetched move, such events are qualified by the Criminal Code as a misdemeanour (Article 661, Code of Criminal Procedure (CCP)).

The whole scenario surrounding the little Madonna did not seem at all convincing to the criminal prosecutor, as he started wondering whether the reddish drops placed on the face of the little Madonna were actually the blood of the owner of the statue. DNA testing seemed perfect to assess the validity of such a hypothesis; a preliminary condition, of course, was a submission of genetic material. Given that the party under investigation refused to do so, issues arose as to the constitutionality of the use of force in this new scenario. More exactly, the question focused on the general provision contained in the Code of Criminal Procedure (Article 224, CPP), which entitles the judiciary to adopt any test instrumental (and mostly useful) to the pursuit of the truth.[2] The answer given by

---

*   I wish to thank Professor Paolo Tonini and Dr Paolo Canessa for their helpful comments. Any mistakes, of course, remain my own.

1   A brief description of the follow-up in the case described in the paper confirms such a hypothesis: see, on this point, *La Repubblica*, 20 January 1998, 23.

2   Notice here that, under Italian law, the Constitutional Court does not exercise a discretionary power of certiorari, but it is the remitting judge who decides, autonomously or under request by the parties, the relevance of the question of constitutionality, as defined by the statute enacted on 11 March 1953, n 87.

the court bears fundamental weight in affecting the current status, as well as the future availability, of DNA in the Italian criminal process. Therefore, it deserves to be carefully examined in this chapter.

Collection of DNA samples

Formal (and informal) procedures

Under Italian law there are several legitimate routes, some 'formal', others 'informal', for acquiring DNA evidence at the pre-trial stage of the criminal process. Only in the first instance are private parties made aware of the performance of the genetic test against them.

This distinction, which emerges from a mix of statutory law and customary rules, can be represented much more clearly starting from the second paradigm: the protagonist here is the leading force behind any criminal investigation in Italy, the Public Prosecutor or Pubblico Ministero (PM), a civil servant from the same judiciary. If he or she wants to narrow the focus of the investigation from the very beginning to a certain direction, the DNA test seems a perfectly suitable means. Assuming that at least a few cells of the human body have been found on the site where the crime was committed, if genetics confirms that the DNA profile matches with the one already collected from cells held by a public or private institution (for instance, the suspect is a drug addict who may have been undergoing treatment in the past and left samples of his or her own blood with a public or private daycare centre), a significant amount of judicial resources would be saved.

According to the informal procedure just described, the PM shall issue an internal order to perform the DNA test, without any formal notice being given to the interested party (Article 359, CPP).[3] If the results achieved confirm a match with a sufficient degree of certainty, according to the most advanced technology and reliable statistics, the prosecutor shall issue a provisional charge, docketing the name of the interested party and the alleged crime within a file officially registered within the criminal courthouse[4] (Article 335, CPP).[5]

---

3   See generally, on this point, Domenici (1995), 372ff. According to Grimaldi *et al* (1995), at 1067ff, the protocol commonly used comprises seven micro-satellite systems (HUMTH01, HUMFES\FPS, HUMF13A1, HUMVWA31, HUMMBP1, MIT-MH26, D21S11).

4   Interview with Dr Paolo Canessa, PM (Florence, 22 November 1997).

5   For the sake of completeness, it should be remembered that there is another informal procedure: having collected some DNA evidence on the crime site, the prosecutor may have restricted the focus of the investigation to a specific range of individuals. If not enough evidence has been collected, the optimal measure that avoids the 'noise' generally surrounding the opening of a formal investigation is to call on each individual separately, soliciting him or her to submit voluntarily a sample of blood, urine, etc. Here, a typical prisoner's dilemma scenario arises: if such parties are unable to define a common strategy in advance, and only one refuses, he or she knows that the Public Prosecutor will focus the investigation even more on him or herself. On the contrary, if innocent, such a party has a full interest in voluntarily submitting samples of DNA materials upon request by the Public Prosecutor, even without the presence of private counsel. In order to be used at trial, the evidence collected needs, of course, to be repeated in a formal way, following the modalities already explained in the text.

This last step corresponds to the opening of the most common formal type of investigation, whose compliance with the adversarial model embodied by the new Code of Criminal Procedure[6] allows the entire body of evidence already collected to be legitimately used later at trial.

The procedure here described requires full notice to the (already formally) accused party, who in turn is required to submit voluntarily the DNA samples collected to the judicially-appointed expert (Article 360, CPP).

The full application of the general rules of criminal procedure here entails a higher standard of protection for the accused party, as confirmed by the fact that the party is given full opportunity to be assisted by his or her lawyer or expert throughout the development of the DNA test. Motivated objections can be raised immediately in a far easier manner in front of the judge designed by the new Code of Criminal Procedure to overlook the pre-trial stage, the Giudice delle Indagini Preliminari (GIP), whose decisions shall be immediately executing (Article 328 of the CCP), although subject to review later at trial.

If private parties are not co-operative, there is an alternative 'formal' route that can be followed. In these circumstances, the main difference is that such parties under investigation, or even a third party qualified as a witness, can be forced to submit some genetic material to the court (Article 392, CPP). Competent in this field is the PM, whose discretionary power is actually quite limited: when the test involved is relevant and its performance could interrupt the trial for more than 60 days (Article 392), as it is likely to be the case of a new DNA test, the chances that the GIP may refuse a request of the test from the prosecutor or any other third party decrease substantially.

Here, we are still in the realm of the adversarial model, given that the interested parties can immediately raise motivated and written objections concerning the mode of performance of the test or, more radically, its relevance in the search for the truth: for instance, religious motivations may lead to a successful objection against the taking of a blood sample. In this case, the machinery of justice can address itself to a collection of urine, hair, etc.

Another successful objection can be raised by minors aged under 14, who are not punishable at all under Italian criminal law. Although we do not yet have case law available on this point, it seems likely that they could be forced to submit DNA material. In their capacity as witnesses, they can be legitimately asked and possibly even forced to co-operate with the judiciary in the search for the truth.[7]

---

6   For a brief outline in English of the new reform of the Code of Criminal Procedure, enacted with the DPR, 22 September 1988, n 447, see Amodio and Selvaggi (1989), at 1211; Del Duca (1991), at 73; Pizzi and Marafioti (1992), at 1; Freccero (1994), at 345.

7   In the case of minors aged between 14 and 18, on the contrary, the investigations and the following request of a DNA exam belongs to the special jurisdiction of the Tribunal for Minors, which will apply the general substantive rules provided for adults by the Code of Criminal Procedure. See generally the Decreto del Presidente della Republica (DPR), 22 September 1988, n 449. Military personnel are under the jurisdiction of the normal courts when a serious crime affecting life or limb has been committed.

Having taken into account all the different variables (factual, human and natural) involved, the PM or the GIP, depending on the type of procedure followed, shall mandate, at their own discretion, the performance of the DNA test. Eventually, the proper degree of force can be used against a recalutrant party by the delegated authority: the local police office (Articles 399 and 132, CPP). In case a sample of blood is needed, the intervention of a certified medical doctor preserves the test from being successfully challenged later on at trial.

Once the results of the test have been achieved, the general rules of criminal procedure apply: secrecy must be imposed on the evidence already collected, unless the PM, in his full discretion, opts to disclose to all individuals who bear a vested interest, starting, of course, with the accused party, the results of any test performed during the investigative stage (Article 329, para 1 of the CCP).

Given the weight of DNA evidence, especially if the test is positive, it is not hard to foresee such transparency. In Italy, however, the whole procedure is affected by the fact that it is not rare to learn directly from the media about the outcome of an important test such as DNA testing. The problem here is that the public at large may become aware of the DNA test results before the lawyers for the indicted party have a chance to look at them. If the latter person has received high visibility and the results of the test are positive, by the time of the trial, the bias against the accused party may have accrued to a dangerous level.

Testing

The appointment of experts

The appointment of an expert for performing the DNA test falls within the realm of the full discretion of the judge. In due course, this choice can be challenged successfully only for selected reasons: for instance, if the appointee is an unlicensed expert or laboratory.

Italy has two major sources of experts entitled to perform DNA tests. A state laboratory performing the test within its own premises is mainly selected in those instances in which the investigators want to verify the genetic material found on the crime site, following the informal procedure described above.

A second pool of experts consists of a list held within the local courthouse. Its members have been selected according to their professional qualification, which must offer sufficient guarantees of expertise in the field of genetics. It is from this list that in all cases of DNA testing the PM shall select one or more names.

Although formally independent and privately remunerated from the public coffer, these experts are mostly employees in a public laboratory (usually a university department). This formal affiliation allows them to shift some fixed costs to the taxpayer. Although several objections can be raised against such a solution in distributive terms, we have to take into account that the low number of DNA tests currently undertaken would not generate sufficient incentives to attract otherwise many experts working in the private sector, despite the fair level of remuneration usually earned.[8] The legitimacy of such allocation of costs can be justified only if we look at the public nature of the task performed in this field.

Cases and modalities of DNA collection

The forthcoming regulation reviewed in the light of the recent intervention of the Constitutional Court

The search for the truth clashes with the privacy of individuals every time a compulsory taking of DNA from a suspected person under investigation is involved.

In the light of Article 2 of the Constitution, which imposes a duty of solidarity,[9] each citizen would have been supposed to comply with an injunctive order such as that described above, unless life, limb or even personal dignity of an individual had been in peril. The constitutionality of this principle was clearly stated by the Italian Constitutional Court in 1986.[10]

With the advent of the DNA test, the Italian legal system has not missed the opportunity to address once again the same delicate compromise. The scenario for a new intervention of the Constitutional Court has been set by the case described at the beginning of this paper.

The relevant provision of the Code of Criminal Procedure (Article 224, CPP) is totally silent when it comes to regulating the extent of the use of force by the judiciary in this field. The court also had to take into account the enactment of the new Code of Criminal Procedure, which has envisioned the protection of (personal) freedom as an absolute priority.[11]

Meanwhile, two other important features of the general landscape have changed: the degree of accurateness attained by the DNA technique in the last few years has been increasing at a fast pace. Correspondingly, there has been much more room for delegating to science (and, more particularly, to genetics) fundamental weight in solving a criminal case that nobody confesses to have committed.

Secondly, the same achievements of the DNA technique have enabled the machinery of criminal justice to adopt several less intrusive means than blood collection (mainly hair, saliva or urine).

These important changes, as well as a much reinforced protection of privacy within the new Code of Criminal Procedure, have almost forced the Constitutional Court to raise the level of protection for private individuals. According to the court, any injunction ordering the taking of DNA material entails

---

8   According to the last (unofficial) data gathered about the use of DNA testing (see Montinaro (1996), n 30, 27 July 1996, 69), the police labs have undertaken the test in more than 2,000 cases, involving about 1,000 crimes. In 65% of the cases the suspected person has accepted a voluntary submission to the test, whereas in 34% of the cases it has been necessary to use force. In the remaining 1% of the cases the judge has refused to overcome the refusal to submit through the use of the proper degree of force.

9   This aspect is raised by Felicioni (1997), at 316.

10 Corte Cost, 24 March 1986, n 54, in Foro it (1987) c 716. For comments, see Mazzacuva-Pappalardo (1986), at 165; Ferraro (1986) at 868ff; Mastropaolo (1987), at 1081ff.

11 Corte Cost, 9 July 1996, n 238, Giust Cost (1996), 2142ff, 2146.

'an invasion in the realm of privacy' so relevant that the power of the judge cannot be fully discretionary,[12] but needs to be regulated as required by Article 13 of the Constitution. Meanwhile, DNA evidence should be barred from being used at all. This outcome has been heavily criticised as excessive, being almost like 'throwing away the baby with the bath water'.[13]

Leaving aside the pragmatic and narrow question of what happens to the test already developed and not yet used at trial,[14] here it seems more important to note that DNA evidence cannot be excluded from playing a role within the Italian criminal process, given its importance in achieving a fair solution.

The temporary compromise reached is that private parties must agree to a collection of genetic material, after being informed that the samples submitted shall be used for the development of such a test. Negative behaviour could seriously turn the outcome of the trial against the refusing party, so it is likely that consent – maybe even implicit – will follow.[15]

Along the same lines recently embraced by the Constitutional Court, any future regulation should focus on the *cases* and *modalities* allowing such relevant invasion in the realm of privacy, opening the door, once again, for the legitimate and widespread use of DNA evidence.[16]

Following some models already in place in other countries, the new proposal – which has not yet reached draft status – should restrict the cases enabling a compulsory taking of DNA samples to investigations related to serious offences,[17] excluding, all misdemeanours.

The qualification of an event as a specific crime, however, is very often quite controversial, delaying the useful acquisition of the DNA results until a final decision on the specific point is taken. The establishment of a minimum penalty threshold would, however, be a smoother way to restrict the use of force to serious crimes.

Secondly, only reasonable grounds – such as a relevant suspicion that leads to a belief that the collection of DNA material is defective – should allow a repeated invasion of privacy.

As far as the *modalities* of the DNA test are concerned, the new legislation envisioned by the Constitutional Court should embrace, once again, some broad guidelines. More precisely, given the current pace of improvements in the technique used, it should not be forgotten that the description of a specific methodology concerning the collection of genetic material from the suspected

---

12 Such consideration is reinforced by the fact that against such, a judicial order cannot be appealed with immediate effect on the performance of the test: a direct appeal can be addressed to the Court of Cassation, normally a court of third instance, without bearing injunctive effects: the point is raised by Vigoni (1996), at 1022ff, 1037.

13 See Ruotolo (1996), at 2151ff, and Dolso (1996), at 3221ff.

14 The status of the tests already taken before the intervention of the Constitutional Court, as far as their use at trial is concerned, is described by Giacca (1997), at 602.

15 This opinion has been clearly endorsed recently by Cass, 3 July 1997, n 2.45812, *Dir Pen e Processo* (1997) 951ff.

16 For a general overview, see Tonini (1997), at 471ff.

17 This is the educated guess of Chiavario (1996), at 20. Along the same lines, see already CPP, Article 266, which legitimates wire-tapping only for investigations related to certain types of crimes.

crimefeasor, as well as the performance of the test, would likely be subject to rapid obsolescence. This is why the adoption of a flexible approach seems preferable: in this light, the legal system should strive for a balance between the efficiency of criminal procedure and the protection of privacy. The use of the best technology available is certainly a professional responsibility of the expert designated by the court.[18]

Finally, a crucial point deserving careful evaluation concerns the proper destination of the genetic material already collected. A dilemma here arises: any perishable item – such as, inevitably, the case of a sample of genetic material – should be destroyed after being used at trial (Article 260, para 3 of the CPP) or, before that time, if the formal deadline of an investigation has expired, without sufficient evidence being gathered by the prosecutor (Articles 406 and 415 of the CPP).

On the contrary, if properly collected, stored and used following the informal procedure previously described (Article 359 of the CPP), the genetic material available could be subject to a new test, at least until it is available in sufficient quantity. New, emerging techniques could be used in those cases, opening the door for a legitimate reopening of the trial.

This implies that the interested person could be targeted by repeated scrutiny every time a new crime is committed. Does the higher statistical probability of DNA matching, whenever a new investigation begins, represent an unfair situation for such a party, even beyond the plain fact that it is a repeated invasion of his or her privacy?[19]

Further improvements in the technique used in the development and interpretation of the DNA test should enable the legal system to reply successfully to such legitimate questions, by reducing the systemic risk of confusion just described. Moreover, the possibility of challenging such practices in front of the pre-trial judge (GIP) works as a counterbalance against any risk of prosecutory intent vis-à-vis the interested parties.

Use of DNA test results in the criminal procedure

Challenges to DNA evidence at trial

Generally speaking, under the previous legal regime, an expert witness was not under a legal obligation to attend the trial and be cross-examined in order to explain the results achieved as well as the proper scientific methodology, unless the results of the test had turned out to be so contradictory, open-ended or unclear as to require some oral clarification.[20]

---

18 The necessity of waiting for more reliable techniques was raised in Italy during the first few years after the introduction of DNA fingerprinting by scientists: see Scorretti-Cortivo-Crestani (1991), at 767ff.

19 For a brief summary of the controversies aroused by this specific point, see Terrosi Vagnoli (1995), at 87. The recent and more refined developments in the use of DNA techniques are explained by Cucurachi *et al* (1994), at 439ff.

20 The point is clearly explained in *ibid*, 433.

The shift from an inquisitorial to an adversarial system of procedure has not only reduced the distance with the common law countries but, more importantly here, has broadened the possibility of challenging the evidence acquired at the pre-trial stage.[21] The discussion between the different parties at trial, much more efficiently ensured at trial through the well-established question and answer model of cross-examination, is the proper and formal stage for raising any doubts about the validity of the alleged results of any scientific test, including, of course, the case of DNA fingerprinting.

All interested parties – defendants, victims, the Public Prosecutor – are entitled at this stage to raise qualified and motivated objections on crucial points, such as: the collection and preservation of DNA material found on the crime site; the procedure used for developing the test; and, of course, the interpretation of the DNA profiles.

The presence of one or more experts appointed by the parties allows judges and juries to master even better the results achieved from the test.

The weight of DNA evidence in influencing the outcome of a trial is certainly far from being trivial, with Italy not far from other foreign legal experiences already very familiar with DNA evidence, mainly in the US and the UK. Fundamental steps in this universal direction are certainly the increased sophistication and reliability of the test, as well as the familiarity of judges and experts with the new achievements of genetics.

The foreign reader should be aware that we operate within the general framework of Article 192 of the CPP, according to which any criminal court is obliged to motivate the logic behind each decision. More exactly, such transparency entails that any judge is required to specify the evidence that has been relevant in influencing the final verdict (Article 546, CPP). An allegedly insufficient or unsatisfactory motivation can, generously as usual under Italian law, be subject to scrutiny on appeal to the court of third instance (Corte di Cassazione) by the prosecutor as well as, of course, the same convicted party.

There are no specific provisions concerning the use of DNA evidence at trial: this implies that the results of the DNA test shall be evaluated in the context of the entire body of evidence collected during the pre-trial stage, although it must be noted that the normal degree of judicial discretion is more and more constrained by genetic evidence, both incucpatory and exculpatory.[22]

A different and truly unique case arises when a party refuses to submit some DNA material to the court and its delegates. Here, a presumption of culpability is not admissible: indeed, we are facing a truly ambiguous behaviour which, although de facto quite influential on the final outcome of the trial, cannot be the only ground for a verdict against the refusing party.[23]

---

21   The literature on this point, comprehensibly, is quite extensive: for instance, see Siracusano et al (1990), at 67ff; more specifically, on the impact of the new model in the area of DNA evidence, see Stalteri (1993), at 189ff, 218.

22   It is almost impossible to give an account of the real weight of DNA evidence in the Italian system of criminal procedure: the only database available, whose files contain all the verdicts of the Supreme Court of Cassation, do not report any case that refers to the use of DNA at trial. This may be due to the fact that it takes many years to get to such third and final stages of jurisdiction. A weak use of DNA fingerprinting in the civil trial is underlined by Taruffo (1995), at 1479ff.

23   See on this point the arguments noted by Vigoni (1996), at 1042ff. More generally, see Ramajoli (1995), at 189.

DNA profiles

Databases and collection

The range of beneficial uses of genetics seems boundless. Inside the boundaries of the legal field, DNA-related information could play a key role not only for a range of helpful screenings on public health, but also for the identification of single individuals for criminal and non-criminal purposes (paternity cases are the most relevant example).

There is a major difference between the collection of DNA samples and DNA profiles. In the first scenario, as noted before, we have to rely on a basic rule that sanctions all kinds of abuses perpetrated in the field of criminal justice during the fundamental stage of the collection of evidence.

In the second case, the recent regulation on data protection applies.[24] This comprehensive statute has implicitly encompassed genetics within its range of application: more precisely, all databases containing relevant pieces of information on the personal identification of an individual – as is certainly the case with DNA profiles – are deemed in conflict with the protection of privacy, a priority openly reinforced by the advent of the new regime.

The nature, private or public, of the entity collecting the relevant data makes a real difference in determining the applicable provision. In the latter case, if the collected data is instrumental to a more efficient system of justice, as in the case of specific information previously acquired in the field of criminal investigation, the new regulation contemplates a broad exemption from the general rule of protection of privacy: this enables each court (including, of course, the office of the Public Prosecution) or the Department of Justice to set up databases instrumental to legitimate public goals (Article 4(d)).

A tighter provision applies to other branches of the state: regardless of the legitimate goals pursued, a specific statute is needed (Article 4(e)).

The new statute is even more rigid vis-à-vis private entities setting up internal databases. It should not be forgotten that we are dealing with data which, given the repetition of certain genetic frequencies within each specific sub-group of the population, could help to identify the racial or ethnic origin of the interested person.

Taking into account that DNA evidence – like any other piece of evidence collected during a criminal trial – can be freely consulted by third parties whose legitimate interest is proved informally in front of the courthouse (Article 116 of the CPP), the forthcoming regulation on DNA evidence would clearly represent a missed opportunity if the legitimate purposes – public health research, scientific publications, criminal investigations, etc – for a relaxation of the protection of privacy were not specified in detail.

Article 22, sub-s (1) of the recent statute on data protection applies here: it requires the open consent of each individual whose personal data has been

---

24 The new statute of 31 December 1996, n 675, has been modelled on the EU Directive 95/46 on privacy. It represents the first comprehensive regulation on data protection.

collected. Secondly, each database must previously receive a seal of legitimacy from the newly-established agency exercising its jurisdiction on data protection.[25]

The delicate compromise achieved between public aims and private entitlements is actually reinforced by the fact that any distorted or totally illegitimate use of the data already collected is deemed a tortious action that falls under a regime of strict liability, as expressly indicated by the above-mentioned statute (Article 18). This should provide a sufficient deterrent against any unsolicited intrusion in the privacy of individuals, even if punitive damages under Italian law are not admitted.

References

Amodio and Selvaggi (1989) 'An accusatorial system in a civil law country: the 1988 Italian Code of Criminal Procedure' 62 Temple University Law Review

Chiavario, M (1996) 'Sul test del DNA parola alle camere' (Il Sole 24 ore), 13 July 1996

Ciallela and Colesanti (1991) 'Il segreto professionale nell'archiviazione informatica di dati sanitari', XIII Riv It Med Leg

Cucurachi et al (1994) 'Minisatellite variant repeat (Mvr-Pcr) nella identificazione personale' XVI Riv It Med Leg

Del Duca, LF (1991) 'An historic convergence of civil and common law systems: Italy's new "adversarial" criminal procedure system' 10 Dickinson Journal of International Law

Dolso, GP (1996) Giur Cost

Domenici (1995) 'Prova del DNA' X Dig IV, Disc Pen

Felicioni (1997) 'L'esecuzione coattiva del prelievo ematico: profili problematici' Cass Pen

Ferraro (1986) 'Il prelievo ematico coattivo e la violenza 'lecita' Cass Pen

Freccero (1994) 'An introduction to the new Italian Criminal Procedure' 21 American Journal of Criminal Law

Giacca (1997) 'In tema di prelievo emativo coatto: brevi note a margine della sentenza della Corte Cost n 238 del 1996' Riv It Dir Proc Pen

Grimaldi et al (1995) 'Guida all'uso forense dei polimorfismi del DNA microsatellite. Criteri per la selezione, liste di polimorfismi e di potenziali candidati' Riv It Med Leg

Mastropaolo (1987) 'Prelievi del sangue a scopo probatorio e poteri del giudice' Riv It Med Leg

Mazzacuva-Pappalardo (1986) 'Prelievo ematico coattivo ed accertamento della verità: spunti problematici' I Giust Pen

---

25 Before the enactment of that reform, a (weak) barrier against the distorted use of data related to the health of the parties was given by the rules of professional responsibility, as confirmed by Ciallela and Colesanti (1991), at 71ff. Nowadays, genetic data can be collected and subsequently used without any special requirement or authorisation only when such data is instrumental to prevention, diagnosis, therapy, scientific research, provision of insurance and public health services.

Montinaro (1996) 'Per le esigenze della polizia scientifica occorrono norme al passo con le nuove tecnologie' *Guida al Diritto (Il Sole–24 Ore)*

Pizzi and Marafioti (1992) 'The new Italian Code of Criminal Procedure: the difficulties of building an adversarial trial system on a civil law foundation' 17 Yale Journal of International Law

Ramajoli, S (1995) *La prova nel processo penale*

Ruotolo, M (1996) 'Il prelievo ematico tra esigenza probatoria di accertamento del reato e garanzia costituzionale della libertà personale' Giur Cost

Scorretti-Cortivo-Crestani (1991) 'I problemi sorti nei primi anni di applicazione del DNA profiling in ambito medico-legale' Riv It Med Leg

Siracusano *et al* (1990) *Manuale di Diritto Processuale Penale I*

Stalteri (1993) 'Genetica e processo: la prova del "dna fingerprint": problemi e tendenze' Riv Trim Dir Proc Civ

Taruffo (1995) 'Le prove' Riv Trim Dir Proc Civ

Terrosi Vagnoli (1995) 'L'identificazione genetica (DNA profiling) nella recente giurisprudenza statunitense' I Giust Pen

Tonini, P (1997) 'Gli atti di disposizione del corpo umano', in Flora, G and Tonini, P (eds), *Nozioni di diritto penale*

Vigoni (1996) 'Corte Costituzionale, prelievo ematico coattivo e test del DNA' Riv It Dir Proc Pen

CHAPTER 9

JAPAN

Professor Toshihiro Kawaide
University of Tokyo

Time in the criminal process at which DNA sampling and testing may occur

Under Japanese law, DNA samples may be taken and tested when the investigation starts. In order for these procedures to take place it is not necessary that either the suspect be arrested, or that criminal charges be filed.

Collection of DNA samples

Procedures

The formalities required in relation to the collection of samples will vary depending on the manner the collection of samples takes. On the one hand, when it is conducted on a compulsory basis, for example, a blood sample from a suspect is taken against his will, a warrant issued by a judge is necessary without exception. On the other hand, when it is conducted on a non-compulsory basis, for example, when the police collect the hairs of a suspect from a garbage can put out by that suspect, no warrant is necessary.

Degree of force

Generally speaking, force that is necessary and reasonable in order to enforce the warrant may be used. For example, if the suspect resists the taking of his or her blood sample, the police can hold his or her body down to suppress resistance and restrain him or her forcibly.

Special requirements for specific groups

According to Japanese law, there is no differentiation between persons in relation to the collection of samples. In effect, therefore, the same rules apply to all people who are suspects.

Testing

Scientific tests carried out on DNA samples

At present, most DNA tests are carried out at institutes that belong to the police. They conduct four kinds of DNA tests, ie, 'MCT118 type test', ' HLADQ type test', 'TH01 type test' and 'PM inspection test'.

Licence requirements

At present, there are no requirements for a testing laboratory to hold a licence in order to carry out DNA tests. However, in practice, all tests for criminal procedure are carried out by competent scientists at police institutes or universities.

Other rules or regulations

The police established a set of internal guidelines for the practice of DNA tests in 1992. They provide for the method of tests and the contents that should be included in the written expert opinion, etc.

Use of DNA test results in the criminal process

Pre-trial

Availability of test results to defence counsel

In Japan's Code of Criminal Procedure the prosecutor is not obligated to reveal the results of the investigations to the defence lawyer at the pre-trial stage. Therefore, it depends on the discretion of the prosecutor as to whether the defence lawyer can know and use the results of DNA tests carried out by the investigating authorities.

During the trial

Admissibility of DNA test results

There are no special rules of evidence for the admissibility of DNA test results. The general rule for the admissibility of scientific evidence applies in the same way. This rule is not statutory but based on judicial precedent. It consists of two judgment factors. One is that the scientific test concerned has a general reliability, and the other is that the test was carried out properly in the case in question. The latter means that the collection, storage and testing of samples must be properly conducted.

There is only one case in which the Supreme Court has decided on the admissibility of DNA test results.[1] The Court ruled in a murder case that the result

---

1   *Saiko-Saibansho Keiji-Hanreishu*, vol 54 No 6, 17 July 2000, 550.

of a MCT118 type DNA test conducted by the police was admissible, because the scientific principle of the MCT118 type test has theoretical accuracy, and the test in this case was conducted in a scientifically exact way by a person who possessed the requisite skills for conducting the test. This decision was basically based on the above general rule.

Besides this, some courts have referred to the possibility of a second testing of samples in judging the admissibility of DNA test results. However, the Supreme Court had not found that it should be a requirement in determining admissibility.

Standard of proof

There is no special standard of proof that applies to DNA evidence. The general rules of evidence apply.

Challenges to DNA evidence by the defence lawyer

Defence lawyers usually challenge DNA evidence by insisting that it does not meet the above-mentioned requirements for the admissibility of scientific evidence. There is one case in which the admissibility of the DNA test result was denied on the ground that the storage and test of the sample, which was hair in this case, had been improper.[2]

Interpretation of DNA test results by the courts

The courts have found in several cases that DNA test results could be an important piece of evidence in establishing a person's guilt, but there still has been no case in which the defendant was found guilty based only on DNA test results. Rather, the courts evaluate DNA test results together with other evidence, or use them as corroborative evidence. In the above-mentioned case, the Supreme Court pointed out that the credibility of the DNA test results should be checked cautiously. In this sense, Japan's courts are still prudent in judging the evidentiary value of DNA test results.

Retention and storage of samples/test results

Japan has a statute dealing with the retention of records of criminal trials (the Finalized Criminal Suit Document Law 1987). This law provides the period for which records of criminal trials must be retained. DNA test results, which usually appear as written expert opinion, must also be retained under this law when they were presented as evidence at trial. The period of retention is from three to 50 years, according to the seriousness of the crime in question. The Public Prosecutor's Office is responsible for their retention.

---

2   *Hanrei-Jihou*, No 1543, 30 June 1995, 181 (Fukuoka Appellate Court).

This law does not apply to DNA samples and test results that were not presented at trial. The internal regulation of the Public Prosecutor's Office provides the period for which they are to be stored.

On the other hand, there are no statutory rules that provide for when samples and test results must be destroyed. However, in the internal guidelines of the police for the practice of DNA tests, the rest of blood samples taken on a warrant must be destroyed after the test has been completed. Thus, the Public Prosecutor's Office and the police can retain and store other samples and DNA test results. However, a so-called DNA database does not yet exist.

Penalties

There are no penalties for unauthorised storage, nor are there direct penalties for using samples or results for unauthorised purposes. However, all public officers, including investigating authorities, have a duty not to disclose secrets learned in the line of duty. If they disclose such secrets without due reason, they are penalised (Article 100 of the National Public Service Law, Article 34 of the Local Public Service Law). DNA data from individuals is, of course, included in these secrets.

Release of DNA test information

Release of stored test results

When DNA test results are objects of the above-mentioned Finalized Criminal Suit Document Law, they can be released to everyone, with some exceptions.

The release of other DNA test results depends upon who requests them. When other investigation authorities request them, the results are released, because all public offices are obligated to co-operate with an investigation (Article 197(1), Code of Criminal Procedure). On the other hand, when other government authorities or private citizens request them, they will not be released because of the duty to protect secrets.

Privacy and DNA test results

There are no special rules on the privacy of DNA test results. The general rules on privacy apply.

CHAPTER 10

NEW ZEALAND

Deborah Lawson and PDG Skegg
University of Otago

Introduction

In 1995, the Parliament of New Zealand enacted the Criminal Investigations (Blood Samples) Act 1995, which commenced by explaining that it was:

An Act:

(a) to make provision for the taking of blood samples for use in criminal investigations; and

(b) to authorise:

(i) the establishment of a databank of information derived from the analysis of blood samples taken from certain persons; and

(ii) the use of information from that databank in criminal investigations; and

(ii) to provide for matters incidental thereto.

The Act was – and is – divided into five parts:

I   Preliminary Provisions (ss 2–4);

II   Obtaining Blood Samples from Suspects (ss 5–24);

III DNA Profile Databank (ss 25–44);

IV Procedures for Taking Blood Samples (ss 45–63);

V   Miscellaneous Provisions (ss 64–82).

Late in 2003, the New Zealand Parliament enacted the Criminal Investigations (Bodily Samples) Amendment Act 2003. Most unusually, it altered the name of the earlier Act; it is now the Criminal Investigations (Bodily Samples) Act 1995. It also changed many references in the 1995 Act to 'blood' (as in 'blood samples') to 'bodily', so the 1995 Act now contains repeated references to 'bodily samples'. In addition, it made many other significant changes to the statute enacted in 1995.

This account focuses on New Zealand law as it is following the coming into force of the 2003 Amendment Act.[1] The section numbers cited are those of the 1995 Act, as amended.[2]

Time in the criminal process at which DNA sampling and testing may occur

Suspect requests

The Act provides that in any criminal investigation in respect of an indictable offence (committed or believed to have been committed), a bodily sample may be taken for the purposes of that investigation from any 'suspect' (s 5). In this context, 'suspect' means any person whom it is believed has committed or may have committed that offence – whether or not that person has been charged with the offence, and whether or not there is good cause to suspect that the person has committed the offence (s 2)). A criminal charge need not have been laid, and the person need not have been arrested.

Section 5 of the Act provides:[3]

Subject to section 72 of this Act, in any criminal investigation in respect of an offence committed or believed to have been committed, a bodily sample may be taken from a suspect, for the purposes of that investigation, on behalf of any member of the police only if:

(a) the offence is an indictable offence; and

(b) either:

   (i) in the case of a suspect who is of or over the age of 17 years, the suspect consents to the taking of that sample in accordance with section 9 of this Act; or

   (ii) in the case of a suspect who is of or over the age of 14 years but under 17 years, both the suspect and a parent of the suspect consent to the taking of that sample in accordance with section 9 of this Act; or

   (iii) the sample is taken under and in accordance with a suspect compulsion order or a juvenile compulsion order; and

(c) the sample is taken in accordance with the procedures set out in Part IV of this Act.

---

1   It is assumed that all of the Amendment Act will have been brought into force before this account is published. A consolidated version of the legislation is available at www.legislation.govt.nz.

2   The headings to the six major divisions of this chapter are those specified by Professor Donald Chalmers in 1997, when this Country Report was first requested (Letter, Chalmers to Skegg, 25 June 1997) and prepared. Ms Kerry Anderson, then Research Assistant in the Faculty of Law, University of Otago, prepared the first draft of the 1997 response to this request. Only a few fragments of this draft have survived subsequent revision and expansion, but the authors of this chapter gratefully acknowledges the assistance received from this earlier account.

3   The section to which reference is made at the beginning of the section is headed 'Other powers and abilities to take bodily samples not affected' (s 72).

A member of the police may request a suspect to give a bodily sample if he or she has reasonable grounds to believe that analysis of the sample would tend to confirm or disprove the suspect's involvement in the commission of the offence (s 6(1)).

There is a detailed consent procedure that must be followed upon making a request for consent to take a bodily sample. The member of the police must hand the suspect a written notice that deals with the following matters:

- the (approved) reasons for seeking the bodily sample (s 7(b)(i) and (ii));

- the consent and consent refusal options and procedures, including a statement that the suspect may wish to consult a lawyer before deciding whether or not to consent (s 7(b)(iii), (iv), (v) and (vi));

- that the sample will be analysed and may provide evidence that may be used in criminal proceedings (s 7(b)(vii));

- the possibility of a suspect compulsion order application being made upon refusal to give consent (s 7(b)(viii));

- a summary of the provisions relating to the procedure for taking the sample and those for analysis and disclosure of the results of the analysis (s 7(b)(ix) and (xi));

- that a suspect may request that the sample be taken in the presence of a lawyer, or another person of the suspect's own choice (s 7(b)(x));

- that the sample and information derived from its analysis will be held by or on behalf of the police (s 7(b)(xii));

- that if the suspect is convicted of a relevant offence (see s 2(1) of the Act) information derived from an analysis of the sample will be held on a DNA profile databank (s 7(b)(xiii));

- the provisions relating to the destruction of the sample and of any information derived from any analysis of the sample (s 7(b)(xiv)); and

- such other particulars as may be prescribed (s 7(b)(xv)).

The first four points must also be explained to the suspect, when making a suspect consent request, in a manner and in language that the suspect is likely to understand (s 6(2)(b)).

The suspect consent procedure outlined in ss 6 and 7 is subject to s 8, which deals with suspect requests to persons under 17 (see below).

Suspect compulsion order

If there is good cause to suspect that the suspect has committed a relevant offence, and he or she has refused to consent to a bodily sample request, a commissioned officer of the police may apply to a High Court judge for an order requiring that suspect to give a bodily sample (s 13(1)).

The 2003 Amendment Act substantially increased the number of relevant offences to which the Act applies (from a previous total of 34 offences, to a new total of 78). These additional offences are in keeping with the criteria applied when the original Act was developed: that the offences should be serious, violent, and indictable, or ones where it is most likely that an offender will leave DNA at the scene.[4]

A relevant offence is (s 2(1)):

(a) an offence against any of the provisions listed in Part 1 of the Schedule; or

(b) an offence against any of the provisions listed in Part 2 of the Schedule; or

(c) an attempt to commit an offence against any of the provisions listed in Part 1 or Part 2 of the Schedule if the offence is not itself specified as an attempt; or

(d) conspiring with any person to commit an offence against any of the provisions listed in Part 1 or Part 2 of the Schedule if the offence is not itself specified as a conspiracy; or

(e) an offence punishable by a term of imprisonment of 7 years or more; or

(f) an attempt to commit an offence of the kind referred to in paragraph (e); or

(g) conspiring with any person to commit an offence of the kind referred to in paragraph (e).

The commissioned officer of the police must set out various particulars in the application, including the facts relied upon to show good cause to suspect (s 13(2)(a)); the reasons why it is considered necessary to obtain a suspect compulsion order (including the facts relied upon to show reasonable grounds to believe that analysis of the sample would tend to confirm or disprove the suspect's involvement) (s 13(2)(b)); and (where possible) the type of analysis likely to be required (s 13(2)(c)).

A High Court judge may make a suspect compulsion order if satisfied that:

- there is good cause to suspect that the respondent has committed the relevant offence to which the application relates (s 16(1)(a)); *and*

- material reasonably believed to be from, or genetically traceable to, the body of a person who committed the offence has been found or is available:

  (i)   at the scene; or

  (ii) on the victim; or

  (iii) from within the body or from any thing coming from within the body of the victim that is reasonably believed to be associated with, or having resulted from, the commission of the offence; or

  (vi) on any thing reasonably believed to have been worn or carried by the victim when the offence was committed; or

  (v)   on any person or thing reasonably believed to have been associated with the commission of the offence (s 16(1)(b)); *and*

- there are reasonable grounds to believe that an analysis of a bodily sample taken from the respondent would tend to confirm or disprove the respondent's involvement in the commission of the offence (s 16(1)(c)); *and*

---

4   Law and Order Select Committee Report on the Bill (www.clerk.parliament.govt.nz /content/SelectCommitteeReports/221bar2.pdf), (hereinafter 'the Report'), p 5.

- the respondent has refused to consent to the taking of a bodily sample in respect of the offence, or a related offence (s 16(1)(d)); *and*

- in all the circumstances, it is reasonable to make the order (s 16(1)(e)).

When considering whether to make a suspect compulsion order, the judge is to have regard to the nature and seriousness of the offence to which the application relates (s 16(2)(a)); any reasons the respondent gives for opposing the order sought (s 16(2)(b)); any evidence regarding the importance of obtaining a sample to the investigation (s 16(2)(c)); and any other matter the judge considers relevant (s 16(2)(d)).

Every suspect compulsion order is subject to conditions included in the order by the judge under s 24A, and any other special conditions included in the order by the judge (s 24(2)).

Every suspect compulsion order must contain:

- the date on which and the place where the sample will be taken (s 24(4)(a));

- a summary of the provisions relating to the methods by which a bodily sample may be taken, the persons who are authorised to take such samples, and a statement that in certain circumstances a judge may specify the method by which a bodily sample is to be taken (s 24(4)(b));

- information about the persons in whose presence the suspect may request that the sample be taken (s 24(4)(c) and (ca));

- a summary of the provisions relating to the procedures for the analysis of samples and the disclosure of the results of the analysis (s 24(4)(d));

- conditions included by the judge under s 24(2) (s 24(4)(e));

- a statement that if the suspect refuses to allow a bodily sample to be taken, a sample may be taken by force (s 24(4)(f));

- a statement that the sample, and any information derived from any analysis of the sample, will be held by or on behalf of the police (s 24(4)(g));

- a statement that if the suspect is convicted of the offence in respect of which the order is made, or a related offence that is a relevant offence, information derived from any analysis of the sample will be held on a DNA profile databank (s 24(4)(h));

- reference to the provision relating to the destruction of the sample and of any information derived from any analysis of the sample and (s 24(4)(i)); and

- such other particulars as may be prescribed (s 24(4)(j)).

DNA databank request

A bodily sample may be taken from a person for the purpose of including that person's DNA profile on a DNA databank only if that person consents (in accordance with s 34 of the Act) or the sample is taken pursuant to a databank compulsion notice; and the sample is taken in accordance with the procedures set out in Part 3 of the Act (s 29).

A member of the police may request anyone of or over 17 years of age to give a bodily sample for the purposes of obtaining a DNA profile for storage on a DNA profile databank (s 30(1)). A person need not be a suspect in relation to any offence for him or her to be asked to give a sample for the DNA databank.

The request for a bodily sample to be taken, and stored on the DNA profile databank, must be accompanied by much of the same information required for requests for bodily samples under Part II of the Act. However, there is no requirement to stipulate an offence in respect of which the request is made, and the member of the police need not have reasonable grounds to believe that analysis of the sample would tend to confirm or disprove that person's involvement in the commission of the offence.

The person must be informed that the purpose of the request is to obtain information that will be stored on a DNA profile databank and that may be used by the police in the investigation of criminal offences (s 30(2)(b)(i)). A person to whom a databank request is made must also be informed that he or she may, at any time before the taking of the sample, withdraw consent to the sampling (s 30(2)(b)(iii)). Additionally, the person must be told that he or she may also withdraw consent (after the taking of the sample) to the subsequent use of the bodily sample, except in certain circumstances (ss 30(2)(b)(vi) and 36).

The notice given to the person providing the sample, for the DNA profile databank, must contain the same information as that accompanying a request for a bodily sample under Part II of the Act (with the variations mentioned in the foregoing paragraph incorporated). It must also outline the provisions relating to the procedure for taking the sample, the procedures for analysing the sample and disclosing the results of the analysis, the use of any DNA profile obtained from the sample, the removal of information from the databank, and the provisions relating to the retention of a sample and DNA profile notwithstanding withdrawal of consent (s 31(b)).

Minors under the age of 17 cannot consent to the taking of a bodily sample (under s 30) for a DNA profile databank (s 32).

There is provision for dual requests for bodily sampling and a databank request (see s 33).

Consent to a bodily sample being taken in response to a databank request is only valid if it is given in writing (and signed by the person giving consent) or if the person's oral consent is recorded on videotape (s 34(1)). There are prescribed procedures for recording such consent, and also for recording any withdrawal of consent (before the sample is taken) (s 34(2) to (5)).

People in custody who are asked to provide a sample for the DNA profile databank are entitled to consult privately with a lawyer about the request (s 35).

There are provisions relating to the withdrawal of consent after a sample has been taken (s 36), and about when a sample may be retained for a time despite the withdrawal of consent (s 38).

DNA databank compulsion notice

A commissioned officer of the police may issue a databank compulsion notice requiring a person to give a bodily sample if the person has been convicted of a relevant offence (as defined in s 2(1)), and if the conviction is one to which this Part of the Act applies under s 4.

The Amendment Act added a retrospective element regarding people to whom DNA databank compulsion notices could be issued (see s 4, as amended).

People convicted of a relevant offence after the commencement of the new provision can be issued with a DNA databank compulsion notice. Additionally, a person convicted of a relevant offence (listed in Part 1 of the Schedule) before the commencement of the new provision may be issued a databank compulsion notice – if he or she was detained (under a sentence of imprisonment) in relation to that conviction, on the date of commencement of s 7 of the Criminal Investigations (Bodily Samples) Amendment Act 2003.

If a databank compulsion notice is issued, the police must (s 39(2)):

- serve the notice on the person to whom it relates by handing the notice to the person; and

- if that person is under the age of 17 years, take all reasonable steps to serve a copy of the notice on a parent or other person having the care of that person by giving him or her a copy of it; and

- explain the contents of the notice to the person being served in a manner and in a language that the person is likely to understand.

The date on which a person may be served with a databank compulsion notice varies according to whether or not the person is detained under a sentence of imprisonment (for the relevant offence in relation to which it is issued).

If the person is not detained, the notice must be served as soon as is reasonably practicable after conviction is entered (s 39(3)(a)), but need not be served before sentencing (s 39(3)(b)). Notice must be served on a date that allows for the taking of a bodily sample:

- on a date later than the 14th day after the date on which the notice is served; *and*

- before the date six months after the date the person's conviction for the relevant offence was entered (ss 39(3)(c) and 39C(3)).

If the person to whom a notice is issued is detained under a sentence of imprisonment, the notice must be served on a date that allows for the taking of a bodily sample:

- on a date later than the 14th day after the date on which the notice is served; *and*

- before the later of the two following dates:

  (i) the date the person is released from being detained under a sentence of imprisonment for the relevant offence; or

  (ii) the date six months from the date on which the conviction for the relevant offence was entered (ss 39(4) and 39C(4)).

The form and content requirements of the databank compulsion notice are similar to those for suspect compulsion orders. Every databank compulsion notice must contain the following particulars:

- the offence in relation to which the notice is issued (s 39A(2)(a));
- a place where, and a date on which, the person is to attend to give a bodily sample (s 39A(2)(b));
- a statement that the person must attend to give a bodily sample at the place and on the date specified, unless agreement is reached with a member of the police that the person may attend at a different place, on an earlier date, or both (s 39A(2)(c));
- a statement that information obtained from the bodily sample will be stored on a DNA profile databank and may be used by the police in the investigation of criminal offences (s 39A(2)(d));
- a statement that the person may request a databank compulsion notice hearing under s 41(1) and a summary of the grounds on which a hearing may be requested under s 41(2) (s 39A(2)(e) and (f));
- a summary of the provisions relating to the methods by which a bodily sample may be taken, the persons who are authorised to take such samples, and a statement that in certain circumstances a judge may specify the method by which a bodily sample is to be taken (s 39A(2)(g));
- a statement that if the suspect refuses to allow a bodily sample to be taken, a sample may be taken by force (s 39A(2)(h));
- information about the persons in whose presence the suspect may request that the sample be taken (s 39A(2)(i));
- a summary of the provisions relating to the procedures for the analysis of samples and the disclosure of the results of the analysis (s 39A(2)(j));
- a summary of the provisions relating to the use of any DNA profile obtained from the sample (s 39A(2)(k));
- any other particulars that may be prescribed (s 39A(2)(l)).

Databank notices issued to home detainees must contain the same information as every other notice – except that, instead of the particulars in s 39A(2)(b) and (c), the notice should include:

- a statement that the person must give a bodily sample at the residence at which the person is detained; and
- a statement that the person and a member of the police may not agree to vary the place, but may agree to vary the date on which the person is to attend to give a sample to a date earlier than that specified in the notice (s 39A(3)(b)(i) and (ii)).

A commissioned officer may state in a notice that a home detainee may give the sample at a place other than the detention residence if the officer is of the view that it is necessary to do so on account of the person's health (s 39A(4)).

Databank compulsion orders issued in relation to people under 17 years of age must include additional particulars, because of the greater vulnerability of younger offenders (s 39B).

Databank compulsion notice hearings

The Act allows a person to whom a databank compulsion notice is issued to request a member of the police to arrange a hearing before a judge, before the date specified in the notice as the date on which the person is to attend to give a sample. A databank compulsion notice hearing may only be requested on one or more of the following grounds:

- the offence (in relation to which the notice has been issued) is not a relevant offence (s 41(2)(a)(i));

- the conviction for the relevant offence (in relation to which the notice has been issued) is not a conviction to which this Part applies (s 41(2)(a)(ii));

- the conviction was quashed before the notice was issued (s 41(2)(b)(i));

- the conviction was quashed after the notice was issued but before the sample was taken and the police have not notified the person that the notice is of no effect as required by s 40(2) (s 41(2)(b)(ii));

- all three methods available for the taking of a bodily sample will cause serious harm to the person's health, on the date specified in the notice (as the date on which the person is to attend to give a sample) (s 41(2)(c));

- the date specified as the date on which the person is to attend does not comply with the dates (in ss 39(3), (4) and 39C) between which bodily samples may be taken under this Part of the Act (s 41(2)(d), (e));

- the person to whom the notice relates was not served with the notice (s 41(2)(f)).

A request for a databank compulsion notice hearing must be in writing and must specify the grounds relied upon (s 41A(1)). If a request is made for a hearing, a bodily sample may not be taken from the person to whom the notice relates – unless a judge at a databank compulsion notice hearing makes a Part III order (s 41A(2)).

There are certain filing and notification obligations on the police and on the registrar of the court when a hearing has been requested (see s 41B).

Sections 41C–44B outline who may appear at a databank notice hearing, what orders the judge can make, including options for varying or imposing conditions on notices, the effect of any change in circumstances before a hearing takes place or is completed, when an order that a notice is of no effect must be made, and the rules in relation to further databank compulsion notices.

Collection of DNA samples

Procedures

Bodily samples may be taken by venous sample, fingerprick sample or buccal sample (s 48(2)).

A venous sample is a sample of venous blood taken in accordance with normal medical procedures. A fingerprick sample is a sample of capillary blood taken, in accordance with normal medical procedures, from the tip of a finger or thumb. A buccal sample is a sample of epithelial cells from inside the mouth taken by a device, or provided by other means, approved for the purpose by the Minister of Justice (s 2(1) and s 4B(1)(b)).

Where bodily samples are being taken as a result of a suspect or databank request, the person from whom the sample is to be taken must be given an opportunity to choose which of the three methods is to be used (s 48(3)). If the sample is to be taken pursuant to a compulsion order or databank compulsion notice, and a judge has not specified the method, the person may choose the method, if he or she is a consenting samplee (s 48(4)(a)). In either of the above cases, where the samplee is consenting, a member of the police may indicate to the person that the police prefer to use a particular sampling method (s 48(6)).

If the person has been given a reasonable opportunity to choose the method and has indicated that he or she has no preference, a member of the police may choose the sampling method (s 48(7)). The provisions conferring the authority to use force are activated if a person, having indicated that he or she had no preference for the sampling method, refuses to allow a bodily sample to be taken after a member of the police has chosen the method (s 48(8)).

If the person refuses to give a sample in compliance with a compulsion order or notice, the sample, if it is taken by force, must be taken by fingerprick sample (s 48(4)(b)).

Where bodily samples are taken pursuant to a compulsion order or databank compulsion notice in which the judge has specified the sampling method, the sample must be taken by that method if the person agrees to give a sample in compliance with the order or notice (s 48(5)(a)). However, if the person refuses to give a bodily sample in compliance with the order or notice, then the sample must be taken by buccal sample if the judge has specified that method because of the person's state of health, or by fingerprick sample in any other case (s 48(5)(b)).

Blood samples (whether a fingerprick sample or a venous sample) must be taken by a suitably qualified person (s 49). In relation to a blood sample, a suitably qualified person means (s 2(1)):

- a medical practitioner; or

- a registered nurse; or

- a medical technologist with a degree in medical laboratory science; or

- a person trained in phlebotomy in accordance with the national standard for training phlebotomists adopted by the Association of Community Laboratories Incorporated.

Kits are provided to the police to facilitate the collection of whole blood or fingerprick samples.[5]

---

5   www.esr.co.nz/features/esr_and_dna/techniques/index.htm (accessed on 28 July 2003). All the contents of each kit are labelled with a unique six-digit barcode. A custom designed software database program uses these barcodes as unique identifiers for the samples as they move through the various stages of analysis, including loading to the databank itself.

If a buccal sample is being taken pursuant to a compulsion order or databank compulsion notice from a person of or over the age of 17 years, he or she may elect to take the sample him or herself under the supervision of a member of the police, or have the sample taken by a suitably qualified person (s 49A(1)).

A suitably qualified person in relation to a buccal sample means (s 2(1)):

- a medical practitioner; or

- any other person suitably qualified to take a blood sample (see above) who has undergone training in taking and dealing with buccal samples in accordance with the training criteria determined by the approved agency.

If a buccal sample is being taken pursuant to a suspect request or a databank request from a person of or over the age of 17 years, the person must take the sample him or herself under the supervision of a member of the police (s 49A(2)).

There are a number of special provisions relating to collecting bodily samples from minors and persons unable to take buccal samples themselves.

When giving a bodily sample, the person is entitled to have a lawyer or another person of the person's choice present (s 50(1)(a)). If the person from whom the sample is being taken is under 17 years of age, that person is also entitled to have a parent or carer present (s 50(1)(b)). The member of the police arranging the taking of the sample is required to ascertain whether the person providing the sample wishes any of the permitted people to be present. If so, the member of the police must ascertain the names of those chosen (s 50(2)(a)), and then must take all reasonable steps to notify these people of when, where, and how the sample is to be taken (s 50(2)(b)(i) and (ii)). The lawyer or any other person chosen (including a parent or carer) is not compelled to attend (s 51(b)). The Act does not compel any suitably qualified person to take a sample (s 51(a)).

Persons permitted to be present when a bodily sample is taken are:

- a member of the police who should (where practicable) be of the same sex as the person from whom the sample is taken (s 52(1)(a));

- the suitably qualified person who is to take the sample, or the member of the police who will supervise the taking of the sample, or a parent taking a buccal sample from a child (s 49A(4)(b) or 6(a)) and the member of the police who will supervise that (s 52(1)(b));

- any person chosen by the samplee pursuant to s 50 (s 52(1)(c) and (d));

- in the case of a suspect under the age of 17 years who has consented to the taking of a bodily sample as a result of a suspect request or a Part 2A request, and who has elected to take a buccal sample him or herself, an independent adult (who may be one of the persons referred to directly above) (s 52(1)(da));

- any person who is for the time being guarding or escorting a samplee who is in custody (s 52(1)(e)).

Subject to the above requirements, the sample should be taken in circumstances affording reasonable privacy to the person from whom the sample is being taken (s 53).

People from whom bodily samples are taken may have their own analyses done. If a venous sample is taken, the person is to be asked whether he or she wants part of the sample to have his or her own analysis done (s 55(1)). If the person wishes to act on this option, the sample is to be divided into two parts, each placed in a separate container and then sealed (s 55(2)). One part of the sample is to be delivered immediately to the person from whom it was taken (s 55(2)(c)(i)). If the person from whom the sample is taken is in custody at the time, one part of the sample must be delivered as soon as is practicable to any person nominated by that person (if the nominated person is not present when the sample is taken) or immediately to any person nominated if that person is present when the sample is taken (s 55(2)(c)(ii)).

If the person declines the option of having his or her own analysis done, or does not respond to the enquiry, then the sample is to be placed in a single container and sealed (s 55(3)). An anti-coagulant may be added (s 55(4)).

If the suspect has a fingerprick sample taken, it is to be placed in a container which is to be sealed as soon as practicable after the sample has dried. People from whom samples are taken must be asked whether they wish to have a second fingerprick sample taken so they can have the sample analysed on their own behalf. It is then to be stored and delivered to the person, as with a venous sample (s 56).

If the suspect has a buccal sample taken, it is to be sealed in a container once it has dried, or placed in a container in a way that allows it to dry (s 56A(2)(a)). People from whom samples are taken must be asked whether they wish to have a second buccal sample taken so they can have the sample analysed on their own behalf (s 56A(2)(b)). If the person responds in the affirmative, the member of the police supervising the taking of the buccal sample must provide the person with the means to take a second buccal sample him or herself (or in the case of a buccal sample being taken from a child, if applicable, provide a parent with the means to take a second buccal sample from the child) (s 56A(2)(c)(i)). Alternatively, the suitably qualified person, with the person's consent, must take a second buccal sample or provide the person with the means to take a sample him or herself (or in the case of a sample being taken from a child, if applicable, provide a parent with the means to take a second sample from the child) (s 56A(2)(c)(ii)). It is then to be stored and delivered to the person, as with a venous or fingerprick sample (s 56A(2)(d)).

There are only two circumstances in which a bodily sample can be taken, pursuant to a compulsion order or databank compulsion notice, if the date specified in the order or notice has passed:

- if a warrant to arrest the person to whom the order or notice has been issued under s 45; or

- if the date has been varied by a judge under s 42, 43, 43A, or 47, to a date later than the date originally specified in the order or notice (s 45AA(1)).

If the person to whom a compulsion order or databank compulsion notice relates, and a member of the police, agree to vary the date specified in the order or notice for the sampling, but for any reason the person does not attend to give the sample on that date, the person may attend to give a sample on:

- the date specified in the order or notice, which may be the date as varied by a judge under s 42, 43, 43A or 47; or

- any other date before the date specified in the order or notice, agreed to by the person to whom the order or notice relates and a member of the police under s 24A(2) or (4)(b) or s 39A(2)(c) or (3)(b)(ii) (s 45AA(2)).

If a compulsion order is made or a databank compulsion notice is issued, a judge may direct the issue of a warrant to arrest and detain the person to whom the order or notice relates, for as long as is reasonably necessary to take a bodily sample, but in no case for longer than 24 hours (ss 45(3) and 45A(2)(b)). Judges cannot direct the issue of a warrant before the date specified in an order or notice for the sampling, except in the limited circumstances specified (s 45(4)). A judge can direct the issue of a warrant on or after the date specified in an order or notice for the sampling if satisfied, on evidence given on oath, that the person has failed to attend to give a sample on the date specified in the order or notice. All reasonable steps must have been taken to serve the person to whom the order or notice relates with the order or notice specifying the date on which the person is to attend to give the bodily sample. If applicable, all reasonable steps must also have been taken to give the person notice of any varying of the date under s 42, 43, 43A or 47 (s 45(5)).

Every warrant issued under s 45 must be in the prescribed form and expires immediately after a sample is taken from the person to whom the order or notice in relation to which the warrant is issued relates (s 45A(1)). Bodily samples taken pursuant to a warrant must be taken in accordance with the order or notice to which the person is subject (although the place and date may be different from that specified) (s 45A(3)). The power to arrest and detain a person, pursuant to a warrant issued under s 45, may be exercised on one occasion only (s 45A(5)).

Degree of force

When a bodily sample is to be taken pursuant to a compulsion order or a databank compulsion notice, a member of the police must do the following (s 54(1)):

- ascertain from the person from whom the sample is to be taken which of the three methods he or she wishes the sample to be taken by way of (unless the method has been specified by a judge) (s 54(1)(a));

- if a method has not been specified by a judge, inform the person that if he or she refuses to give a bodily sample, then a member of the police may use or cause to be used reasonable force to assist a suitably qualified person to take a fingerprick sample (s 54(1)(b));

- if a judge has specified the method by which the sample is to be taken, inform the person that, despite the judge's specification, if he or she refuses to give a bodily sample, a member of the police may use or cause to be used reasonable force to assist a suitably qualified person to take a fingerprick sample (s 54(1)(c));

- if a judge has specified that because of the person's state of health, the bodily sample must be taken by way of a buccal sample, inform the person that if he or she refuses to give a bodily sample, a member of the police may use or cause to be used reasonable force to assist a suitably qualified person to take a buccal sample (s 54(1)(d)).

If the person refuses to give a sample, the member of the police may act in accordance with the information given to the person pursuant to s 54(1) (s 54(2)).

If a member of the police exercises the power conferred by s 54(2), that member of police must provide a written report of the exercise of that power to the Commissioner of Police no later than three days afterwards (s 54(3)).

No civil or criminal proceedings may be laid against any person using force in accordance with the statutory entitlement (s 79(1)). However, that provision does not apply 'with respect to any proceeding on the ground of any negligent act or omission in the taking of any blood sample' (s 79(2)).

Special requirements for specific groups

Children and young people

The Act provides many special rules and requirements concerning children and young people. In this context, a child is a person of or over the age of 10 years but under the age of 14 years (s 2(1)). Other provisions deal with young people of or over the age of 14 years but under the age of 17 years (referred to here as juveniles).

Pursuant to s 5, suspect requests can be made to suspects who are juveniles; however, the consent of both the suspect and a parent of the suspect must be given in accordance with s 9.

The general suspect request procedure applies to juvenile suspects, with modifications set out in s 8(2) to take account of their greater vulnerability. The modifications relate mainly to informing both the juvenile and a parent of their rights with respect to giving, refusing or withdrawing consent; involving parents in the procedure; and the related amendments to the requisite suspect request notice.

Sections 6 and 7 outline the general procedure, and the form and content of the notice, for making a suspect request. However, by virtue of s 8(1), nothing in s 6 applies in respect of a suspect who is a child or who was a child at the time the offence was committed. Section 8(1A) provides:

> However, a suspect who is a child or was a child at the time an offence in relation to which he or she may not be lawfully prosecuted (being an indictable offence other than murder or manslaughter) was committed, may consent to the taking of a buccal sample as a result of a Part 2A request.

Section 24C is important in relation to Part 2A requests. It provides that:

> (1) Subject to section 72, in a criminal investigation in respect of an indictable offence committed or believed to have been committed by a suspect who is a child or was a child at the time the offence was committed and in relation to which that suspect may not lawfully be prosecuted, a buccal sample may be taken from that suspect, for the purposes of the investigation, on behalf of any member of the police, only if –

(a) both the suspect and a parent of the suspect have consented to the taking of a buccal sample under section 24G; and

(b) the sample is taken in accordance with the procedures set out in Part IV.

(2) Every reference in this Part to an indictable offence for which a suspect may not lawfully be prosecuted is a reference to an indictable offence other than murder or manslaughter.

A member of the police may request that a suspect give a buccal sample if (s 24D):

- there is good cause to suspect that the suspect has or may have committed an indictable offence for which the suspect may not lawfully be prosecuted (because the suspect is a child or was a child at the time the offence was committed); *and*

- the suspect is a person under 17 years of age in relation to whom an application for a declaration for care or protection may be made[6] if the suspect's involvement in the offence tends to be confirmed by the analysis of a buccal sample; *and*

- a member of the police has reasonable grounds to believe that analysis of a buccal sample from the suspect would tend to confirm or disprove the suspect's involvement in the commission of the offence.

Police have specific obligations to inform suspects of certain matters when making a Part 2A request. The procedure, form and content of the applicable notice bear some resemblance to that for a suspect request, with the modifications incorporated into juvenile requests. Additionally, the police must inform the person that the sample will be analysed and may be used to make an application for a declaration that the suspect is in need of care and protection, but may not be used to prosecute the suspect for any offence (s 24E(ix)). Broadly similar provisions to the general scheme outline the valid consent procedure, the withdrawing of consent and the forwarding of the buccal sample to an approved agency (ss 24G–24I).

Largely comparable to the requirements for a suspect compulsion order are the criteria applying for a juvenile compulsion order, if the suspect may lawfully be prosecuted for that offence (being an offence of murder or manslaughter in the case of a suspect who is a child or was a child at the time the offence was committed) (s 18(1)(b)). In the case of a suspect 14 years or older at the time of the offence, consent to a suspect request must have been refused either by the suspect or a parent, or both (s 18(1)(c)).

Much the same procedures as those for a suspect compulsion order follow the making of such an application, again with slight variations to account for the greater vulnerability of the juvenile suspect (see ss 18–23). Extra protections generally relate to extra persons who must be notified of proceedings and decisions, and who may appear and adduce evidence at hearings regarding juvenile compulsion orders.

---

6   See the Children, Young Persons and Their Families Act 1989, s 14(1)(e). ('In the case of a child of or over the age of 10 years and under 14 years, the child has committed an offence or offences the number, nature or magnitude of which is such as to give serious concern for the well-being of the child.')

The prohibition against the publication of the respondent's name in compulsion order applications is stronger in relation to juveniles. (It extends to the names of their parents or caregivers, and permits almost no exceptions (s 19) – by way of contrast to regular suspect compulsion order applications (cf s 14)).

Juvenile compulsion orders must contain a statement that as well as a lawyer or other person of the suspect's own choice, a juvenile suspect may have a parent (or other person having the care of them) present at the taking of the sample (s 24(4)(ca)).

Minors under the age of 17 years cannot be requested to, and are not here capable of, consenting to provide a sample for the DNA profile databank (s 32).

There is a special procedure for the issue and service of databank compulsion notices in relation to those under 17 years of age, with slight variations concerning serving notice on a parent or other person having care of the person, and informing suspects that a parent or other person having care of the suspect is entitled to request a databank compulsion notice hearing under s 41(3) (s 39B).

The extra requirements involved in issuing and serving databank compulsion notices to suspects under the age of 17 years gives such suspects additional grounds for requesting a databank compulsion notice hearing, if those requirements are not met (s 41(2)(g), 41(3)). Juveniles are also allowed to have more people appear and adduce evidence at a databank compulsion notice hearing than a suspect 17 years of age or more (s 41C).

Finally, there are special rules and requirements relating to the methods by which bodily samples may be taken from suspects under the age of 17 years, and regarding who may be present when bodily samples are taken.

Bodily samples taken pursuant to a Part 2A request can only be taken by buccal sample (s 48(1)). A child may choose to:

- take a buccal sample him or herself under the supervision of a member of the police; or

- have the sample taken by a suitably qualified person; or

- choose to have the buccal sample taken by a parent under the supervision of a member of the police (s 49A(4)).

If a child is unable to take a buccal sample him or herself due to disability or injury, that child may only elect to have the buccal sample taken by a parent under the supervision of a member of the police, or by a suitably qualified person (s 49(6)). A bodily sample cannot be taken from a child as a result of a Part 2A request if the child is unable to take the buccal sample him or herself due to disability or injury, and has not made an election under s 49(6) (s 49(7)). A parent cannot be compelled to take a buccal sample from his or her child (s 51(c)).

If a buccal sample is being taken from a juvenile, he or she may elect to take the sample him or herself under the supervision of a member of the police, or have the buccal sample taken by a suitably qualified person (s 49A(3)).

When a bodily sample is taken from a suspect under the age of 17 years, a suspect who has consented to the taking of a sample as a result of a suspect request or a Part 2A request and who has elected to take a buccal sample him or herself may have an independent adult present. Such a suspect must not take a buccal sample him or herself unless an independent adult is present and the suspect has confirmed, in the presence of that independent adult, that he or she has elected to take a sample him or herself.

Prisoners and home detainees

Suspects who are already in custody, and to whom a suspect or databank request is made, are entitled to consult privately with a lawyer about the request (ss 12(1) and 35(1)). However, nothing in these provisions prevents the taking of such measures as are reasonably necessary to prevent the suspect from escaping or from damaging any property, or to ensure the safety of the suspect or of any other person (ss 12(2) and 35(2)).

If the respondent is serving a sentence of imprisonment by way of home detention ('home detainee'), a suspect or juvenile compulsion order or a databank compulsion notice must include the condition that the respondent must give a bodily sample at the residence at which he or she is detained (ss 24A(4)(a) and 39A(3)(b)(i)). However, a judge may include a condition in a compulsion order (or a commissioned police officer may state in a databank compulsion notice) that a home detainee give a sample at a place other than the residence at which he or she is detained, if of the view that it is necessary to do so on account of the respondent's state of health (ss 24A(5) and 39A(4)).

Databank compulsion notices must be served to persons detained under a sentence of imprisonment on a date that allows for the taking of a bodily sample later than the 14th day after that on which the notice is served and before the later of the two following dates:

- the date the person is released from being detained under a sentence of imprisonment for the relevant offence; or

- the date six months from the date on which the conviction for the relevant offence was entered (ss 39(4) and 39C(4)).

Section 46 outlines special rules in relation to persons in custody attending to give bodily samples pursuant to compulsion orders or databank compulsion notices. Persons having custody of, or responsibility for, people to whom this section applies must cause them to attend at the place where, and on the date on which, the bodily sample is to be taken (s 46(2)). Any agreement reached between a person to whom this section applies, and a member of the police, to vary the place where, or the date on which, a sample is to be taken, is of no effect unless it has been approved by the person having custody of, or responsibility for, the person to whom this section applies (s 46(4)).

Similarly, any agreement reached between a home detainee and a member of the police to vary the date on which a sample is to be taken, is of no effect unless it has been approved by the probation officer supervising the home detainee (s 46A(1)). If a condition has been included in the suspect compulsion order or databank compulsion notice, whereby it is necessary for the home detainee to attend at a different place to give a bodily sample (on account of his or her health), the police must as soon as is practicable, give the Department of Corrections notice of the need for the home detainee to leave his or her place of detention (s 46A(2) and (3)).

When requesting a databank compulsion notice hearing, the same grounds apply in relation to prisoners and home detainees (s 41).

If a person detained under a sentence of imprisonment for the relevant offence (in relation to which the notice was issued) requests a hearing, and the later of the two dates before which the sample must be taken has passed before an application has been made, before the matter has been considered by a judge or before consideration is complete, a hearing must be completed as if that date had not been reached (ss 43A(1)(b) and 43A(2)(a)). The judge must make an appropriate order under s 42, and may, if applicable, vary or include any condition in a databank compulsion notice under s 42 or 43.

If a person detained in a penal institution refuses to give a bodily sample, a prison officer may (on a request made by a member of the police) use or cause to be used reasonable force to aid a member of the police to assist a suitably qualified person to take a fingerprick sample from that person (or a buccal sample if so specified by a judge because of the state of the person's health) (s 54(3)).

People with health problems and people who cannot take buccal samples themselves

If the judge is satisfied that it is necessary, on account of the respondent's state of health, the judge may impose, on a suspect or juvenile compulsion order, the condition that a bodily sample not be taken unless it is taken by a particular method specified in the order by the judge, and an independent medical practitioner (approved by the judge) certifies that the method will not cause serious harm to the person's health (s 24A(1)).

A databank compulsion notice hearing may be requested on the ground that all three methods available for the taking of a bodily sample will cause serious harm to the person's health on the date specified in the notice (as the date on which the person is to attend to give a sample) (s 41(2)(c)):

> If a judge is satisfied, at a databank compulsion notice hearing, that the ground has been proved, pursuant to s 42(2) the judge must –
>
> (a) if he or she believes on reasonable grounds that the state of the person's health is unlikely to change, make an order that the databank compulsion notice is of no effect; or
>
> (b) if he or she believes on reasonable grounds that the taking of a bodily sample by a particular method will not cause serious harm to the person's health if taken on a date other than the date specified in the databank compulsion notice –
>
>   (i) make a Part III order; and
>
>   (ii) vary the notice by specifying a new date on which the person to whom a notice relates is to attend to give a bodily sample that need not be a date in accordance with the applicable date set out in s 39C(3)(b) or 4(b); and
>
>   (iii) vary the notice to require the sample be taken by a particular method.

A judge must not vary a databank compulsion notice in these circumstances unless an independent medical practitioner (approved by the judge) certifies that the taking of the sample by the method specified will not cause serious harm to the person's health on the new date specified (s 42(3)).

If a person who may elect to or 'must' (s 49A(2)) take a buccal sample him or herself is unable to do so due to disability or injury, the buccal sample must be taken by a suitably qualified person (s 49A(5)).

There are also references in the Act to the overall reasonableness of making compulsion orders and varying or imposing conditions on databank compulsion notices (ss 16(1)(e) and 43(1)(c)). In deciding whether or not to make a suspect compulsion order, there is a requirement to consider any reasons given by the respondent for opposing the making of the order (s 16(2)(b)).

Testing

Scientific tests on DNA samples for use in criminal proceedings

A Crown Research Institute, the Institute of Environmental Science and Research Limited (ESR), carries out DNA profiling on samples submitted by the police. The technique applied by the ESR for use in criminal proceedings is Short Tandem Repeat (STR) Profiling. This type of analysis has replaced the earlier methods known collectively as RFLP (restriction fragment length polymorphism). The specific method currently in use at ESR examines 10 STR loci (sites) and in addition includes ameliogenin, a test to determine the sex of the source of the sample. Other DNA profiling samples are available on a case by case basis, such as Y chromosome STR profiling and mtDNA profiling.[7]

The ESR describes steps in the process as follows:[8]

(1) Recover cellular material (blood, semen, saliva, etc) from the crime stain or reference sample.

(2) Extract the DNA. Positive and negative controls are used at this stage.

(3) Clean and quantitate the DNA. (An assessment of how much DNA is present. Controls are used to verify DNA concentration at this stage.)

(4) Select and amplify the targeted loci using polymerase chain reaction (PCR). (PCR is a process in which a specific DNA fragment is copied a large number of times to permit easy, routine analysis.) Further positive and negative controls are introduced.

(5) Sort the general fragments according to size, using either manual or automated electrophoretic techniques. Additional controls and markers are used at this stage.

(6) The DNA profile of each sample is determined by two analysts independently. The results from control samples are validated prior to crime sample results being reported.

---

7   ESR, personal communication. The authors are most grateful to staff at ESR (and especially Dr Jill Vintiner, the scientist responsible for the DNA Databank) for their helpfulness in answering questions, and (given the long gestation period of this Country Report) advising on which earlier answers required updating to reflect developments in the intervening years.

8   See www.esr.co.nz/features/esr_and_dna/techniques/index.htm (accessed on 28 July 2003).

(7) The results from the reference samples are compared with those from the crime samples which indicate from whom a sample may or may not have come. Statistical analysis is carried out on appropriate samples.

Licence requirements

No licence is required for the laboratory or technician that carries out the test. However, ESR has had its forensic facilities accredited by the American Society of Crime Laboratory Directors, Laboratory Accreditation Board (ASCLD/LAB), a United States-based forensic laboratory accreditation organisation.[9]

To receive accreditation, there must be additional compliance with an international standard for forensic DNA analysis. This is set by the DNA Advisory Board to the US Federal Bureau of Investigation.[10]

ESR has quality assurance procedures in place, including the preparation of and adherence to written procedures, participation in regular quality assurance trials, regular audits of the laboratory, staff, and procedures, training programmes for staff, and participation in Accreditation Programmes.[11]

Other rules or regulations

The Act (see especially Pt IV) governs police and ESR working methods in relation to DNA sampling and testing, including the taking of reference samples for specific investigations and the taking of samples from individuals for inclusion on the National DNA Databank. There are no regulations promulgated under the Act that deal with DNA testing.

Some of those who made submissions on the Amendment Bill had concerns regarding possible contamination of DNA samples and the potential this has to lead to wrongful verdicts.[12] However, having visited the testing site and seen how DNA samples are stored, tested and processed, the Parliamentary Select Committee expressed confidence that ESR has minimised the potential for contamination at the processing stage.

Procedural and operational safeguards include:

• a specific workplace for each task in the testing and sampling process;

• separate non-amplified and amplified DNA areas (the inner core being maintained under negative air pressure to contain amplified material);

• control and maintenance of differential air pressures throughout the facility to allow the changes in air pressure to draw extraneous DNA particles away;

• a heavy duty airtight ceiling and interlocked motor-driven door;

• a 'single pass' air-conditioning system which ultra filters the air before returning it outside the facility, eliminating biological contaminants from being returned to the outside environment;

9   ESR, pers comm.
10 ESR, pers comm.
11 ESR, pers comm.
12 The Report, p 12.

- DNA samples being fully self-contained before going into the instrument room;
- the lobbies/air locks to the instrument room being flooded with ultra violet light at the end of each day to denature any extraneous DNA particles and biological contaminants.[13]

The Committee was of the view that any amendments which sought to reduce the potential for contamination at the crime scene would be outside the scope of the Bill, so made no recommendations about this matter.[14]

Use of DNA test results in the criminal process

Pre-trial

Availability of DNA test results to defence counsel

Any record of the analysis of the bodily sample taken by the police, and any record of a comparison between this and the analysis of material found at the scene (or found in any of the other circumstances mentioned in s 57(1) s 57(1)(a): see below), must be made available to the person from whom the sample was taken, or that person's lawyer, as soon as practicable (s 59).

As mentioned above, people from whom bodily samples are taken are also permitted to make arrangements for their own analyses of the sample (ss 55–56A). In addition, the Act provides (s 57):

(1) If –

    (a) material reasonably believed to be from the body of a person who committed an indictable offence has been found –

        (i)   at the scene of the offence; or

        (ii) on the victim of the offence; or

        (iii) from within the body or from any thing coming from within the body of the victim of the offence that is reasonably believed to be associated with, or having resulted from, the commission of the offence; or

        (iv) on any thing reasonably believed to have been worn or carried by the victim when the offence was committed; or

        (v) on any person or thing reasonably believed to have been associated with the commission of the offence; and

    (b) a bodily sample is taken pursuant to Part II of this Act from any person in respect of that offence; and

    (c) the person from whom the bodily sample is taken is charged with that offence, or a related offence, –

then, if practicable, a part of the material sufficient for analysis shall, at the request of the person so charged, be made available to him or her or to any other person nominated by him or her.

---

13   The Report, pp 12–13.
14   The Report, p 13.

(2) Sub-section(1) applies with all necessary modifications to a buccal sample taken as a result of a Part 2A request if an application is made for a declaration that the suspect from whom the buccal sample is taken is in need of care or protection on the ground set out in section 14(1)(e) of the Children, Young Persons, and Their Families Act 1989.

During the trial

Admissibility of DNA test results

Evidence obtained as a direct or indirect result of a bodily sample taken from a person pursuant to the Act is admissible, even though any person chosen to be present during the taking of the sample was not in fact present – if all reasonable steps had been taken to notify that person (s 69).

Where a person refuses to allow a bodily sample to be taken from him or her, following the making of a suspect or juvenile compulsion order, evidence of that refusal may be given – unless the prejudicial effect of the admission would outweigh its probative value (s 70(1)(a)–(c)). The relevant provision continues (s 70(1)(d)):

> The court or jury may draw such inferences (if any) from the fact of refusal as appear to the court or, as the case may be, the jury to be proper in the circumstances, taking into account any evidence given by or on behalf of the person who refused to consent to the taking of the bodily sample.

A judge may (but is not required to) tell the jury in such a proceeding that there may be good reasons for the person's refusal to allow the taking of a bodily sample (s 70(2)).

No DNA profile that is derived from any bodily sample taken pursuant to the Act, and stored on a DNA profile databank, is admissible as evidence against that person in criminal proceedings (s 71(1)) – except in the following circumstances:

- where a bodily sample is taken pursuant to Part II of the Act, and the proceedings are for the offence in respect of which the sample was taken, or for a related offence (s 71(2));

- in any proceedings on an application for a compulsion order (s 71(3));

- where there is evidence (other than a DNA profile) that relates to the use of any DNA profile in the course of any criminal investigation, if that evidence would otherwise be admissible (s 71(4)).

Other rules of evidence

There are no special rules of evidence that deal with DNA evidence: it is the same as any other expert evidence and is subject to the normal evidential principles (for example, prejudicial effect outweighing probative value, unfairly obtaining the sample, breach of procedure).

The Act is regarded as a code. Bodily samples may be taken from suspects only if certain conditions are met, and thus there must be strict compliance with the conditions, restraints and procedures. Unsurprisingly, there have been many cases in which the defence has challenged the admissibility of DNA evidence, on the ground of non-compliance with the detailed statutory requirements.

The factors that are said to point to a strict compliance approach include:[15]

- the strict prohibition in s 5 against the taking of a sample from a suspect, except ('only if') in the circumstances specified in paras (a), (b), and (c) of that section (cf s 72(c));

- the absence of any 'reasonable compliance' provision like that in the 'breath and blood testing' regime in transport legislation (formerly the Transport Act 1962; now the Land Transport Act 1998); and

- the fact that, apart from the limited terms of s 69 ('Non-attendance of [respondent's chosen] persons not to affect admissibility of evidence'), there is no general dispensation provision.

In *R v T* (1998),[16] the Court of Appeal adopted the view that unless a particular breach of the Act was minimal 'in the sense that the Crown demonstrates that it can have no material impact upon the statutory process and therefore the rights of the subject', the consequent unlawfulness must lead to the exclusion of the evidence of the bodily sample.

Breaches which have rendered bodily samples inadmissible include one where an investigating officer was present during the taking of the sample (in contravention of original s 52(2)(a))[17] and one where police made no effort to comply with the specified juvenile suspect request procedure when dealing with a 15 year old.[18]

In *R v Shaheed* (2002),[19] the Court of Appeal dealt with a case which involved an extraordinary number of breaches of the Act. The police took the first sample inappropriately and this sample later led to them matching the suspect with an abduction and a rape. From that match the police gathered identification evidence and a further blood sample, so as to charge the suspect with the abduction and the rape. None of the DNA evidence could be admitted, because it all hinged upon that first sample, the taking of which involved numerous and serious breaches of the Act:

- The police did not comply with the notice and information requirements or the consent procedure.

- The police had compelled the suspect to provide the first sample when he had simply been charged with offensive behaviour. (He was threatened with a compulsion order if he refused to give the sample, although there was no legal basis for such an order when he had simply been charged with offensive behaviour).

---

15 See *Adams on Criminal Law*, Looseleaf CI5.05 11-26 (6 February 2003).

16 [1999] 2 NZLR 602, 613.

17 *R v L* 9/4/98, Randerson J, HC Auckland T277/97. Section 52(2) was repealed by the 2003 Amendment Act, so there is now no prohibition on investigating officers being present during the taking of samples.

18 *R v A* (2000) 20 FRNZ 205.

19 [2002] 2 NZLR 377.

- The sample was not taken in accordance with the statutory procedures: the respondent was not given the opportunity to consult with a lawyer, or have a lawyer, a medical practitioner, and another person present when the sample was taken (as allowed under the 1995 Act).

- The police could not legitimately have made a 'suspect request' to the suspect pursuant to the Act, as offensive behaviour is not an indictable offence and a blood sample could have had no relevance to proof of the commission of offensive behaviour.

The Court of Appeal judged that the connection between the initial significant breach and the evidence obtained from the second sample was 'real and substantial'. The fact that the second sample was obtained pursuant to a lawful suspect compulsion order did not cure or mitigate the earlier breaches.[20]

The New Zealand Bill of Rights Act 1990 includes a 'right' to be secure from unreasonable search and seizure.[21] The Court of Appeal decided, by a majority, that in relation to breaches of this Act the *prima facie* rule of exclusion of evidence should no longer apply in determining the admissibility of evidence obtained as a result of a more than trivial breach. Questions of admissibility are to be decided by a balancing process in which, as a starting point, appropriate and significant weight is to be given to the fact that there has been a breach of the right to be secure against unreasonable search and seizure.

Applying this approach, the court held that the substantial breach of the respondent's right to be secure against unreasonable search and seizure was not outweighed by countervailing factors, such as the seriousness of the crimes with which he was charged and the reliability and centrality to the prosecution case of the DNA evidence. In view of the serious breach of the New Zealand Bill of Rights Act 1990, and the major departures from the strict requirements of the Criminal Investigations (Blood Samples) Act 1995, exclusion of the DNA evidence from the second sample was upheld.

Standard of proof

On an application made under the Act, questions of fact are determined by the judge on the balance of probabilities (s 68).

Challenges to DNA evidence by defence counsel

DNA evidence is subject to the same challenges as any other evidence. In addition, there is sometimes scope for specific objections. Depending on the circumstances, these may concern contamination of the sample, failure to follow testing techniques, challenges to accuracy or reliability, and examination of statistical accuracy.

---

20   This account of *R v Shaheed* relies very heavily on the summary in *Adams on Criminal Law*, Looseleaf CI5.05 11–26(a)–(b) (6 February 2003).

21   New Zealand Bill of Rights Act 1990, s 21 (but note also ss 4–6).

Retention and storage of samples and test results

Destruction of samples and test results

The bodily sample, every record of any analysis of the sample, and all information linking the person tested with the sample, must be destroyed by the police (generally as soon as practicable) if:

- 12 months expire and the person is not charged with the offence referred to in the request for a sample, or charged with a related offence; or

- the person is charged within the 12-month period but the charge is withdrawn or the person is acquitted (whichever happens first); or

- the person is convicted, but the offence is not one of those listed in the Schedule to the Act, and the appeal period for that particular conviction has expired (s 60).

If the person is convicted of one of the offences listed in the Schedule to the Act, the blood sample and related records and identifying information must be destroyed in accordance with the time requirements specified in the Act (s 60(2)). However, DNA profiles that may lawfully be retained on the DNA profile databank need not be destroyed (s 60(3)).

There is special provision for disposing of buccal samples taken pursuant to a Part 2A request (s 61A).

Only the following information may lawfully be stored on a DNA profile databank (s 26):

- any DNA profile derived from a bodily sample taken pursuant to Part II of the Act ('Obtaining Bodily Samples from Suspects'), where (a) the person is convicted of the offence in respect of which the sample was taken, or a related offence; and (b) the offence is one listed in the Schedule to the Act; or

- any DNA profile derived from a bodily sample taken from any person pursuant to Part III of the Act ('DNA Profile Databank'), unless the person has withdrawn consent (in terms of s 36).

Storage of DNA test results and samples

The samples are stored by the ESR, a Crown Research Institute.

The samples are held in a secure and controlled manner by ESR, under the terms specified in the Act and in accordance with accreditation requirements. They are held at the Databank Unit or other laboratories under conditions that preserve the DNA.[22]

The ESR is the guardian of the databank, on behalf of the New Zealand Police. By August 2003, the databank was storing approximately 35,000 profiles. Of these, some 8,500 (ie, roughly one-quarter) had been obtained pursuant to compulsion orders.[23]

---

22   ESR, pers comm.
23   Dr Jill Vintiner, ESR, pers comm, August 2003.

In addition, the ESR was storing approximately 6,000 profiles from crime scenes, victims, etc.[24]

Conditions are selected as the most appropriate for liquid blood, a blood-stained card or a buccal swab. DNA in a liquid blood sample is kept stable by freezing the liquid blood sample. DNA on a blood-stained card is kept in a dark and dry, cool place (not refrigerated). Cotton swabs containing buccal samples are stored in polypropylene tubes in envelopes in a dark and dry, cool place. A new device has been also been approved for buccal sampling. ESR intends to use a foam tipped applicator for buccal swabs in conjunction with a special kind of card designed for collecting, storing and purifying nucleic acids (see the Criminal Investigations (Bodily Samples: Approved Agency and Buccal Sample Device) Notice 2003, SR 2003/334).[25]

The storage time is limited by the statutory requirements discussed above.

Penalties for unauthorised use

It is an offence, punishable by imprisonment for a term not exceeding three years, to gain or attempt to gain access to the database or a bodily sample, or to disclose any information on the databank, or to use a bodily sample, in contravention of the Act (s 77(2)). Any person who publishes a name or particular in contravention of the Act is liable to a fine not exceeding $1,000 (s 77(3)).

The following are also offences, punishable by a maximum of three years' imprisonment (s 77(2)(a)–(c)):

- knowingly to falsify a DNA profile stored on a databank by the addition, deletion or modification of any information in the profile;

- knowingly to provide false information with the intent that it should be stored on a DNA profile databank; and

- knowing that one is not authorised to do so, to add to (or delete from) a DNA profile databank any information relating to any person.

Penalties for unauthorised storage

The Commissioner of Police is required to ensure that all appropriate samples are destroyed (s 60); no penalties are prescribed by the Act for breach of this requirement. ESR assist police compliance with the Act by notifying them when samples and 'records of any analysis of any such sample' (s 60) are due for destruction.[26]

---

24 Ibid.
25 Dr Janina Savage, ESR, pers comm, December 2003.
26 ESR, pers comm.

Release of DNA test information

Special rules

Section 59 of the Act provides that:

> If any bodily sample taken pursuant to this Act is analysed on behalf of any member of the police, a copy of –
>
> (a) any record of that analysis; and
>
> (b) any record of any comparison made between that analysis and any analysis of any material of the kind referred to in section 57 of this Act –
>
> shall be made available, as soon as practicable, to the person from whom the sample was taken or to his or her lawyer.

Release of stored test results

The only purposes for which DNA profiles stored on the databank will be released are:

* for forensic comparisons in the course of a criminal investigation;

* to make the information available, in accordance with the Privacy Act 1993, to the person to whom the information relates;

* for the purpose of administering the DNA profile databank (s 27(1)).

Information that does not identify any person may be released (s 27(2)).

Access to and disclosure of any information for the purposes of applications for compulsion orders, the issuing of a databank compulsion notice, the making of a Part III order, or for the prosecution of an offence against s 77(2), is not prohibited by s 27.

Privacy and DNA test results

If an application has been made for a suspect compulsion order, the respondent's name may not be published, nor any particulars that may lead to the identification of the respondent, unless (a) at the time, the respondent is charged with the offence or a related one (and there is no name suppression order in place) or (b) a High Court judge, by order, permits such publication (s 14(1) (2)).

Conclusion

As requested, this country report has sought to answer a series of questions posed by the editor. No attempt has been made to provide an account of a vast number of relevant cases,[27] or to provide an explanation of the evolution of this aspect of New Zealand law. Scholars or practitioners interested in the latter issue should not overlook the explanatory note that accompanied the initial Criminal Investigations (Bodily Samples) Amendment Bill, or the extensive commentary provided by the Select Committee in its report on the Bill.[28] Both contain much useful information, even though further changes were introduced before the legislation was enacted.

Law as stated current to May 2005.

---

27 For an account of many of them, see *Adams on Criminal Law*.
28 See n 4, above.

CHAPTER 11

SOUTH AFRICA

Professor L Meintjes-Van der Walt
Rhodes University

Introduction

Rapid progress in the mapping and sequencing of the human genome has resulted in a vast increase in knowledge of fundamental molecular biology and medicine. Applications of DNA analysis have recently been extended to forensic investigations and consequently a profusion of questions have arisen with regard to the collection of samples and methodological standards, the reliability and interpretation of results, and regulation of testing in general.[1]

Despite attempts to draw attention to the applicability of DNA fingerprinting evidence in South Africa,[2] and despite the existence of suitable testing laboratories,[3] the use of extremely small crime samples as a source of DNA for forensic investigation only began in South Africa in 1995 and was both accepted[4] and challenged in court in the same year.[5]

Collection of samples

Arrested persons

Enabling legislation

Section 37 of the Criminal Procedure Act 1977[6] makes specific provision for the taking of the necessary steps in order to ascertain whether the body of an arrested person has 'any mark, characteristic or distinguishing feature or shows any condition or appearance'. However, the section prohibits police officials from taking any blood, and blood samples may only be taken by a registered medical

---

1   See Goodwin and Meintjes-Van der Walt (1997), at 151–73.
2   See Böhm and Taitz (1986), at 662.
3   See Böhm, Taitz and van Helden (1987), at 307.
4   *S v Nondala* (unreported, Eastern Cape Division CC 20–95).
5   *S v Smile* (unreported, Eastern Cape Division CC 61–93); evidence given by Captain PJ Hennop at 1162–63, 1188, 1190 and 1191 in the record of the case indicated how long these techniques have been employed by the South African Police Services Forensic Department; *S v Motloutsi* (unreported, Cape Provincial Division CC 48–95).
6   Act 51 of 1977.

practitioner or a registered nurse. This requirement is set out in ss 37(1)(c) and 37(2)(a) of the Criminal Procedure Act 1977. These sections do not seem wide enough to include the removal of tissue. A sample of blood or the root of a hair would be sufficient for running a forensic DNA test, and therefore it is submitted that extraction of tissue cannot be justified.

Refusal or resistance to the taking of a blood sample

It is of interest to note that in countries such as the UK and Zimbabwe, the refusal to furnish a blood specimen is a criminal offence. This is not the position in the Criminal Procedure Act. However, this does not mean that an arrested person is entitled to refuse to submit to a sample of his or her blood being taken. It is difficult to imagine that a person would consent to a sample of blood being taken for the purpose of analysis if he or she has a right to refuse such permission. This would make the provisions of ss 37(1)(c) and 37(2)(a) meaningless and absurd. It must also be noted that ss 37(1)(c) and 37(2)(a) give a medical practitioner or a nurse the right to take a blood sample. This right of a practitioner simply cannot exist side by side with the right an accused may have to refuse. Thus, the right of a medical practitioner implies that there is a correlative duty on the accused to allow a blood sample to be extracted from his or her body.

The use of force against an accused who resists an attempt to have his or her blood taken

In *S v Binta*,[7] the then Cape Supreme Court (now the High Court) was faced with the question of whether a refusal to allow the taking of a blood sample, being a mere omission, could constitute the crime of obstructing the course of justice. Although the court found in favour of the accused, this did not prevent Ackermann J from concluding that the police were entitled 'to use such force as is reasonably necessary to achieve this end [the taking of a blood sample]',[8] even if it is 'against the wishes of the detainee'.

This poses the question of whether the use of reasonable force by the police to subdue a resisting accused would constitute a violation of the individual's right not to be subject to cruel, inhuman or degrading treatment.[9]

It is fair to assume that the test of reasonableness, which the courts have developed and now apply wherever appropriate when called upon to pronounce on the validity of an arrest or search, is a true reflection of society's notion of fair play and decency. The use of reasonable force has thus become acceptable in law enforcement procedures such as arrest and seizure.[10] If the state cannot exercise this power in regard to blood tests, this would have far-reaching consequences for law enforcement in general. Not only would valuable evidence be lost, but it would also prevent the police from using reasonable force in regard to the taking of fingerprints. This, in turn, would put one of the most successful methods of

---

7   (1993) 2 SACR 553 (C).
8   *Ibid*, 562b. See also *S v Kiti* (1994) 1 SACR 14 (E), 20a.
9   See s 12(1) of the Constitution of the Republic of South Africa, Act 108 of 1996.
10 See Van der Mescht (1996), at 286, 291.

detecting criminals out of reach of the police. It is submitted that such a paralysis of law enforcement is contrary to the values the Constitution seeks to nurture. Instead, the purposive approach to constitutional interpretation demands that a value judgment[11] should be made, which cannot be determined only by legal rules, but must also take into account the interest of the community in crime detection.[12]

There can be no doubt that the use of reasonable force contemplated by Ackermann J in *Binta's* case to ensure the taking of a blood sample from a drunken driver, whether he or she actively or passively resists an attempt to take such a sample, is consistent with the values for which the Constitution stands. In this regard, the reasoning of Claassen J in *Huma's* case,[13] that the forceful taking of fingerprints for purposes of a criminal investigation is a reasonable and necessary limitation of the right in the interests of the administration of justice, is, it is submitted, persuasive. In particular, the judge had the following to say about the taking of blood samples: 'Although I am dealing with an accused unwilling to submit to fingerprint taking, the analogy with the forced taking of blood samples is self-evident.'[14]

The position of a police official vis-à-vis a medical practitioner or nurse who refuses to take a blood sample when requested thereto

The proviso to s 37(1)(c) clearly states that a police official is not entitled to take a blood sample. However, the same section empowers a police official to take such steps, including the use of force that is reasonably necessary, to ascertain whether the body of an arrested person has any distinguishing feature or shows any condition. Read in conjunction with s 37(2)(a), these steps include the authority to request a medical practitioner to take a blood sample. It is submitted that Ackermann J in *Binta's* case[15] did not mean that the police would also be entitled to use force against a medical practitioner or nurse to ensure the taking of a blood sample. I submit that the omission by the said practitioner or nurse would, however, constitute the crime of obstructing or defeating the ends of justice, since it is the duty of the police to investigate an alleged offence.

---

11   The nature of this test has been elegantly stated by Van Dijkhorst (1994), at 128 as follows:
      In my view one must apply the purposive approach to interpretation of our Constitution, determining from it as a whole what was the aim of Chapter 3 and its constituent sections individually, what problems and aspirations did it seek to address, and what does it have in mind for our society. In short, what are the values and norms our society cherishes and intends to uphold. This approach does not mean that in some or many instances this will not result in a 'generous' interpretation. It will, but that is not the starting point.

12   In *S v Mayekiso* (1996) 2 SACR 298 (C), Van Rerner J held that in exercising its discretions to admit evidence obtained in violation of a fundamental right, a court must weigh up the need for the protection of fundamental rights with the community's interest in procuring justice.

13   *S v Huma* (2) (1995) 2 SACR 411 (W).

14   *Ibid*, 419b.

15   (1993) 2 SACR 553 (C).

The right to privacy and the results of DNA testing

In *Sapat v Directorate for Organised Crime and Public Safety*,[16] the accused sought an order directing the respondents to destroy the forensic expert's affidavit, because much of the applicants' argument in respect of the relief sought turned on a breach of the applicants' right to privacy with regards to the implications the DNA records could have in respect of membership of medical aid scheme employment applications. The expert's affidavit, however, revealed the limited purpose for which DNA has been used, and the limited access to DNA records and the identification of the donors.[17]

Military personnel, minors, prisoners and incompetent adults

Consent

The collection of hair, blood or tissue samples for DNA testing should, in all the abovementioned categories, require the consent of the individuals or their guardians.

The decision in *C v Minister of Correctional Services*,[18] dealing with blood samples taken from a prisoner for an HIV test, is illuminating. Kirk-Cohen J laid out parameters within which an HIV test could be performed. He held that, generally, informed consent was a prerequisite for testing a person for HIV. An individual, he found, could consent to an HIV test only if he or she understood the object and purpose of the test, understood what a positive result could entail, had time and place to reflect on the information received concerning the test, and had the free occasion to refuse to submit to the test.[19] I submit that it is likely that informed consent may also be required in cases of the collection of samples for DNA testing purposes.

This view is also strengthened by the fact that the Constitution of South Africa entrenches the right to freedom and security of person.[20]

The Biology Unit of the Police Forensic Science Laboratory currently does not make use of a criminal intelligence database (this is a database where the DNA profiles of convicted felons are placed and linked to the identity of the particular person).

Involuntary collection

Involuntary collection of hair, blood or tissue samples could be deemed to be in breach of certain fundamental rights of the individual entrenched in the

---

16 (2000) 2 BCLR 200 (C).

17 *Ibid*, 207J.

18 (1996) 4 SA 292 (T).

19 *Ibid*, 301.

20 Section 12(2) of the Act 108 of 1996 particularly states: 'everyone has the right to bodily and psychological integrity, which includes the right ... (c) not to be subjected to medical or scientific experiments without their informed consent.'

Constitution of the Republic of South Africa.[21] The 1996 Constitution, *inter alia*, entrenches the rights to dignity,[22] privacy[23] and the right to bodily and psychological integrity, which includes the right:[24]

- to make decisions concerning reproduction;

- to security and control over one's body; and

- not to be subjected to medical or scientific experiments without one's informed consent.

The right to privacy, which in South African law derives from the right to dignity,[25] is closely intertwined with the right to bodily and psychological integrity. In *S v A*, Botha AJ stated that an infringement upon an individual's right to privacy constituted an impairment of his or her *dignitas*, regardless of the information gleaned from such an infringement.[26] The then-Appellate Division characterised the right to privacy not only as protecting the interest in avoiding disclosure of personal matters, but more generally in protecting against 'intrusions upon the personal privacy of another'.[27] In South Africa, the Constitutional Court in *Bernstein v Bester*[28] appeared to echo these developments by emphasising the connection between the common law and the constitutional right to privacy, and underscored the importance of the rights to autonomy and dignity:

> The scope of privacy has been closely related to the concept of identity and it has been stated that rights, like the right to privacy, are not based on a notion of the unencumbered self, but on the notion of what is necessary to have one's own autonomous identity. ... In South African common law the right to privacy is recognised as an independent personality right which the courts have included within the concept of *dignitas*. [A] breach of privacy can occur either by way of an unlawful intrusion upon the personal privacy of another, or by way of unlawful disclosure of private facts about a person.[29]

By emphasising the relationship between privacy, dignity and autonomy, this judgment suggests that the zone of privacy protected in South Africa could include protection from intrusions into personal decision-making.

The Bill of Rights, Chapter 2 of the 1996 Constitution, binds all organs of state.[30]

These rights are not absolute. Section 36 of the 1996 Constitution permits limitations that are contained in a law of general application, and that are reasonable and justifiable given, *inter alia*, the nature of the right, the importance

---

21 Act 108 of 1996.

22 *Ibid*, s 10.

23 *Ibid*, s 14.

24 *Ibid*, s 12(2).

25 *Jansen van Vuuren v Kruger* (1993) 4 SA 842 (A), 849E–F.

26 *S v A* (1971) 2 SA 294 (T).

27 *Financial Mail (Pty) Ltd v Sage Holdings Ltd* (1993) 2 SA 451 (A), 462E–F; *Jansen van Vuuren v Kruger* (1993) 4 SA 842 (A), 849.

28 (1996) 4 BCLR 449 (CC) (Ackermann J). Justices Chaskalson P, Mahomed DP, Madala, Langa, Mokgoro, Sachs, and Ngoepe AJ concurred.

29 (1996) 4 BCLR 449 (CC), 65F, 68E, 68F, citing *Financial Mail (Pty) Ltd v Sage Holdings Ltd* (1993) 2 SA 451 (A), 462F.

30 Act 108 of 1996, s 8(1).

of the limitation, its nature and extent, and the availability of less restrictive means to achieve the objective of the restriction. The rights to privacy or the right to bodily or psychological integrity are thus not absolute. Both could be limited in certain instances.

Testing

Introduction

In South Africa, the Biology Unit of the Police Forensic Science Laboratory is the primary laboratory specialising in DNA testing for prosecution purposes. The Laboratory for Tissue Immunology at Groote Schuur Hospital in Cape Town also tests DNA evidence in criminal cases on request.

DNA tests used in South Africa

Standard blood typing

The ABO blood-group system was the first polymorphic system used in forensic typing. The four major blood groups, A, B, AB and O, are characterised by three alleles comprising six genotypes (AA, AO, BB, BO, AB and OO), the frequencies of which may be associated with a particular population. Although in forensic cases, blood typing is used with confidence only in excluding suspects from an investigation, it remains a preliminary screening procedure to eliminate any of several suspects, as it is less costly and more expeditious than DNA analysis. At the Police Forensic Science Laboratory, the classical blood grouping and enzyme tests have now been replaced by DNA typing.

Reverse dot blot hybridisation

This method is designed to detect differences in the DNA sequence of a specified coding locus. Considerable sequence variation exists in the human leucocyte antigen (HLA) DQAI gene located on chromosome 6.[31]

Polymorphism occurs as single-base substitutions in the gene, giving rise to four alleles and three subtypes of type 1 and 4 alleles. Oligonucleotide probes have been designed[32] for each of these variants, making use of classical DNA hybridisation technology. A commercial, standardised test kit has been developed,[33] which makes use of the reverse dot-blot hybridisation method.

Use of this test requires amplification of the DNA by means of the polymerase chain reaction (PCR). Primers complementary to the sequences flanking the DQAI gene are labelled with biotin tags and used to amplify this region. The method then employs the reverse of the hybridisation procedure used in VNTR typing. The test kit provides nylon strips on which are fixed oligonucleotide probes

---

31   See Gyllensten and Erlich (1988), at 7652–56.
32   See Erlich and Bugawan (1989), at 193.
33   Ampli Type PM – DQAI PCR Amplification and Typing Kits (Perkin-Elmer).

complementary to each of the seven possible alleles. The amplified test DNA is incubated with the probes on the strip, and it will only hybridise to the probe if there is an exact sequence match. Thus, more than two different alleles should be detected under the correct conditions. The blot is washed to remove unbound DNA and a streptavidin-horseradish peroxidase conjugate is added, which binds to the biotinylated DNA. The peroxidase enzyme converts a colourless substrate to a blue precipitate that is visible as a dot on the strip. The HLA DQAI type is determined by the number of blue dots appearing on the strip.

Until recently, this was the only polymorphic locus tested using the PCR in forensic investigation. The introduction of the new Polymarker amplification system, which types five additional polymorphic loci,[34] has vastly increased the discriminatory power of PCR DNA typing. In South Africa, the combined results of the HLA test and the five Polymarkers provide an average discriminating power of one in 280,000 for Asians, one in 220,000 for Caucasians, one in 300,000 for Africans and one in 230,000 for 'Coloureds'. These figures are based on the current database used by the Police Forensic Science Laboratory (compiled by Major Christo Weitz and Olga Phillips, July 1994). This database is in the process of being expanded. (The database is an anonymous unlinked database, ie, the DNA profile cannot be traced back to a specific individual.)

VNTR (Variable Number of Tandem Repeats) profiling

The study of VNTR loci has been widely applied in forensics. Profiling the HLA/PM and the D1S80 typing systems are used by the Police Forensic Science Laboratory in disputed casework. The HLA/PM typing is also employed in routine criminal casework.

Short tandem repeats occur in both coding and non-coding regions of the genome. They consist of stretches of DNA containing arrays of two to five bases, which are repeated several times. The DNA flanking the repeat regions is highly conserved, and, by using the polymerase chain reaction (PCR), primer DNA can target specific repeat regions and amplify them for analysis. This entails synthesising millions of copies of the specified gene or fragment of DNA from the original DNA preparation. The PCR involves a series of cycles in which the DNA, combined with a cocktail of reagents needed to replicate the target sequence, is subjected to a range of discrete temperatures. The first stage is denaturation of the DNA by incubation at 94 degrees and 60 degrees. This enables the primer oligonucleotides in the cocktail to anneal or hybridise to the template DNA. These primers are complementary to sequences flanking the target region and help to 'kick-start' the polymerase enzyme that synthesises the new DNA. The second step in this stage is extension of the DNA. The temperature is raised to 72 degrees, which is the optimum temperature for the activity of the synthesising enzyme, and new deoxyribonucleotides are added to either strand, according to the template sequence. Thus, in one cycle, the number of copies of the target sequence is doubled. This series of temperature changes continues from 30 to 35 cycles, amplifying the target DNA approximately a millionfold.[35]

---

34 The low-density lipoprotein receptor (LDLR), glycophorin A (GYPA), haemoglobin G gammaglobin (HBGG), a specific allele on the D7S8 locus and group component (GC).

35 See Saiki (1989), at 7.

The amplified DNA is then separated by means of electrophoresis and the sizes of the STR alleles are determined. The number of repeats in a STR is highly variable. Consequently, allele sizes vary considerably among individuals, making these excellent markers for identification. Furthermore, the frequencies of allele sizes vary between races and ethnic groups,[36] making STRs effective discriminating markers in population-genetics analyses. Resolution of STRs employs a multiplex system where several loci are amplified and electrophoresed at once. Previously, four loci are used in the UK,[37] two of which[38] have been identified as ideal for reliable standardisation of the technique among European forensic laboratories.[39]

The high level of resolution achieved with this system, coupled with the vast array of possible loci to be analysed, explains why it is extremely rare to find two unrelated individuals sharing the same two alleles. Furthermore, the speed and efficiency of analysis means that this technique will rapidly become a formidable forensic tool.

STR (Short Tandem Repeats) typing, has been used routinely in casework since November 1997. The STR system used most frequently by the South African Police Service Forensic Science Laboratory is the AmpFISTR Profiler Plus PLR Amplification kit. This is a 10 locus STR system.

Laboratory standards for equipment, personnel and protocols

The use of precision equipment is mandatory in DNA testing and the correct calibration of these machines is paramount in ensuring accurate, reliable results. Regular testing of equipment should form part of a rigorous quality-control programme.[40] At present, there are, however, no uniform standards imposed upon forensic facilities that function in the public and private sectors.

The standards of the Scientific Working Group for DNA Methods and Analysis (SWGDAM) of the US, and the American Society for Crime Laboratories Accreditation Board, are applied by the Police Forensic Science Laboratory. The South African National System (SANAS) has to date drafted but finalised standards for laboratories which wish to be accredited in this field. Separating procedures and competency of personnel should also be tested on an ongoing basis by a National Forensic Council, which can be established through legislation.[41]

---

36 See Evett et al (1996), at 398–407; Lee et al (1996), at 43–48.
37 HUMVWFA31/A, HUMTHO1, HUMF13A1 and HUMFES/EPS.
38 HUMVWFA31/A, and HUMTHO1.
39 See Andersen et al (1996), at 83–93.
40 In S v Motloutsi (unreported, Cape Provincial Division CC 48-95), 36–42, maintenance of the thermocycler used in typing evidentiary material was challenged by the defence when it was discovered that components essential to ensuring consistent temperature changes were unavailable at the time of testing. Furthermore, once the machine was tested, it was discovered that the 4°C storage facility was not functional.
41 See below the section on 'The establishment of a Forensic Science Council'.

Statistical issues and population genetics

Once a match has been declared between the crime sample and that of the suspect, the significance of the match is determined by estimating the frequency with which that profile would occur at random in the population.[42] This requires a knowledge of the frequency with which the alleles represented occur within a population. This calculation is of particular importance, as DNA typing cannot claim to prove without doubt the genetic identity of two samples. Typing evidence, with the aid of population genetics statistics, can merely indicate that the two samples are unlikely to have originated from different persons.

The need to establish DNA typing frequency databases, which are adequately representative of all ethnic groups within a population, has been emphasised.[43] Previously, the frequency database established for the South African population failed this requirement. Established from 'convenience samples'[44] taken from four broadly defined races,[45] the database lacks frequency estimates for several HLA DQAI genotypes in the Asian population.[46] Thus, in the case of an Asian suspect typed for one of these genotypes, the HLA locus, which comprises one-sixth of the composite profile,[47] must be omitted from the frequency estimates.[48] The consequence of this is a large increase in the probability of a coincidental match between the suspect and the crime sample. This is no longer the case as the frequency database has been updated.

As indicated above, the use of DNA profiling in the context of the criminal justice process raises issues ranging from the technical aspects of the procedure, to questions about population data and statistics. In South Africa, there has been a paucity of reported judgments dealing with these aspects of DNA evidence. It is against this background that the recent judgment of *S v Maqhina*[49] should be seen in its preparedness to scrutinise genetic evidence.

---

42 This is called the match probability and describes the statistical probability with which a randomly selected person will have a DNA profile that matches the crime sample.

43 See Lewontlin and Hartli (1991), at 1745–50; Weir (1996), at 497–500.

44 Samples were taken from individuals, because they were easily obtainable. This was confirmed by Major Christo Weitz in his testimony in *S v Motloutsi* (unreported, Cape Provincial Division CC 48–95) 130: '[D]ie hoeveelheid bloedmonsters wat daar is, is nie werklik die verspreiding van die bevolking … nie … [E]k het besluit om dit nie volgens verhouding te verdeel nie, maar wel alle monsters te laat analiseer en die databasis te gebruik.' ('The number of blood samples used was not really representative of the population … I decided not to divide them according to proportions … but to analyse all the samples and use them for the database.') (My translation.)

45 'Asian', 7%; 'Caucasian', 30%; 'Coloured', 18%; and 'Black', 45% of the total 565 samples.

46 See *S v Motloutsi* (unreported, Cape Provincial Division CC 48–95), 136–37: '[D]it meen as ek by Asiërs kom op die oomblik gee ek hulle die voordeel in die saak en ek gebruik glad dan nie die genotipe in die berekening nie … [O]p die oomblik moet ons nog besluit … as daar 0% voorkom, kan ons 'n minimum waarde van 5% of 2% daarstel wat sekere persone gebruik, maar ons het nog nie 'n waarde daargestel nie.' ('[T]hat means that when it comes to Asians, I give them the benefit of the doubt and I do not take into account the genotype. At this stage we must decide that if 0% is present, whether we can determine a minimum value of 5% or 2% as some people do. We have not yet set a value.') (My translation.)

47 In many criminal cases, where small samples from blood or hair are retrieved from the crime scene, the HLA locus and five polymarker loci are used: see above n 33.

48 The prosecution chose not to rely on DNA evidence in *S v Motloutsi* (unreported, Cape Provincial Division CC 48–95) based on this incomplete database.

49 (2001) 1 SACR 241 (TPD).

The facts were, briefly, the following: two accused were jointly charged with murder. Only the facts that relate to the second accused are relevant to this discussion. The second accused contended that he was not involved in the murder. He alleged that he had at all relevant times been working on a neighbouring property and had no knowledge of the charge of murder against him. The prosecution case against the accused in question rested entirely on the results of DNA testing.

Based on the results of the DNA profiling conducted at the South African Police Services Forensic Science Laboratory, it was held that neither of the accused could be eliminated as the source of the DNA found on the knife with which the deceased had been stabbed. DNA testing of genetic material found on the trousers worn by the second accused on the date of the murder revealed that the deceased could not be eliminated as the source of that DNA. This result of the DNA profiling was used by the forensic expert of the prosecution to estimate the statistical frequency of achieving such a result in a reference population.[50]

The main thrust of the judgment concerns the role of expert witnesses and the procedures that should be followed in the process of scientific analyses. Van Oosten J reiterated the particular responsibility borne by expert witnesses towards the court, and emphasised this duty especially in circumstances where the court does not possess the expertise and facilities to draw appropriate inferences.[51]

During the course of the judgment, the shortcomings of the DNA evidence *in casu* were enumerated:

- the state neglected to prove the reliability of the databases used for the statistical calculation;[52]

- the methodology of the statistical calculation was also not proved by the prosecution.[53]

The other deficiencies relating to the DNA evidence were based on points highlighted by the expert witness for the defence:

- the control samples taken from each of the two accuseds both indicated a match between the genotype at five of six loci. The difference found at only one of the loci is not discriminating enough to properly differentiate between the two;[54]

---

50 To illustrate how the result obtained by DNA testing was expressed as certain statistical values, the honourable judge cited the example of the genetic material from the deceased found on the second accused's trousers, which, based on the black population, translates into a frequency of one in every 16,549 persons having a genotype combination such as that of the second accused. Van Oosten J then continued to say that, based on this result, the possibility that the deceased deposited the genetic material on the accused's trousers *could not be ruled out* (nie uitgeskakel kan word nie). (See 248i–j and not as reported in the headnote, the possibility that the deceased deposited the genetic material on the second accused's trousers could not be established.)

51 (2001) 1 SACR 241 (TPD), 251h–i.

52 *Ibid*, 248j–249a.

53 *Ibid*, 249a–b.

54 *Ibid*, 250c–e.

- the course of action followed by the expert of the Forensic Science Laboratory did not follow appropriate standard protocols;[55]

- certain control procedures prescribed by the manufacturer of the HLA polimarker test were not followed;[56]

- the colour dot result of the polimarker test with regard to one of the loci was no longer visible and therefore it was impossible to determine whether it had existed at all;[57]

- the prosecution expert neglected to run certain duplicate tests which, according to the defence expert, made it impossible to determine the reliability of the test;[58]

- the Forensic Science Laboratory is not an accredited laboratory.[59]

In the light of the above, the court held that where an accused's guilt depended solely on the results of scientific analyses, it is of paramount importance that not only the testing procedure, but also the controls applied, should be conducted and recorded with such care that it can be verified by an objective expert and ultimately the trial court.[60]

The facts in *S v Maqhina* serve to illustrate vividly the problems that could arise in the interpretation of DNA evidence. A six locus HLA-polimarker test was used. The control samples taken from both of the two accused were found to match at five of the six loci. The only difference found by the prosecution expert was at one locus, which, as the defence expert indicated, was not sufficient to distinguish between accused one and accused two. These results were then reflected in the report as indicating that both of the accused could not be excluded as depositors of the blood found on the murder weapon. What can the significance of such a conclusion be? What does it prove? If a particular accused person is the source of the DNA, then a DNA sample from that accused and the crime scene sample should have the same profile. Where, however, as *in casu*, the DNA crime scene sample and the samples from both accused exhibit the same genotype, such evidence does not take the prosecution case any further.

Even in circumstances where the forensic sample and the sample from a particular accused have the same genotype, there may be other hypotheses that could account for the matching profiles. These alternatives should be considered. One possibility could be laboratory error arising from either mistakes in labelling or handling samples, or from cross-contamination of samples. Another possibility is that despite the fact that the genotypes match, the forensic sample came from another individual, such as a close relative of the accused or even an unrelated person who happens to have the same profile.[61]

---

55 *Ibid*, 250f.
56 *Ibid*, 250h.
57 *Ibid*, 250i–251b.
58 *Ibid*, 251c.
59 *Ibid*, 251c–d.
60 *Ibid*, 251h–i.
61 See Devlin and Roeder (1997), at 724.

With sufficient genetic markers all individuals, except identical twins, should be distinguishable, but this ideal is not always attainable, especially not where a limited number of loci is used in forensic testing. *In casu*, there was only a match in respect of five genetic markers. Harlan Levy, in his book *And the Blood Cried Out*, observes:

> This statement [that no two individuals other than identical twins should have the same DNA], absolutely true as a matter of scientific fact, can be highly misleading if it leads us to believe that the power of DNA analysis lies in its ability to identify and analyse all the characteristics of DNA unique to each individual. Science does not yet have the power.[62]

According to the facts of *Maqhina*, samples from both accused exhibited the same genotype as the profile from the crime scene sample. The fact that the only evidence against the second accused was that his profile in respect of five markers matched that of the crime scene sample (as well as the first accused's genotype) could in all probability be an example of where mere coincidence is responsible for the match. The procedure commonly followed is to estimate the relative frequency of the incriminating genotype in a suspect population. The frequency with which particular alleles are revealed in the population can be determined by constructing relevant databases. Principles of population genetics can then be applied to combine the estimated allele frequencies into an estimate of the probability that a person born in the population will have that multi-locus genotype. This, however, was not proved in *Maqhina*. As observed in *Maqhina*, the different methods used to calculate random match probabilities, as well as measures applied to express the probative value of the DNA evidence, is fraught with contradictory and opposing views. Suffice to say that within the confines of this discussion, DNA laboratory results divorced from evidence in regard to these aspects are meaningless.

Use of DNA test results in the criminal process

Admissibility of DNA evidence

South Africa, unlike the US,[63] does not have special rules of evidence that control the admissibility of scientific evidence. Section 225 of the Criminal Procedure Act states that whenever it is relevant in criminal proceedings to determine whether the accused has any 'characteristic or distinguishing feature', evidence of such characteristic or distinguishing feature, including the result of any blood test, is admissible.[64] Generally, DNA evidence will be admitted, and the issue to be determined by the trier of fact goes to the weight that should be attached to such evidence. In South Africa, DNA profiling is now accepted as a robust and reliable technique. Many of the problems in the past have either been rectified or

---

62   (1996) 26.

63   Rule 702 of the Federal Rules of Evidence provides:

> If scientific, technical or other specialized knowledge will assist the trier of fact to understand the evidence or to determine a fact in issue, a witness qualified as an expert by knowledge, skill, experience, training or education, may testify thereto in the form of an opinion or otherwise.

64   Act 51 of 1977, s 225(1).

the attacks were based on techniques no longer in use. *S v Maghina* (2001)(1) SACR 241(T) serves as a good example of the latter point, as the STR DO-Alpha profiling system.

The assessment of the probative value of DNA evidence

It is trite law that a court is not bound by expert evidence. It is the court that ultimately assesses the cogency of the expert's evidence in the contextual matrix of the case with which it is seized.[65] Within the confines of the facts of *Maqhina*, this case has not only attempted to illustrate some of the pertinent issues involving DNA evidence. The discussion also illustrated that the significance or implications of a match between two DNA samples cannot be evaluated in a vacuum. While the DNA evidence must be evaluated within the context of other evidence, the statistics relate to specific claims or hypotheses about the origin of the DNA samples. If DNA from an evidence sample and DNA from a suspect share a profile that has a low frequency in the population, this suggests that the sample came from the same person. However, as illustrated in *Maqhina*, the possibility also remains that the match is only apparent – and that an error has occurred and that the profiles coincide because of inadequate laboratory performance. This, in turn, emphasises the need for quality control and assurance, laboratory accreditation, proficiency tests and confirmatory testing.

DNA evidence is not unlike the evidence of other expert witnesses, in that the court does not usually have an independent means by which it can verify the witnesses' conclusions. This hinders compliance with the injunction by Schreiner JA in *R v Nksatlala*:

> [A] court should not blindly accept and act upon the evidence of an expert witness, even of a finger-print expert, but must decide for itself whether it can safely accept the expert's opinion. But once it is satisfied that it can so accept it, the court gives effect to that conclusion even if its own observation does not positively confirm it.[66]

Where rival experts' opinions diverge, the problem becomes compounded by the fact that the court, with no access to its own independent expert, would have to rely 'upon doubtful factors such as the rival witnesses' reputations and experience'.[67]

In South Africa, the Police Forensic Science Laboratory is the primary laboratory specialising in DNA testing for prosecution purposes. Although independent laboratories[68] are becoming available for confirmation testing, the current situation could, in addition to the complexity of the technique, have an effect on the capacity of the defence to challenge DNA typing results. DNA typing is, by and large, used in the investigation of violent crimes. The accused persons are often from the less affluent sectors of society, and therefore in need of legal aid defence counsel. In other jurisdictions, time and monetary constraints have compelled such defence lawyers to believe that any challenge of DNA results will be futile, thereby encouraging their clients to plead guilty.

---

65 *S v M* (1991) 1 SACR 91 (T), 100a.

66 (1960) 3 SA 543 (A), 546d–e.

67 *S v Malindi* (1983) 4 SA 99 (T), 104h–105a, quoted by Le Roux, J from Hoffmann and Zeffert (1981), at 86.

68 The Laboratory for Tissue Immunology at Groote Schuur Hospital also tests DNA evidence in criminal cases on request.

Currently, the defence is entitled to pre-trial docket disclosure, but this usually only includes the results of the tests. It is proposed that the defence should be entitled to sufficient pre-trial disclosure, not only of the DNA results but also of the statements and records made by the expert with regard to the procedure followed in the particular case.

Storage of samples/test results

Police Forensic Science Laboratory

Blood samples are put on Guthrie paper with envelopes in the case files. All stains are cut out and placed in the case file. DNA extractions are stored in –70°C fridges. Access control to case files and exhibits exists, and only authorised personnel (examiners) have access. Case files are also individually sealed once the specific examiner has completed his or her examinations. Case files may not be destroyed without specific instructions from a court of law. This very rarely occurs. Unauthorised access to case files or information on a case file is a criminal offence.[69]

Release of information

Police Forensic Science Laboratory

Specific details of a case are only released to the specific investigating officer or the state prosecutor in the particular case. Staff are not allowed to divulge any information to a third party or the media.

The establishment of a Forensic Science Council

On the initiative of the Police Forensic Science Laboratory, interested parties have been approached to investigate the establishment of a Forensic Science Council through legislation. Such a council will have the responsibility of regulating standards applied by forensic practitioners and setting minimum standards. It is also proposed that such a council would, *inter alia*, have the following functions:

- the registration and certification of forensic science practitioners in the various disciplines of forensic science;

- the regulation of accreditation for forensic science facilities;

- management of proficiency testing of facilities and/or members;

- inspection and auditing of forensic facilities;

---

69 The Human Tissue Act (No 65 of 1983), which governs the removal of tissue, blood or gametes from the bodies of both living and dead persons for therapeutic uses, specifically criminalises the acquisition or use of tissue, blood or gametes in any manner or for any purpose other than is permitted by the Act.

- approving and monitoring the management of databases containing information from intimate samples, especially with regard to ethical and human rights issues;

- investigation of malpractices by forensic practitioners or institutions and taking corrective action;

- making proposals to improve the legal infrastructure with regard to all issues pertaining to forensic court evidence in order to facilitate the prompt and effective use of forensic evidence by the South African judicial system, without violating the constitutional rights of individuals;

- act as an educational and training qualification authority.

A Forensic Council will not only promote co-operation between laboratories and encourage the harmonisation of technical standards within South Africa, but will also ensure that findings made and presented to courts of law are made according to acceptable principles and standards required by the forensic community within South Africa. It will assist the judicial process by having consensus on issues such as standards applied in forensic science and the competency of experts rendering their services to the prosecuting and defence lawyers.

Law as stated current to May 2005.

References

Andersen, J et al (1996) 'Report on the Third EDNAP Collaborative STR Exercise' 78 Forensic Science International

Böhm, L and Taitz, J (1986) 'The DNA fingerprint: a revolutionary forensic identification test' 103 South African Law Journal

Böhm, L, Taitz, J and van Helden, P (1987) 'The implementation of DNA fingerprinting as a forensic identification test in South Africa' 104 South African Law Journal

Devlin and Roeder (1997), 'DNA profiling: statistics and population genetics', in Faigman et al (eds), Modern Scientific Evidence, St Paul, MN: West Publishing

Erlich, HA and Bugawan, TL (1989) 'HLA class II gene polymorphism: DNA typing, evolution and relationship to disease susceptibility', in Erlich, HA (ed), PCR Technology, Principles and Applications for DNA Amplification, New York: Stockton Press

Evett, IW et al (1996) 'Establishing the robustness of short-tandem-repeat statistics for forensic applications' 58 American Journal of Human Genetics

Goodwin, J and Meintjes-Van der Walt, L (1997) 'The use of DNA evidence in South Africa: powerful tool or prone to pitfalls?' 118 South African Law Journal

Gyllensten, UB and Erlich, HA (1988) 'Generation of single-stranded DNA by the Polymerase Chain Reaction and its application to direct sequencing of the HLA-DQA Locus' 85 Proceedings of the National Academy of Sciences

Hoffmann, LH and Zeffertt, D (1981) The South African Law of Evidence (3rd edn), Durban: Butterworths

Lee, LD *et al* (1996) 'Valuation of a frequency database for four STR loci for use in casework in the Strathclyde Police Forensic Science Laboratory' 79 Forensic Science International

Levy, H (1996) *And the Blood Cried Out*, New York: Basic Books

Lewontlin, RC and Hartli, DL (1991) 'Population genetics in forensic DNA typing' 254 Science

Saiki, RK (1989) 'The design and optimisation of the PCR', in Erlich, HA (ed), *PCR Technology, Principles and Applications for DNA Amplification*, New York: Stockton Press

Van der Mescht, HL (1996) 'The influence of the Interim Constitution upon the taking of a blood sample of a person arrested for drunken driving' South African Journal of Criminal Justice

Van Dijkhorst, J (1994) in *De Klerk v Du Plessis* 6 BCLR 124

Weir, BS (1996) 'The second National Research Council Report on forensic DNA evidence' 59 American Journal of Human Genetics

CHAPTER 12

SPAIN

Professor Carlos M Romeo-Casabona,* LLD, MD,
Professor Aitziber Emaldi-Cirión,** LLD, Amelia Martín-Uranga,**
LLD and Pilar Nicolás-Jiménez, LLD

Introduction

There is no specific provision in the Spanish legal system to expressly regulate
DNA analysis as a means of proof in criminal trials.[1] There is no regulation of the
taking of the previous biological sample (operation), or of the genetic analyses of
these samples or the storing of the results in databases.

There is, however, an Organic Law[2] in which everything concerning personal
data stored in automated files is regulated.[3] This law must be taken into account
today and, naturally, by future law governing this matter. There are also certain
landmarks in the establishment and admission of genetic evidence in criminal
trials in Spain, such as the attempts that have been made to regulate this – which
will be listed below – among which we may underline the Draft Bill (Borrador de
Anteproyecto de Ley) regulating DNA databases, which may help us to gain an
accurate idea of the way in which the regulation of these matters will follow in
Spain in the immediate future.

We must not forget several pronouncements of the Council of Europe urging
the Member States to establish regulations for all these matters, in accordance
with its recommendations. In 1991, during the meeting of the ad hoc Committee
of Experts in Advances in Biomedical Sciences (CABI), the Council of Europe
made a number of recommendations on the use of DNA analysis within the
framework of criminal justice systems:

*   Professor in Criminal Law; Director, Inter-University Chair BBVA Foundation – Provincial
    Government of Biscay in Law and the Human Genome, University of Deusto and
    University of The Basque Country.
** Researchers, Inter-University Chair BBVA Foundation – Provincial Government of Biscay
    in Law and the Human Genome, University of Deusto and University of The Basque
    Country.
1   In general, there is not an appropriate provision in the Spanish legal system to regulate the
    corporal interventions as a means of proof in criminal trials, as has been emphasised by the
    Constitutional Court (Ruling 207/1996, 16 December). In this ruling, the court analysed
    how many fundamental rights could be limited or restricted by these interventions.
2   An Organic Law (Ley orgánica) requires approval by a qualified majority.
3   Ley Orgánica 15/1999, 13 December, de Protección de Datos de Carácter Personal.

- Recommendation (92)1 of the Council of Europe on the use of DNA within the framework of the criminal justice system;

- Resolution of 9 June 1997 on the exchange of DNA analysis results, in which the Member States are invited to consider the creation of national databases of DNA, in accordance with common and compatible regulations, to facilitate the exchange of data among Member States.

In Spain, some of the attempts made to regulate this special kind of expert testimony assessment have been the following:

- White Paper 122/000090, put forward on 3 March 1995 by the Popular Parliamentary Group before the Board of the Spanish House of Commons (Congreso de los Diputados), on the 'use and examination of DNA analysis evidence within the framework of criminal law and in the investigation of paternity', which followed very closely the Council of Europe's Recommendation (92)1 on the use of DNA within the framework of the criminal justice system. This motion was turned down on the basis of it being considered very imprecise in its regulation, because: it did not deal, despite its title, with the investigation of paternity; it did not distinguish between sample files and DNA analysis results files; and it referred to the Code of Criminal Procedure as a legal ground. Nevertheless, and although it had quite a few points to improve, its passage – with certain changes – would have been very positive as a starting point. The above-mentioned Parliamentary Group was at that moment in the Opposition and in a minority in the House of Commons. In short, the government adduced that it would be preferable to draw up a more extensive and complete law on the matter;

- Green Paper 162/000242 of 5 May 1998, put forward, too, in the Spanish House of Commons by the Popular Party's Parliamentary Group: '[a] Green Paper in which the government is urged to include in the Spanish legal system a regulation on the use of DNA analysis within the framework of criminal law and in the investigation of paternity.' In this Green Paper, too, mention was made of the Council of Europe's Recommendation (92);

- Draft Bill regulating DNA databases (the second and last versions of which are dated January 2000). At this moment it is maybe the most important document on this matter in Spain. Nevertheless, it is still a draft and it will be long before it can be taken into consideration. Let us just say that it aims to meet the need for regulation – by means of a law and in a coherent way – of DNA analysis and of the storing of resulting data in databases or computer files, a need mainly derived from the importance of these matters in criminal inquiry.

Thus, until this Draft Bill becomes law – and it would be advisable for it to be an Organic Law, since certain fundamental rights might be limited or restricted with these kind of practices – we may say that at this moment there is a real legal loophole in Spain on this matter.

It must be taken into account that Organic Law 15/1999, mentioned above, refers to 'personal data'; its scope does not include biological material itself or biological samples.

The legal loophole in Spain extends to the storage of samples, and also to the procedures to obtain them.[4] A White Paper (161/001817) was put forward on 29 November 2002 by the Socialist Parliamentary Group before the Spanish House of Commons on the 'creation of the DNA Profiles National Agency'.

Despite this, these kinds of tests are actually being undertaken in Spain, even without the necessary legal ground, although they do always have the previous consent of the subject allowing them. The Spanish jurisprudence relies on certain Articles of the Code of Criminal Procedure ('CCP') (to be precise, Articles 339 and 478.1 of the CCP), which in fact do not regulate this possibility, unless they are interpreted in an excessively extensive and not very advisable way. This is a practice that the most specialised Spanish doctrine has been systematically criticising for years. All this might change in the immediate future, however, since at present a working party has already been established in the Ministry of Justice to produce a new Code of Criminal Procedure, in which all these practices, that is, the use within criminal trials of the new scientific techniques of genetic identification and examination, will doubtless be regulated.

Some of the State Security Forces, too, have been developing databases with the results of genetic analyses for several years. This experience seems to be producing very good results, but is also devoid of the necessary legislative provision. Two ministerial orders are the sole legal support for these databases, which is by any reckoning insufficient, given the deficiencies of these two orders in regulating a matter like the one we are dealing with, if the sensitive nature of the data kept in those databases is considered. The regulatory texts mentioned above are: the Ministerial Order of 26 July 1994, by which files containing personal data (including those containing DNA profiles of subjects) managed by the Home Office (Ministerio del Interior) are regulated; and the Ministerial Order of 7 March 2000, which regulates the automated file for genetic identification of biological traces (ADNIC) in the General Directorate of the Spanish Civil Guard (Dirección General de la Guardia Civil).

Time in the criminal process at which DNA sampling and testing may occur

DNA samples must be obtained during the instruction stage, when the court proceeds to the verification of the offence and the ascertainment of the offender (Article 339, CCP). Once a charge of an offence exists, the judge will admit the expert testimony when, in order to know or estimate some fact or important circumstance in the case, scientific or artistic knowledge is necessary or convenient (Article 456, CCP). Thus, both actions – sampling and testing – will take place during the summary stage.

Although in Spain evidence must be examined in the oral trial, in the immediacy of the decision making court, so that the requirements of immediacy, contradiction, orality and publicity are met, we come across tests like the one on DNA, which by nature cannot be carried out while the oral trial is being held

---

4   See below under the heading 'Retention and storage of samples/test results'.

because they would bring it to a halt. That is why they are carried out before (as anticipated evidence) and the report prepared by the experts is produced in the oral trial. If it is considered as pre-constituted evidence, the experts must attend the oral trial to ratify their report, except if they belong to the National Institute of Toxicology, in which case this ratification in the plenum is not necessary.[5]

Collection of DNA samples

Procedures

Given the lack of regulation for this kind of expert assessment in Spain, it is necessary to obtain the passive subject's informed consent, that is, it is necessary that the subject be willing to give the samples on which DNA tests will be carried out.

It is also necessary for these tests to be ordered by the judge trying the case or directing the inquiry, by means of a 'motivated resolution',[6] in which the judge explains the need and proportionality of taking such a measure.

Degree of force

There is no obligation in the Spanish legal system to undergo these kinds of tests, and if a person refuses to consent to the obtaining of biological samples for a DNA test, no physical force or coercion can be used against him or her. If this happened, the proof would be considered illegally obtained and it would have no value as evidence.

Special requirements for specific groups

There are no special regulations applying to specific groups of people. By this we mean that there are no specific groups (minors, prisoners, disabled, etc) to which special regulations might be applied with regard to this matter.

Testing

Scientific tests on DNA samples for use in criminal proceedings

Regions or loci of the Short Tandem Repeat (STR) type are analysed. The number of regions or loci depends on the commercial kit used, varying on a range from eight to 15 (SGM, Profiler Plus, Codifiler, Identifiler, Powerplex 16).

---

5   Decisions of the Spanish Supreme Court of Justice of 4 February 1991, 14 June 1991, 7 February 1992, 26 February 1993, 17 May 1994, 14 February 1996 and 6 June 1997.
6   Resolución motivada: text of a judgment, laying out the reasons for the decision (TN).

Licence requirements

There is no legislation regulating this matter. There is no body in Spain to take charge of carrying out a real control on these centres, or on the professionals working in them, through an accreditation system. Despite the fact that there is no such body or legal regulation of the matter, laboratories do carry out, on their own initiative, a number of periodic controls.

The laboratories that carry out this kind of analysis in Spain belong to the GEP-ISFG – the Spanish-Portuguese Group in the International Society of Forensic Genetics. All of them take into account the ISFG recommendations, which, among other things, establish the conditions and requirements that both appraisers and centres or laboratories must fulfil.

The above-mentioned Draft Bill regulates the creation of a National Agency of DNA profiles, that would be in charge of these laboratory accreditations and of many other matters related to genetic evidence.

Other rules or regulations

There are no other regulations in the Spanish legal system.

Use of DNA test results in the criminal process

Pre-trial

Availability of test results to lawyers for the accused

Counsel for the defence has total access to the other party's evidence in order to prepare his or her client's defence on equal terms. He or she may even appoint an expert to participate too in the carrying out of the DNA analysis.

During trial

Admissibility of DNA test results

The judge will admit the expert testimony when, to know or estimate some fact or important circumstance in the case, scientific or artistic knowledge is necessary or convenient (Article 456, CCP), as happens in the case of DNA evidence, which, as we have explained, would be placed within the evidence of opinion in general. At no point is the DNA evidence considered in particular.

This kind of appraisal may also be carried out at the request of one of the parties in the trial. However, it will be the judge who will, in such cases, determine its relevance, and who will ultimately have the say in whether the appraisal will or will not be carried out.

Other relevant rules of evidence

There are no other regulations on this matter in the Spanish legal system.

Standard of proof

There are no specific regulations on DNA evidence, since it forms part of the evidence of opinion in general. DNA evidence in the criminal framework will, predictably, be specifically regulated in the new Code of Criminal Procedure that is being drawn up.

Challenges to DNA evidence by the lawyer for the accused

The DNA evidence can be challenged first by claiming that the biological samples have been obtained without his or her client's consent and outraging the latter's fundamental rights (personal safety, privacy, etc).

Secondly, counsel for the defence may disagree with the results of the analyses and propose a contra-analysis. Before this, he or she is also entitled to name an appraiser that will take part in the analyses together with the ones appointed by the judge.

Thirdly, he or she can ask for the appraisers who carried out the analyses and submitted the report to attend the oral trial to ratify it and explain their conclusions, and he or she, alone or assisted by another expert, can rebut these conclusions.

Finally, counsel for the defence can appeal against a conviction that took into account DNA evidence if he or she understands that fundamental rights of the defendant have been violated (Article 850.1, CCP).

Judicial interpretation of DNA test results

There are no regulations in the Spanish criminal procedural law on the valuation of the evidence of opinion, therefore, the general rule established for the rest of the evidence will apply. Thus, the court will weigh in good conscience the evidence heard in the oral trial (Article 741.1, CCP). This Article establishes the system of free valuation of evidence. This does not mean free decision; it means that the valuation must deal with the evidentiary result verified in the oral trial. Finally, the valuation of evidence must be done in accordance with the principles of fair comment, that is, the evidentiary result must be reasoned and justified in the 'statement of proved facts'.

Indeed, the DNA evidence is not decisive in estimating whether the defendant is guilty or not guilty. It will only complement other proof: that is, it will have to be taken into account together with the rest of the evidence adduced in the case.

Judicial directions concerning DNA evidence

Expert testimonies, and this includes DNA evidence, do not bind the court with their conclusions. Nevertheless, the courts are aware of the great importance of these tests, of their great discrimination and identification capacities, and of the great deal of certainty they provide. They are also aware that this evidence derives from technical and scientific knowledge and therefore is quite objective. Thus, this evidence will be given special consideration in relation to other more subjective or less conclusive evidence, even when the law does not make this mandatory.

Retention and storage of samples/test results

To date there is no specific rule in the Spanish legal system governing the retention and storage of DNA samples. As we have said, Organic Law 15/1999 only refers to 'data', not to biological samples (as 'physical support of information').

Laboratories where this kind of analysis takes place have a great number of these samples and do not know exactly what to do with them, since there is no law to determine where they should go.

In relation to 'data' (DNA fingerprints), Article 22.2 of the Organic Law 15/1999 must be taken into account, which states:

> The capture and processing, with police purposes, of personal data by the security forces and bodies without the consent of the people affected are limited to those cases and categories of data that were necessary to prevent an actual danger to public security or to repress criminal breaches. The data must in those cases be stored in specific files set up with that particular purpose, which must be classified in categories according to their reliability.

This article could be applied to data already existing, but it does not provide a legal basis to obtain new DNA profiles. Thus, there is a legal loophole in relation to the obtaining of test results.

As explained in the introduction, the scientific police and the Spanish Civil Guard are in fact storing DNA profiles resulting from the analyses they carry out (the police, for example, use CODIS – the Combined DNA Index System).

These files have no legal regulation. They only have the Ministerial Order of 26 July 1994 and another of 7 March 2000 as legal grounds. These two orders, however, given their short extension, do not regulate this matter in the way it should be done.

Work is being carried out in the Ministry of Justice on this matter and, as we have explained above, a Draft Bill regulating DNA databases has been produced, which would actually regulate in a proper and complete way all of these matters.

Destruction of samples and test results

There is no regulation in Spain determining the storing or the destruction of the samples or data resulting from a DNA test.

Nevertheless, when the law is passed that will regulate all these matters and that will obviously also regulate the destruction or deletion of the data, it will have to take into account what is said in the Organic Law 15/1999 of 13 December, which, in Article 22.4, establishes that:

> ... personal data, registered with police purposes, will be deleted when they are not necessary for the enquiries that caused their storing. For this purpose, the age of the person concerned and the nature of the data stored, the need for keeping the data until the completion of a certain enquiry or procedure, the final court judgment – especially if it is of acquittal, pardon, rehabilitation and prescription of liability – the lapsing of the period during which prosecution may be brought, will all be especially considered.

To consider how the regulation of this matter will be in Spain in the immediate future, we may turn to Article 20 of the Draft Bill, where it is said that the data will be deleted from the files once the conviction is spent, when the offence that caused the action has lapsed – in the case of non-convict indictees – and also after the death of the person to whom they refer. As we can see, the option has been taken to fix time limits according to a number of circumstances, instead of establishing objective time limits of 10 years, 15 years, etc.

Place and condition of storage

There is no regulation of this matter.

Penalties for unauthorised use

According to Article 44.4b of the Organic Law 15/1999 of 13 December, 'Protecting Personal Data', the communication or transfer of personal data (among which DNA fingerprints can be included) in cases different from those in which they are allowed is considered a very serious violation.

The sanctions contemplated for very serious violations attract heavy fines.

On the other hand, the 1995 Penal Code typifies in Articles 197 and following some behaviours regarding illicit transfer of personal data, establishing penalties of imprisonment that may range from one to five years, depending on the illicit act and the person who committed it.

Penalties for unauthorised storage

In accordance with Article 44.3.a of the Organic Law 15/1999, the establishment of files of public ownership, or initiating the capture of personal data for those files without the warrant of a general disposition published in the Official Gazette of the Spanish State[7] or relevant official journal, is a serious violation. The sanction will be a fine ranging from 50,000 to 100,000,000 pesetas.

Release of DNA test information

Special rules

There are no specific regulation on this matter in the Spanish legal system.

Release of stored test results

Before personal data may be revealed, it is mandatory that the subject consents (Article 11.1 of the Organic Law 15/1999), except if certain circumstances occur (Article 11.2). Some of these circumstances are relevant in the matter we are considering:

---

7   *Boletín Oficial del Estado*: published daily, laws come into effect as of the date of their publication in this journal (TN).

- when the transfer is allowed by law;
- when the recipient is the Ombudsman, the Attorney-General or the judges or courts or the Court of Auditors, in the exercise of its powers;
- when the transfer is carried out between public administrations with historic, statistical or scientific purposes.

According to the Draft, that is, the regulation currently under preparation, genetic data contained in police files can, during the course of criminal investigations, be transferred to the courts, to the Attorney-General, and to the State Forces and Bodies of Security, who can proceed to the processing of this data without the consent of the person concerned.

Privacy and DNA test results

There are no specific rules with regard to this kind of data.

It is laid down, however, in Article 9 of the Organic Law 15/1999 – where files containing personal data are regulated as a whole – that:

> The person responsible for the file, and, where appropriate, the person in charge of its processing must take the necessary technical and organisational measures to guarantee the safety of the personal data and prevent their alteration, loss, processing or unauthorised access.

In the following article (Article 10), the person responsible for the file and those taking part in any stage of the processing of the personal data are obliged to keep them secret, a duty that still exists after their relations with the person to whom the data refers – or, where appropriate, with the person responsible for him or her – finish.

Article 199 of the Spanish Penal Code must also be taken into account. According to this Article (point 1):

> he/she who revealed somebody else's secrets, of which he/she has knowledge owing to his/her profession or his/her professional relations, will be punished with prison for one to three years and a penalty of six to 12 months.

and in point 2:

> the professional who, failing to perform his/her duty of caution and secrecy, disclosed another person's secrets, will be punished with prison for one to four years, penalty of 12 to 24 months and specific disqualification from that profession for a period of two to six years.

Postscript

The reform caused by the Law 15/2003, 25 November, amending the Penal Code

The organic Law 15/2003, 25 November, amending the country's Penal Code, has modified the Criminal Justice Law. With the adoption of this Law, a legal provision has been made for the use of DNA profiling in criminal processes.

Spain was one of the few remaining European countries not to have legislated the use of these techniques in criminal evidence, despite experts' view that regulation was needed, in view of the repercussions for the fundamental rights of the individuals concerned. The recent law reforming the Penal Code addresses the most salient features in three very short sections, closely reflecting the preparatory work carried out by the Ministry of Justice in 1999 and 2000 aided by a committee of experts. However, in taking this route a more detailed regulation of this type of evidence and a specific legal regime for data bases of DNA profiles of convicted persons have been deferred to a later date and this has resulted in a lack of legal cover for existing police files, which would appear not to be covered adequately by Spain's Data Protection Act of 1999.

Provisions are made for two separate situations in the First Final Disposition of Law 15/2003. The first refers to the taking of prints or biological remains for testing that might throw light on the crime under investigation. A new paragraph is added under article 326 of the Criminal Justice Law, which stipulates that a judge will take, or ask the Judicial Police or Forensic Doctor to take, all necessary steps to ensure that the samples are obtained, kept and examined in such a way that their authenticity is guaranteed (the 'chain of custody'). A new Third Additional Disposition is added in the Criminal Justice Law to this end, according to which, the government (Justice and Interior Ministries) is instructed to prepare the necessary Royal Decrees covering the structure, make-up, organisation and operation of the National Commission on Forensic Use of DNA, a body entrusted with the important missions of certifying and coordinating testing laboratories, drawing up protocols, establishing the conditions for the secure keeping of samples, confidentiality, etc. In truth, this entire issue has been left virtually wide open.

The second situation, refers to the obtaining of biological samples from a suspect for DNA profiling, when the profile is required as part of evidence. A second new paragraph is added in article 326 of the Criminal Justice Law. According to this new provision, a judge, with good reason, may order inspections, check-ups and examinations of a suspect's body as long as these are 'proportional and reasonable'. Here, the very brief wording of the regulation may well result in significant gaps which cannot be remedied in all cases by the principles of proportionality and reasonableness that the law seeks to use as its basis. There is no mention, for example, as to whether coercion, including physical force, may be used if a suspect refuses to be examined. Similarly, there is no reference to the legal consequences of refusal, whether biological samples can be taken to establish a suspect's DNA profile for all crimes or offences, what the profiles – and biological samples – will be used for, etc.

Most of these questions will eventually be resolved through interpretation (with all the dilemmas this poses for legal certainty), but the lawmakers could and should have seized the opportunity to clarify matters.

Law as stated current to May 2005.

CHAPTER 13

UNITED KINGDOM

Dr Graeme Laurie
School of Law, University of Edinburgh

Introduction

This chapter details the current legal provisions and professional guidelines governing the use of genetic testing and DNA samples in the administration of criminal justice in the UK. It covers the provisions that operate in the three main jurisdictions of the UK, which have instituted laws in this area. These are England and Wales, Northern Ireland and Scotland. For each jurisdiction, the chapter is further divided into sections that together address all of the questions posed in the questionnaire (upon which this report is based) on the uses of DNA testing in criminal trials. However, because of the overlapping nature of some of the provisions that apply in the three jurisdictions, and notably the provisions relating to the collection, storage, disposal and release of samples and information derived from samples, it has not been possible to answer the questions in the order asked in the questionnaire. Instead, part 1 of the chapter deals with each jurisdiction in turn, arranging each division as follows: s 1 deals with the time in the criminal process when sampling and testing may occur and the powers available to take samples; s 2 deals with the use of DNA test results in the criminal process; s 3 outlines any special rules that apply to specific groups; and s 4 relates to provisions surrounding the destruction of samples. Part 2 of the chapter concerns the national DNA database and the laws and guidance surrounding the collection, storage, security and access rules operative throughout the UK.
The law is stated as at 1 January 2003.

Updates to this chapter from 1 January to May 2005 were prepared by Gerard Porter, Arts and Humanities Research Council (AHRC) Research Centre for Studies in Intellectual Property and Technology Law, University of Edinburgh, Scotland.

England and Wales

Time in the criminal process at which DNA sampling and testing may occur and powers to take and use samples

In England and Wales, a distinction is drawn between 'intimate' and 'non-intimate' samples. DNA evidence can be derived from samples falling into either category. The power to obtain such samples varies, however, depending on the category into which the samples fall. The relevant legislation is the Police and

Criminal Evidence Act 1984 (PACE),[1] as amended by the Criminal Justice and Public Order Act 1994 (CJPOA), the Criminal Procedure and Investigations Act 1996, the Criminal Evidence (Amendment) Act 1997 and the Criminal Justice and Police Act 2001.

The provisions of PACE are supplemented by the Code of Practice for the Identification of Persons by Police Officers (Code D of the statute). The Codes of Practice contained in PACE have been prepared by the Home Secretary and brought into operation by a statutory instrument approved by resolution of both Houses of Parliament. The binding force of the Codes is not clear-cut, and s 67 of PACE provides that a failure on the part of any person to adhere to the provisions of the Codes will not *per se* render that person liable to any criminal or civil proceedings. Nonetheless, under s 67(11), a breach of PACE can certainly be taken into account in subsequent civil or criminal proceedings against the police or others involved in the investigation and prosecution of crime. Furthermore, it is established under this section that in *any* proceedings the Code of Practice shall be admissible and shall be taken into account if it is thought by the court to be relevant to any question arising in those proceedings. This means, therefore, that the fact that a Code has not been followed can result in evidence being excluded from a trial at the discretion of the court.

Intimate and non-intimate samples: definitions

The definition of 'non-intimate sample' contained in s 65 of PACE has been widened by s 58 of the CJPOA.[2] A *non-intimate sample* means:

(a) a sample of hair other than pubic hair;

(b) a sample taken from a nail or from under a nail;

(c) a swab taken from any part of a person's body including the mouth but not any other body orifice;

(d) saliva;

(e) a footprint or a similar impression of any part of a person's body other than a part of his or her hand.

Before any sample is taken, the subject must be informed of the grounds on which the relevant authority has been given, including, where appropriate, the nature of the suspected offence.[3]

Where hair samples are taken, for the purpose of DNA analysis, the suspect should be permitted a reasonable choice as to the part of the body from which he or she wishes the hair to be taken. When hairs are plucked they should be plucked individually unless the suspect prefers otherwise, and no more should be plucked than the person taking the sample reasonably considers necessary for a sufficient

---

1   See, generally, Zander (1995).

2   As Seabrooke and Sprack note, this is of considerable importance because a DNA profile can be obtained from some non-intimate samples and the police powers to obtain non-intimate samples are wider than the powers to obtain intimate samples. See Seabrooke and Sprack (1996), at 99.

3   Code of Practice [5.11B].

sample.[4] Hairs should be plucked with the root, for it is in the root that the useful DNA material is found. Although the hair and its root are different entities, it is permissible to pluck hairs so that the root is also excised and to analyse the DNA of the resulting material.[5] It is not the case that s 63 permits the taking of only one non-intimate sample.[6]

An *intimate sample* means:

(a) a sample of blood, semen or any other tissue fluid, urine or pubic hair;

(b) a dental impression;

(c) a swab taken from a person's body orifice other than the mouth.

Under s 62(9) of PACE, as amended by the Criminal Justice and Police Act 2001, intimate samples may only be taken by a registered medical practitioner or a registered nurse. Paragraph 5.3 of the Code of Practice also provides that dental impressions may be taken by a registered dental practitioner.

Obtaining intimate samples

This is dealt with by s 62 of PACE, as amended. Section 62(1) provides that an intimate sample may be taken from a person in police detention only:

(a) if a police officer of at least the rank of inspector authorises it to be taken; and

(b) if the appropriate consent is given.

The meaning of 'appropriate consent' is provided by s 65. 'Appropriate consent' means:

(i) in relation to a person who has attained the age of 17 years, the consent of that person;

(ii) in relation to a person who has not attained that age but has attained the age of 14 years, the consent of that person and his or her parent or guardian; and

(iii) in relation to a person who has not attained the age of 14 years, the consent of his or her parent or guardian.

An officer of any rank can seek such consent; it need not be one of at least the rank of superintendent.

Under s 62(1A), an intimate sample may be taken from a person who is not in police detention, but from whom, in the course of the investigation of an offence, two or more non-intimate samples suitable for the same means of analysis have been taken which have proved insufficient. This is so, however, only if (a) a police officer of at least the rank of inspector authorises the sample to be taken, and (b) the appropriate consent within the meaning of s 65 is given. An insufficient sample is one that is not sufficient either in quantity or quality for the purpose of enabling information to be provided for the purpose of a particular form of analysis (eg, DNA analysis). An unsuitable sample is one that, by its nature, is not suitable for a particular form of analysis.[7]

---

4   Code of Practice, Note 5C.
5   *R v Cooke* [1995] 1 Cr App R 318; PACE, s 63A(2).
6   See PACE, s 63A(2).
7   Code of Practice, Note 5B. Under s 65(2) of PACE, as amended by the Criminal Justice and Police Act 2001, references to a sample proving insufficient includes where this is a consequence of loss, destruction, contamination or damage to the whole or part of the sample, and where the sample produced no results or produced results some or all of which must be regarded, in the circumstances, as unreliable.

For the purposes of both s 62(1) and 62(1A), a police officer may only give authorisation of the taking of an intimate sample if he or she has reasonable grounds (a) for suspecting the involvement of the person from whom the sample is to be taken in a recordable offence, and (b) for believing that the same will tend to confirm or disprove his or her involvement.

A 'recordable offence' is defined by reference to the National Police Records (Recordable Offences) Regulations 1985.[8] This is very broad and covers *any* offence punishable by imprisonment. In addition, the three statutory instruments outline specific statutory offences that also fall within the definition.

Crucial to these provisions is the need for valid consent to be obtained from the person from whom a sample is to be taken. Contrast this with the Scottish position (below). If consent is not obtained, there is no provision to 'take' an intimate sample. However, under s 62(10), the court or jury can draw an adverse inference from a refusal if no good cause is shown for the refusal. Under paragraph 5.2 of the Code of Practice, a person should be warned, before being asked to give an intimate sample, that if he or she refuses without good cause his or her refusal may harm his or her case if it comes to trial. Little guidance has been given by the courts as to what demonstrates 'good cause'. In *R v Cooke*, there is a tentative suggestion that a needle phobia may be good cause to refuse consent.[9]

Obtaining non-intimate samples

This is governed by s 63 of PACE, as amended. These provisions start with the premise that non-intimate samples may not be taken without written consent. However, they go on to provide exceptions to this and so accord the police wider powers in respect of non-intimate samples, as compared with intimate samples. Importantly, where the taking of non-intimate samples is authorised without consent, the Code of Practice permits the use of reasonable force.[10]

The circumstances in which a non-intimate sample may be taken without consent are when (a) the person from whom the sample is to be taken is in police detention or is being held in custody by the police on the authority of a court,[11] and (b) an officer of at least the rank of inspector authorises it to be taken without the appropriate consent.[12] Similarly, a non-intimate sample may be taken from a person without consent if (a) he or she has been charged with a recordable offence or informed that he or she will be reported for such an offence, and (b) either he or she has not had a non-intimate sample taken from him/her in the course of the investigation of the offence by the police, or he or she has had a non-intimate sample taken from him/her but either it was not suitable for the same means of analysis or, though so suitable, the sample proved insufficient.[13] An insufficient sample is one that is not sufficient either in quantity or quality for the purpose of enabling information to be provided for the purpose of a particular form of

---

8   SI 1985/1941, as amended by SIs 1989/694 and 1997/566.
9   *R v Cooke* [1995] 1 Cr App R 318, 329F.
10   Code of Practice [5.6].
11   Police and Criminal Evidence Act 1984, s 63(3)(a).
12   *Ibid*, s 63(3)(b).
13   *Ibid*, s 63(3A).

analysis. An unsuitable sample is one which, by its nature, is not suitable for a particular form of analysis.[14] Finally, a non-intimate sample may be taken without consent if the person from whom the sample is to be taken has been convicted of a recordable offence.[15] It should be noted that in the main this only applies to persons convicted of recordable offences after the date on which s 63(3B) came into force, which was 10 April 1995. However, in light of amendments made by the Criminal Evidence (Amendment) Act 1997, samples can now be taken from persons in custody or detained under mental health provisions who were convicted prior to this date if their crimes were of a particularly serious nature and they remain incarcerated (see below).

It must be borne in mind that samples can only be taken without consent if the officer authorising the taking of the samples has reasonable grounds (a) for suspecting the involvement of the person from whom the sample is to be taken in a recordable offence, and (b) for believing that the sample will tend to confirm or disprove his or her involvement.[16]

It should also be noted that even if a non-intimate sample cannot be 'taken' under s 63, an adverse inference may still be drawn at common law from the refusal to give a sample.[17]

Requiring subjects to attend to provide samples

Under s 63A(4) of PACE, a power exists to require an individual to attend at a police station to give a sample when he or she is neither in police detention nor in custody. The conditions are: (a) the person has been charged with a recordable offence or informed that he or she will be reported for such an offence and either he or she has not had a sample taken from him or her in the course of the investigation of the offence by the police, or he or she has had a sample so taken from him or her but either it was not suitable for the same means of analysis or, though so suitable, the sample proved insufficient. Alternatively, (b) the person has been convicted of a recordable offence and either he she has not had a sample taken from him or her since the conviction, or he or she has had a sample taken (before or after his or her conviction) but either it was not suitable for the same means of analysis, or, though so suitable, the sample proved insufficient. A time limit is imposed on this power. If the person required to attend falls into category (a), he or she must be requested to attend within one month, beginning with the date of the charge or of the date that he or she is informed that he or she will be reported for an offence, or one month beginning with the date on which the 'appropriate officer' is informed of the fact that the sample is not suitable or is insufficient.[18] The 'appropriate officer' is the officer investigating the offence with which the person is charged or as to which he or she was informed that he or she would be reported.

---

14   Code of Practice, Note 5B.
15   Police and Criminal Evidence Act 1984, s 63(3B).
16   *Ibid*, s 63(4).
17   See *R v Smith* (1985) 81 Cr App R 286.
18   Police and Criminal Evidence Act 1984, s 63A(5)(a) (as amended by s 4 of the Criminal Evidence (Amendment) Act 1997).

If the person falls into category (b) above, the time limit is one month beginning with the date of the conviction or one month beginning with the date on which the 'appropriate officer' is informed of the fact that the sample is not suitable or is insufficient.[19] The 'appropriate officer' is the officer in charge of the police station from which the investigation of the offence of which the person was convicted was conducted.

In both cases, a requirement to attend to give a sample shall provide the person at least seven days in which to attend, and may direct him or her to attend at a specified time of day or between specified times of day.[20] Failure to attend gives a constable the power to arrest without warrant.[21]

Taking samples: miscellany

Keeping records

Under paragraphs 5.9 and 5.10 of the Code of Practice, a record must be made as soon as practicable of the reasons for taking a sample or impression and of its destruction. If force is used to obtain a sample, a record shall be made of the circumstances and those present. If written consent is given to the taking of a sample or impression, the fact must be recorded in writing. If a warning is given that refusal to provide a sample can lead to an adverse inference in court, a record must be made. A record should also be made of the fact that a person has been informed that a speculative search may be carried out on samples. A speculative search means that a check may be made against other samples and information derived from other samples contained in records or held by or on behalf of the police or held in connection with or as a result of an investigation of an offence (Note 5D of the Code of Practice). This has implications for the establishment and maintenance of DNA databases, discussed below.

Warnings

Note 5A of the Code of Practice suggests the following warning should be given to a subject who refuses to give a sample: 'You do not have to [provide this sample, allow this swab or impression to be taken] but I must warn you that if you refuse without good cause, your refusal may harm your case if it comes to trial.'

Procedures

Any power to take a sample, which is exercisable in relation to any person, may be taken in a prison or other institution to which the Prison Act 1952 applies.

Paragraph 5.12 of the Code of Practice provides that:

Where clothing needs to be removed in circumstances likely to cause embarrassment to the person, no person of the opposite sex who is not a medical practitioner or nurse shall be present (unless in the case of a juvenile or a mentally

---

19 Police and Criminal Evidence Act 1984, s 63A(5)(b).

20 *Ibid*, s 63A(6).

21 *Ibid*, s 63A(7).

disordered or mentally handicapped person, that person specifically requests the presence of an appropriate adult of the opposite sex who is readily available) nor shall anyone whose presence is unnecessary. However, in the case of a juvenile this is subject to the overriding proviso that such a removal of clothing may take place in the absence of the appropriate adult only if the person signifies in the presence of the appropriate adult that he prefers his absence and the adult agrees.

Use of DNA test results in the criminal process

Pre-trial disclosure

It is trite law that the prosecution must disclose to the defence any evidence which it intends to use in the case against the accused. A more controversial issue, however, is the question of access to material that is not to be used.

The Criminal Procedure and Investigations Act 1996 has reformed the law in England and Wales on pre-trial disclosure concerning material that does not form part of the prosecution's case. Under s 1, the scope of the Act is laid out to include all cases in which the accused is committed for trial on indictment and/or cases where he/she pleads not guilty in a summary trial. If the accused intends to plead guilty in a summary trial the disclosure rules do not apply. Presumably, in such cases, the common law position remains (on which see *R v Keane* [1994] 1 WLR 746). In s 2 of the Act it is made clear that its provisions extend to material of all kinds and in particular to information and objects of all descriptions, clearly, therefore, including DNA samples and any information derived from them.

Prosecutor's primary duty of disclosure

Section 3 provides that the prosecutor must (a) disclose to the accused any prosecution material that has not previously been disclosed to the accused and which, in the prosecutor's opinion, might undermine the case for the prosecution against the accused, or (b) give to the accused a written statement that there is no material of a description mentioned in paragraph (a). The duty is discharged either by giving a copy of the material to the accused or providing him or her with a reasonable opportunity to inspect the material: ss 3(3) and 3(5). Material need not be disclosed if it is in the public interest not to do so. A court order to this effect is required: s 3(6). Note that this duty arises only in respect of material that is likely to undermine the prosecution's case. This is significantly narrower than the previous common law position, which allowed disclosure of all 'relevant' material. This would, nevertheless, certainly include DNA profiles and reports that were of no use to the Crown.

Defence's duty to respond

In circumstances where the prosecution has discharged its primary duty of disclosure, s 5 of the 1996 Act requires the defence in a trial on indictment to serve on the court and the prosecution a written defence statement setting out the nature of the defence and indicating the matters on which he or she takes issues with the prosecution and the reasons why he or she does so. This does not apply, however, if the prosecution has not discharged its primary duty. Under s 6, the defence can voluntarily offer a written defence statement to the court and prosecution.

The defence's right to request additional disclosure

Under s 7 of the Act, if the defence has made a defence statement, then the prosecutor must disclose to the accused any prosecution material that has not previously been disclosed to the accused and that might be reasonably expected to assist the accused's defence, as disclosed by the defence statement already given. Alternatively, the prosecution can give a written statement to the defence that there is no material of a description given above. Under sub-section (3), 'prosecution material' is defined as 'material which is in the prosecution's possession and came into his possession in connection with the case for the prosecution against the accused, or which, in pursuance of a Code under the Act (Part II), he has inspected in connection with the case for the prosecution against the accused'. Once again, public interest can be claimed to refuse disclosure.

Section 8 gives the accused the right to apply to the court for an order requiring the prosecutor to disclose material which the defence has reasonable cause to believe might reasonably be expected to assist their case, but which they consider has not been disclosed by the prosecution. This right is subject to a public interest argument by the prosecution. The requirement that the defence show that the material can 'reasonably be expected to assist their case' means that spurious fishing expeditions will not be permitted under this section.

Section 9 ensures that the duties of disclosure of the prosecution continue throughout the trial, and requires that the prosecution keep under review the question of whether there is any evidence that undermines its own case or might assist the defence. Similarly, under ss 14 and 15, the court must, in the course of a trial in which disclosure has been denied on the grounds of public interest, keep under review the question of whether there is a continuing public interest that precludes disclosure.

Code of Practice

Part II of the 1996 Act requires the Home Secretary to produce a Code of Practice to guide those investigating crime in relation to the treatment of unused material obtained in investigations. The Code operates to ensure, *inter alia*, that (a) where a criminal investigation is conducted, all reasonable steps are taken for the purposes of the investigation and, in particular, all reasonable lines of inquiry are pursued, (b) the police record, retain and make material available to the prosecutor, (c) if disclosure is requested by the prosecution, the defence is given the material, and (d) the prosecutor is given a written statement that the prescribed tasks of the Code have been complied with.

The Act also provides that the Code may include a number of provisions relating to:

(a) the responsibilities of police officers carrying out prescribed activities in accordance with the Code;

(b) the form in which information is to be recorded;

(c) the manner in which, and period for which, records and material are to be retained;

(d) the time, form and manner in which material is to be revealed to the prosecution.

The first version of the Code was produced by the Home Office and became effective on 1 April 1997. The effect of non-compliance with the Code is the same as for the Codes under s 26 of PACE (see above).[22]

During trial

On the question of the use of DNA evidence during a trial, the first point to note is that no special standard of proof applies to this type of evidence. Historically, however, and like most jurisdictions, the English and Welsh courts have experienced a period of almost unquestioning acceptance of DNA evidence. However, in recent years, the Court of Appeal has begun to reflect on this position.

In the case of *R v Doheny and Adams*,[23] the Court of Appeal laid down the following procedures that are to be adopted in England and Wales where DNA evidence is to be led:

(1) The scientist should adduce the evidence of the DNA comparisons between the crime stain and the defendant's samples together with his or her calculations of the random occurrence ratio.

(2) Whenever DNA evidence is to be adduced, the Crown should serve on the defence details as to how the calculations have been carried out that are sufficient to enable the defence to scrutinise the basis of the calculations.

(3) The Forensic Science Service (which is responsible for maintaining the national DNA database (see below, under Northern Ireland)) should make available to a defence expert, if requested, the databases upon which the calculations have been based.

(4) Any issue of expert evidence should be identified and, if possible, resolved before trial. This area should be explored by the court in the pre-trial review.

(5) In giving evidence the expert will explain to the jury the nature of the matching DNA characteristics between the DNA in the crime stain and the DNA in the defendant's sample.

(6) The expert will, on the basis of empirical statistical data, give the jury the random occurrence ratio; that is, the frequency with which the matching DNA characteristics are likely to be found in the population at large (see further, *R v Adams*, below).

(7) Provided that the expert has the necessary data, it may then be appropriate for him/her to indicate how many people with the matching characteristics are likely to be found in the UK or a more limited relevant sub-group, for example, the caucasian, sexually active males in the Manchester area.

---

22 For general comment on the 1996 Act, see Niblett (1997).
23 [1997] 1 Cr App R 369.

(8) It is then for the jury to decide, having regard to all the relevant evidence, whether they are sure that it was the defendant who left the crime stain, or whether it is possible that it was left by someone else with the same matching characteristics.

(9) The expert should not be asked his or her opinion on the likelihood that it was the defendant who left the crime stain, nor when giving evidence should he or she use terminology that may lead the jury to believe that he or she is expressing such an opinion.

(10) It is inappropriate for an expert to expound a statistical approach to evaluating the likelihood that the defendant left the crime stain, since unnecessary theory and complexity deflect the jury from their proper task.

(11) In the summing-up, careful directions are required in respect of any issues of expert evidence and guidance should be given to avoid confusion caused by areas of expert evidence where no real issue exists.

(12) The judge should explain to the jury the relevance of the random occurrence ratio in arriving at their verdict and draw attention to the extraneous evidence that provides the context that gives the ratio its significance, and to that which conflicts with the conclusion that the defendant was responsible for the crime stain.

(13) In relation to the random occurrence ratio, a direction along the following lines may be appropriate, tailored to the facts of the particular case:

> Members of the jury, if you accept the scientific evidence called by the Crown this indicates that there are probably only four or five white males in the United Kingdom from whom the semen stain would have come. The defendant is one of them. If that is the position, the decision you have to reach, on all of the evidence, is whether you are sure that it was the defendant who left that stain or whether it is possible that it was one of that other small group of men who share the same DNA characteristics.

The prosecutor's fallacy dismissed

In the case of *R v Doheny and Adams*, the Court of Appeal also took the opportunity to settle once and for all the problem of the 'prosecutor's fallacy' surrounding the conclusions that can legitimately be drawn from statistical data concerning DNA evidence.[24] As the court pointed out, the following reasoning has frequently been commended to juries in a number of cases by prosecuting counsel, judges and expert witnesses:

(1) only one person in a million will have a DNA profile that matches that of the crime stain;

(2) the defendant has a DNA profile that matches the crime stain;

(3) therefore, there is a one in a million to one probability that the defendant left the crime stain and is guilty of the crime.[25]

---

24 For commentary, see Balding and Donnelly (1994). See also Redmayne (1995).

25 *R v Doheny and Adams* [1997] 1 Cr App R 369, 372–73.

However, such reasoning is fallacious and led to a successful appeal conviction in Deen.[26] Rather, the appropriate conclusion in such circumstances where one person in a million has a DNA profile that matches that obtained from the crime scene is that there are likely to be 26 men in the UK who could produce a positive match. As the court pointed out: '[i]f no fact is known about the defendant, other than that he was in the United Kingdom at the time of the crime, the DNA evidence tells us no more than there is a statistical probability that he was the criminal of one in 26.'[27]

The court went on to state that the significance of the DNA evidence will depend critically upon what else is known about the suspect. Thus, for example, if he has a credible alibi placing him at the other end of the country at the time of the crime, then it will be highly improbable that he can be responsible for the crime, despite his DNA match. However, if he was in the vicinity of the crime and there is a match, then it will seem to be almost incredible that two of only 26 men in the country with a matching DNA profile would be in the same place at the same time. The court stated:

> The reality is that, provided there is no reason to doubt either the matching data or the statistical conclusion based upon it, the random occurrence ratio deduced from the DNA evidence, when combined with sufficient additional evidence to give it significance, is highly probative.[28]

Expert opinion

In R v Doheny, the court specifically rejected the appropriateness of the practice of asking the DNA expert if he or she is satisfied beyond reasonable doubt on the DNA evidence that the accused is the person who left the crime stain. This is a question of fact for the jury to be decided by them on the basis of not only the DNA evidence, but also all other relevant evidence that is led.[29] As was stated: '[t]he judge should [leave] it to the jury to weigh, on the one hand, the cogent DNA evidence coupled with the other evidence identifying the appellant as the potential assailant against, on the other, the defendant's evidence and that of his alibi witnesses.'[30]

As it was, the trial judge's summing-up was to the effect that if the jury accepted the Crown's random occurrence ratio, then the accused was guilty. That said, it is now established that there is nothing to prevent a successful conviction solely on the basis of properly established DNA evidence.[31]

In Doheny, the court also expressly disapproved the practice of multiplying the result of a multi-locus probe test with the results of a single locus probe test in

---

26 DNA processing is discussed by Taylor CJ in Transcript of Proceedings, R v Deen (21 December 1993).

27 R v Doheny and Adams [1997] 1 Cr App R 369, 373. See also R v Hassett [1999] EWCA Crim 1481.

28 The random occurrence ratio is a measure of the frequency with which the matching DNA characteristics are likely to be found in the population at large: R v Doheny and Adams [1997] 1 Cr App R 369, 374.

29 Ibid, 378.

30 Ibid.

31 R v Adams [1996] Criminal LR 898.

order to obtain the random occurrence ratio. In the present case, the result of doing so was to produce a random occurrence ratio of one in 40 million. Independently, however, the single locus probe yielded a result of one in 6,900 and the multi-locus probe had a ratio of one in 840. Unfortunately, the nature of the multi-locus probe test is such that it can identify bands of DNA that are the same as those identified by the single locus probe. To multiply the results together can therefore give an inaccurate ratio and should not be done. The court specified that the jury should only have been given the random occurrence ratio produced by the single locus probe and the blood group occurrence ratio. They could also have been told of the result of the multi-locus probe test and that it could have an effect of increasing the random occurrence ration, *but only* to an indeterminate extent.

In *R v Adams*,[32] the appellant was charged with rape. The Crown's case relied entirely on expert evidence connected with a DNA profile obtained from semen found on the complainant. This was the first such case to do so. At trial the defence were permitted to lead evidence on the Bayes Theorem, which is a means of looking at non-statistical matters in statistical terms to assess a situation in terms of uncertainty. The accused was convicted. He appealed on the grounds that (a) DNA evidence itself is inconclusive and inadequate to found the entirety of a prosecution case, and (b) the judge failed to sum up properly the expert's opinion in relation to Bayes Theorem. In the Court of Appeal, both grounds of appeal were rejected. The court found:

> no principle of law that DNA evidence is in itself incapable of establishing guilt ... [t]here is ... nothing inherent in the nature of DNA evidence which makes it inadmissible in itself or which justifies a special, unique rule, that evidence falling into such a category cannot found a conviction in the absence of other evidence.[33]

On the question of reducing the issues in the case to a statistical issue to be determined by reference to the Bayes Theorem, the court took the opportunity to dispute the value of such an approach and to reject its validity for future cases:

> whatever the merits or demerits of the Bayes theorem in mathematical or statistical assessments of probability, it seems to us that it is not appropriate for use in jury trials, or as a means to assist the jury in their task. In the first place, the theorem's methodology requires ... that items of evidence be assessed separately according to their bearing on the accused's guilt, before being combined in the overall formula. That in our view is far too rigid an approach to evidence of the type that a jury characteristically has to assess, where the cogency of (for instance) identification evidence may have to be assessed, at least in part, in the light of the strength of the chain of evidence in which it forms part. More fundamentally, however, the attempt to determine guilt or innocence on the basis of a mathematical formula, applied to each separate piece of evidence, is simply inappropriate to the jury's task ... to introduce Bayes Theorem, or any similar method, into a criminal trial plunges the jury into inappropriate and unnecessary realms of theory and complexity deflecting them from their proper task.[34]

---

32   [1996] 2 Cr App R 467.
33   *Ibid*, 469–70.
34   *Ibid*, 481–82.

The court quashed the conviction on the grounds that the trial judge's directions to the jury on the Bayes Theorem had left them without adequate guidance as to how to evaluate DNA evidence in the light of non-DNA evidence, and a retrial was ordered.

At retrial, the accused was once again convicted and appealed on the grounds that if the Crown is permitted to adduce statistical evidence regarding the random occurrence ratio of a DNA profile, then the defence should equally be permitted to lead appropriate Bayesian evidence to show how such figures could be reduced in giving effect to the probabilities attached to non-scientific, non-DNA evidence. The appeal was heard before the Lord Chief Justice Lord Bingham of Cornhill, Mr Justice Potts and Mr Justice Butterfield on 16 October 1997.[35]

The court relied on the strong criticism of the use of Bayes Theorem in *R v Adams* and *R v Doheny and Adams* (above), and held that it considered reliance on this sort of evidence to be 'a recipe for confusion, misunderstanding and misjudgment, possibly among counsel, probably among judges and almost certainly among jurors'. Such cases should be approached along conventional lines. It is for the jury how they set about their task and it is no court's function to prescribe the course that their deliberations should take. Juries will not be assisted in their task by reference to a complex approach which they are unlikely to understand fully and even more unlikely to apply accurately. In other words, the clear message here is that expert evidence should not be led in an attempt to influence juries into believing that a 'scientific' method for decision-making can be applied to their task at hand.

Admissibility of DNA evidence

In *R v Cooke*,[36] the Court of Appeal seemed to affirm the power of the courts to admit DNA evidence in a trial even when it has been obtained outside the provisions of ss 62 and 63 of PACE. On the question of the fairness of admitting tainted evidence, s 78 of PACE states:

(1) In any proceedings the court may refuse to allow evidence on which the prosecution proposes to rely to be given if it appears to the court that, having regard to all the circumstances, including the circumstances in which the evidence was obtained, the admission of the evidence would have such an adverse effect on the fairness of the proceedings that the court ought not to admit it.

(2) Nothing in this section shall prejudice any rule of law requiring a court to exclude evidence.

However, in *Cooke*, the court took the view that fairness of proceedings involves both fairness to the accused and fairness to the public good, and that in some circumstances – such as those of the case where the dispute related to the means used to extract the sample rather than the accuracy or strength of the evidence – contravention of s 62 or s 63 might not bar admission of the evidence. Some doubt

---

35 *R v Adams (No 2)* (1997) *The Times*, 3 November.
36 [1995] 1 Cr App R 318.

is cast on this by *R v Nathaniel*,[37] where the Court of Appeal took the view that to use samples which had been retained in breach of statutory duty was inherently unfair, and held that the evidence should not have been produced at trial. As Lord Taylor CJ said:

> To allow that blood sample to be used in evidence ... when the sample had been retained in breach of statutory duty and in breach of the undertakings to the [accused] must in their Lordships' view have had an adverse effect on the fairness of the proceedings.[38]

Moreover, in the most recent decision of *R v Attorney General's Reference (No 3 of 1999)*,[39] the House of Lords held that DNA evidence obtained as a result of an investigation prohibited under the old s 64(3B)(b) of PACE, prompted by the illegal retention of DNA evidence under s 64(1), was still subject to the discretionary power of the trial judge under s 78(1) to exclude such evidence if it would be unfair to admit it.[40] However, when it comes to the use of evidence that is very reliable and probative, such as DNA profiles, the courts have, in the past, been reluctant to exclude it as evidence, even if it has been acquired in circumstances of illegality. The approach that the courts have adopted towards the interpretation of s 78 tends to be one of a balancing of competing and conflicting interests.[41] Thus, as Grevling has pointed out: '[t]here is now some support for the view that s 78 tolerates a degree of unfairness in the proceedings, despite its effect on the accused, if the case for admissibility is sufficiently strong to override these concerns.'[42]

This seems to be particularly the case when the nature of the evidence involves DNA profiles which are, in the main, accepted as very 'strong' evidence indeed.

Privilege

In *R v R*,[43] it was held that a sample of the defendant's blood that was provided by him for DNA analysis to his general practitioner for the purposes of criminal defence proceedings was an item 'subject to legal privilege' under s 10(1)(c) of PACE. As a result, legitimate objection could be lodged to the leading of evidence on the sample itself or an expert's view on it by the prosecution. On the facts of the case, the defendant had given the sample on the understanding that it would be

---

37　[1995] 2 Cr App R 565.

38　See also *R v Payne* [1963] 1 WLR 637, in which the accused was induced into providing a specimen of blood under the pretence that it was necessary in order to determine whether he was ill. In reality, the sample was required to determine if he was unfit to drive. The Court of Appeal was categoric that the evidence should be excluded. This is, of course, a pre-PACE case, and the interpretation that has been given to s 78 of PACE (see above), which involves the courts in a balancing exercise to determine the overall 'fairness to proceedings' of admitting evidence, may make future DNA cases less clear-cut; see *R v Cooke* [1995] 1 Cr App R 318.

39　[2001] 1 Cr App R 34.

40　The robustness of this provision to withstand human rights challenges was also confirmed by the House in this case, albeit *obiter*, where their Lordships gave the clear message that the judicial discretion was not only 'fair' but also in keeping with the practice under the European Convention on Human Rights of leaving questions of admissibility of evidence to national law.

41　See, for example, *R v Khan* [1995] QB 27; *R v Smurthwaite* [1994] 1 All ER 898.

42　See Grevling (1997), at 680–81.

43　[1995] 1 Cr App R 183.

examined by the expert to help with his defence. Thus, it was not obtained under PACE and so no question could arise of the prosecution being entitled under the statute to produce in evidence the blood sample. Because the court held that the sample was an 'item subject to privilege', it meant that there was no discretion to admit material (or opinion) based on or derived from the privileged circumstances without the defendant's consent.

Special rules for specific groups

Military personnel

The Police and Criminal Evidence Act 1984 (Application to the Armed Forces) Order 1997 (SI 1997/15) applies certain provisions of PACE to the investigation of offences conducted by a service policeman under the Army Act 1955, the Air Force Act 1955 or the Naval Discipline Act 1957, and to persons held in arrest in connection with such investigation. Certain modifications to PACE are also incorporated in the Order, but these do not change the substance of the PACE provisions. The Order applies wherever an investigation takes place. For the purposes of the Order, a 'service policeman' means a member of the Royal Naval Regulating Branch, the Royal Marines Police, the Royal Military Police, the Royal Air Force Police or the staff of the Royal Air Force Provost Marshal.

Sections 62–65 of PACE are extended to service investigations. The Order allows the taking of samples with consent only when an individual is under arrest or when two or more intimate samples have been taken in the course of an investigation and these have proved to be unsuitable or insufficient. The provisions for taking non-intimate samples apply as above. Authorisation is to be given by 'an authorising policeman'. Samples can be taken for a 'serious service offence' as opposed to a 'recordable offence', and any intimate samples can be taken by either a medical practitioner or a member of a service medical authority. A 'serious service offence' means an offence under any of the service discipline Acts that cannot be dealt with summarily or which appears to a service policeman to be serious. The service discipline Acts are the Army Act 1955, the Air Force Act 1955 and the Naval Discipline Act 1957.

The Armed Forces Act 1996 further provides in s 11 that samples can be taken by a service policeman, for the purposes of recording information, without the need for consent if the subject has been convicted of an offence in service disciplinary proceedings. In other words, arrest is not a prerequisite; only successful conviction. The power arises only if no sample has been taken since conviction or a previous sample has proved to be insufficient in terms of quantity or quality. Reasonable force may be used in extracting a sample.[44]

Only samples of hair (other than pubic hair) or a swab from the mouth can be taken.[45] The hair sample can be plucked by the roots provided that no more hairs are plucked than is reasonably considered to be necessary for a sufficient sample.[46]

---

44 Armed Forces Act 1996, s 11(5).
45 *Ibid*, s 11(2).
46 *Ibid*, s 11(6).

A time limit is imposed under s 11(4) of the Act. A sample may not be taken after the end of a three-month period beginning either with the date of conviction if no sample has previously been taken or, if a previous sample has proved to be insufficient, with the date on which a service policeman is informed of this fact.

Within the meaning of this section, the term 'service policeman' has the same meaning as above under the 1997 Order. A 'service disciplinary proceeding' means (a) any proceedings before a court-martial or a standing civilian court under the 1955 Acts or the 1957 Act; (b) any proceedings before a disciplinary court constituted under s 52G of the 1957 Act; and (c) any proceedings by way of summary trial under s 52D of that Act.

Prisoners and mentally abnormal offenders

The Criminal Evidence (Amendment) Act 1997 operates to extend the categories of person from whom non-intimate samples can be taken under s 63 of PACE. Section 1(2) of the 1997 Act inserts s 63(9A) into PACE to substitute s 63(10). It states the following:

> Subsection (3B) above shall not apply to any person convicted before 10th April 1995 unless he is a person to whom section 1 of the Criminal Evidence (Amendment) Act 1997 applies (persons imprisoned or detained by virtue of pre-existing convictions for sexual offences etc).

Section 63(3B) states that non-intimate samples can be taken without consent if a person has been convicted of a recordable offence, but this has only ever been possible when the persons were convicted after the section came into force (10 April 1995). The effect of the above amendment is that samples may be taken from persons who were convicted of a recordable offence *before* 10 April 1995 when that offence was one specified in Schedule 1 to the 1997 Act (see below) *and* he or she is serving a sentence of imprisonment at the time when a sample is sought or is detained under the Mental Health legislation (Part III of the Mental Health Act 1983) in pursuance of an (interim) hospital order or a transfer direction given at a time when he or she was serving a sentence of imprisonment in respect of the offence in question.[47] It has been estimated that there are some 5,900 offenders in Prison Service establishments and over 2,000 mentally disordered offenders to whom these provisions apply.[48]

The offences with which s 1 is concerned are sexual offences, offences of indecency and violent offences. Examples from Schedule 1 thus include any offence under the Sexual Offences Act 1956 (with the exception of offences under s 30, 31 or 33–36), any offence under s 1 of the Indecency with Children Act 1960, any offence under s 1 of the Protection of Children Act 1978, murder, manslaughter, false imprisonment, kidnapping, a range of offences under the Offences Against the Person Act 1861 and contraventions of the Firearms Act 1968 and the Theft Act 1968. This is not an exhaustive list.

The Act also allows non-intimate samples to be taken from persons without appropriate consent if they are persons detained following acquittal on grounds

---

47 Criminal Evidence (Amendment) Act 1997, ss 1(3) and (4).
48 See Home Office Circular 27/1997.

of insanity or a finding of unfitness to plead.[49] Such a person must be detained under Part III of the Mental Health Act 1983 in pursuance of an order made under (i) s 5(2)(a) of the Criminal Procedure (Insanity) Act 1964 or s 6 or 14 of the Criminal Appeal Act 1968 (unfitness to plead), or (ii) s 37(3) of the Mental Health Act 1983 (power of magistrates' court to make a hospital order without convicting the accused). In addition, the order must have been made on or after the date of the passing of the 1997 Act in respect of a recordable offence (19 March 1997). It is only in respect of offences contained in Schedule 1 that samples can be taken from persons detained before that date. If a sample can be taken under these provisions, then the sample may be taken in the hospital in which the subject is detained.[50]

In real terms, these provisions make a special case of prisoners and mentally abnormal offenders held for certain categories of crime in that they extend the powers of the police to take non-intimate samples without consent and using reasonable force. The Prison Service readily agreed to co-operate with these measures and has provided all necessary assistance to the police, including the provision of lists of offenders who fall to be tested under the Act. These lists arrange the names of prisoners in the order of earliest release date to avoid the eventuality of a prisoner being released before a sample is taken. Guidance on approaching the prisons and those charged with the care of mentally abnormal offenders is offered by the Home Office in its Circular HOC 27/1997. There, a draft letter is proffered that can be sent to inmates explaining the procedures and requesting their consent. It is also explains that samples can be taken without consent. In the case of prisoners, the Circular advises that: '[w]here a prisoner offers violence to resist the taking of a sample, prison officers when called upon by attending police officers will assist with the restraint of the prisoner in order that the sample may be taken' (paragraph 11). In the case of mentally disturbed offenders who refuse, the advice given is that it might be necessary for the patient's clinical team to be involved in taking the sample by force. In such cases, discussion with the Responsible Medical Officer should be undertaken in order to decide whether and how the sample should be taken (paragraph 14). That said, the advice given in paragraph 11 still applies, but is to be read in conjunction with paragraph 14 (paragraph 16).

Minors

Where a person (whether detained at a police station or not) is required to consent to the taking of a sample and that person is a juvenile, then an appropriate adult must consent on his or her behalf. The fact of such consent must be recorded in writing.

Section 3 of the 1997 Act also inserts s 63A(3B) into PACE, which states the following:

> Where the power to take a non-intimate sample under section 63(3B) above [without consent] is exercisable in relation to a person detained in pursuance of directions of the Secretary of State under section 53 of the Children and Young Persons Act 1933 the sample may be taken at the place where he is so detained.

49 Criminal Evidence (Amendment) Act 1997, s 2, inserting s 63(3C) into PACE.
50 *Ibid*, s 3, inserting s 63A(3A) into PACE.

Thus, samples may be taken from young offenders at young offenders' institutions. This serves to emphasise the point that no special case is made of samples taken from minors. Nevertheless, the 1997 Home Office Circular stresses that particular care should be exercised when taking DNA samples from the small number of children and young persons caught by the provisions of the Act.

The purpose of the 1997 Act is to assist the government in the establishment of its national DNA database (see below). After the amendments to PACE by the Criminal Justice and Public Order Act 1994, it became apparent that many offenders would not be registered on the database because the power to take samples for such purposes only applied to those convicted after 10 April 1995. For 'serious' offences, the 1997 Act now removes this problem.

Police officers

In 2001, the Home Secretary approved an agreement of the Police Advisory Board for England and Wales requiring that new police officer recruits provide a DNA sample as a condition of appointment.[51] The purpose of this requirement is to eliminate police officers from the investigative process when a senior investigating officer genuinely believes that innocent contamination of a crime scene may have occurred. The DNA samples are stored in the Police Elimination Database (PED), established on 2 February 2000.

As requested by the Home Secretary, in 2002 the Police Regulations 1995 were amended to make provision for the taking of DNA samples as a condition of appointment. The Police (Amendment) Regulations 2002 inserts reg 20A into the Police Regulations 1995, which stipulates that every member of a police force, except members appointed following transfer from another police force, shall have a sample taken on appointment (reg 20A(1)). 'Samples' are defined as: a sample of hair, other than pubic hair, complete with roots; saliva; or a swab taken from the mouth (reg 20A(4)). The samples taken or the information derived from such under reg 20A are to be kept separate from the samples taken under s 63 of the Police and Criminal Evidence Act 1984 (reg 20A(2)). Finally, the samples taken from police officers, or the information derived from the samples, including all copies and records of such, are to be destroyed when the police officer ceases to be a member of the particular force, except when he or she transfers to another force (reg 20A(3)).

The Home Office also notes that any processing of DNA samples within this context would need to comply with the Data Protection Act 1998. For instance, new recruits will have to provide explicit consent, in writing, to the processing of the data, and such consent will have to be given in the knowledge of the precise reasons for and the means of providing a sample, the details of subsequent testing procedures, the circumstances in which the information is to be used, and procedures governing disclosure of test results.[52]

---

51 Home Office Circular 41/2001, *Requirement for New Recruits to Provide a DNA Sample as a Condition of Appointment and Changes to the Police Attestation.*

52 *Ibid.*

International Criminal Court

Under Schedule 4 to the International Criminal Court (Scotland) Act 2001, the legislature has given effect to Article 93.1(a) of the ICC Statute, which states that the ICC can request assistance from a state party in identifying an individual in whom it has an interest. Upon receiving such a request from the ICC, Scottish Ministers must first ensure that alternative means of identifying an individual have been exhausted. If these means are inconclusive, the Ministers must inform the ICC of such, and if the ICC wishes to proceed with the request, the Ministers may nominate a court to order the taking of evidence necessary for identification, such as a sample of hair. If the court orders that the person attend a police station to provide the evidence and he or she fails to comply, the court may order his or her arrest and the evidence can be taken without consent (s 49).

In tandem with the Scottish Act, the International Criminal Court Act 2001 (UK) similarly provides for the taking of fingerprints or non-intimate samples in response to a request from the ICC for assistance in acquiring evidence to ascertain the identity of a person. In this respect, the provisions of Schedule 4 regulating the taking of fingerprints and non-intimate samples apply (s 34(1)). Schedule 4 deals with matters such as the granting of orders to provide evidence by the courts (ss 2 and 3), consent to the taking of evidence (s 4) and circumstances in which evidence may be taken without consent (s 5). Under s 34(1) and Schedule 4, 'non-intimate samples' and 'fingerprints' have the same meaning as under s 65 of the Police and Criminal Evidence Act 1984.

Terrorism

Schedule 15 to the Terrorism Act 2000 specifically provides that ss 62 and 63 of PACE do not apply to a person arrested or detained under the terrorism provisions. Moreover, s 62(1A) does not apply to non-intimate samples taken under paragraph 10 of Schedule 8 to the Terrorism Act.

Schedule 8 establishes a separate DNA gathering and testing regime applicable to persons suspected of terrorism. Under paragraph 10(3) of this Schedule, a non-intimate sample may be taken from a detained person only if it is taken by a constable with the appropriate consent given in writing or, under sub-paragraph (4), if the person is detained at a police station and a police officer of at least the rank of superintendent authorises the sample to be taken, or the person has been convicted of a recordable offence on or after 10 April 1995.

An intimate sample may be taken from the detained person under paragraph 10(5) only if he or she is detained at a police station, the appropriate consent is given in writing, a police officer of at least the rank of superintendent authorises the sample to be taken, and the sample is taken by a constable or a registered medical or dental practitioner acting under the authority of a constable. Such authority can be given if the officer reasonably suspects that the person has been involved in an offence under s 40(1)(a) of the Terrorism Act and reasonably believes that the sample will tend to confirm or disprove such involvement, or is necessary in order to assist in determining whether he or she falls within s 40(1)(b) of the Terrorism Act.

Before any sample is taken, the person must be informed under paragraph 11(1)(a) that the sample may be used for the purpose of being checked against other samples, as outlined below. Under paragraph 11(1)(b), if a non-intimate sample is taken with written consent, or taken without consent on the basis of the person having been convicted of a recordable offence after 10 April 1995, the reasons for taking the sample must also be given to the person. Under paragraph 11(2), if an intimate or non-intimate sample is taken on the basis of authorisation, the person shall be informed that authorisation has been given, of the grounds upon which it has been given and, where relevant, the nature of the offence in which it is suspected that he or she is involved.

Paragraph 13 of Schedule 8 to the Terrorism Act provides that where appropriate written consent to the taking of an intimate sample from a person is refused without good cause, in any proceedings against that person for an offence, the court and/or jury may draw such inferences from the refusal as appear proper in determining whether to commit for trial or whether there is a cause to answer or in determining whether that person is guilty of the offence charged.

According to paragraph 14(2) (as amended by s 84 of the Criminal Justice and Police Act 2001), samples taken under the Act (or the Act's predecessor, Prevention of Terrorism (Temporary Provisions) Act 1989), and information derived from those samples, may now be retained and used for purposes of a terrorist investigation or for purposes related to the prevention or detection of crime, the investigation of an offence or the conduct of a prosecution. It is further provided under sub-paragraph (3) that a check may be made against such samples under s 63A(1) of PACE or 63(1) of the Police and Criminal Evidence (Northern Ireland) Order 1989, for the purpose of a terrorist investigation, or for purposes related to the prevention or detection of crime, the investigation of an offence or the conduct of a prosecution.

When applied to a person detained in England or Wales, the terms 'appropriate consent', 'insufficient', 'intimate sample', 'non-intimate sample' and 'sufficient' have the same meaning as that given by s 65 of PACE.

Destruction of samples

Formerly, there was a clear obligation under s 64 of PACE to destroy fingerprints and samples taken from an individual if that individual was later acquitted of the offence in respect of which they were taken, or where a decision was later made not to prosecute the individual for that offence. Section 82 of the Criminal Justice and Police Act 2001 removes this obligation, making England and Wales (and Northern Ireland) the only jurisdictions within which it is possible to maintain samples indefinitely on the national database, regardless of whether a suspect is found to be innocent, or whether a decision is made not to prosecute after samples have been taken.

The background to the changes made to s 64 of PACE by s 82 of the Criminal Justice and Police Act 2001 can be found in the decisions of the Court of Appeal and the House of Lords in *Attorney General's Reference (No 3 of 1999)*. In this case, after a burglary and rape, a DNA profile of the perpetrator was found and placed on the national DNA database. Some months later, the defendant was arrested and charged with an unrelated offence of burglary. Although acquitted, the defendant's DNA profile in relation to the latter offence was retained (illegally, under the then-existing provisions of PACE). Eventually a match was made between the first and second DNA profiles, leading to the defendant being charged with offences in regards to the prior burglary and rape and the taking of fresh DNA samples.

The Court of Appeal held that there was no discretion on the part of a trial judge to allow the admission of evidence derived from a sample obtained from a person on an earlier occasion who had been acquitted in respect of the earlier charge, and which should have been destroyed. On appeal to the House of Lords, however, the decision of the Court of Appeal was reversed, with the House of Lords holding that although the sample clearly should have been destroyed once the defendant was acquitted under s 64 of PACE, and the existing s 64(3B)(b) prohibited the use of samples for the purposes of any investigation, the section did not contain any language to the effect that evidence obtained as a result of the prohibited investigation shall be inadmissible.[53] The section therefore had to be read in conjunction with s 78(1) of PACE, which provides a discretionary power in the trial judge to exclude evidence if it would be unfair to admit it.

Now, under s 64(1A)(a) of PACE (as amended by s 82 of the Criminal Justice and Police Act 2001), where samples are taken from a person in connection with the investigation of an offence, they are expressly allowed to be retained after they have fulfilled the purposes for which they were taken, but cannot be used by any person except for the purposes related to the prevention or detection of crime, the investigation of an offence or the conduct of a prosecution.[54] This includes allowing any check to be made under s 63A(1) or (1C) against it or any information derived from it, meaning that if a match is made between a sample at a later crime scene and a sample of an individual cleared of an earlier offence, the police will be able to use this information in the investigation of the later crime.

The legality of these provisions was soon challenged under the terms of the Human Rights Act 1998. In *R (S and Marper) v Chief Constable of the South Yorkshire Police*,[55] a 12-year-old boy who had been acquitted of attempted robbery and another claimant who had been arrested and charged with harassment (but not prosecuted) objected that the new powers under the 2001 Act violated their right to respect for private life (Article 8) and represented discrimination in the protection of their human rights as innocent persons (Article 14). The Court of Appeal dismissed both grounds of review. While the court acknowledged that the retention of samples was a real interference with private life under Article 8(1), it was not substantially so. Moreover, that interference was justified by, and proportionate to, the need to protect the public from the consequences of crime, as

---

53   The House of Lords refused to read s 64(3B)(b) in conjunction with s 64(3B)(a), which states that if a DNA sample is not destroyed as required under s 64(1) of PACE, it may not be used in evidence against the person entitled to its destruction. Of course, on the facts of the case, it was not the profile obtained from the second burglary upon which the prosecution relied, but a fresh profile taken from the defendant, after the second burglary profile had allowed the police to match the defendant's profile with that of the perpetrator of the burglary and rape with which he was eventually charged. In holding this, the House of Lords also rejected the Court of Appeal's decision in *R v Weir* 144 SJ LB 222, 26 May 2000.

54   Section 64(1A)(a), as amended by the Criminal Justice and Police Act 2001, s 82.

55   [2003] 1 All ER 148.

provided by Article 8(2). As regards Article 14, the comparator to assess whether there had been any discrimination in the protection of the claimants' rights was *not* between the claimants and all other innocent parties not in the database (as had been argued), but rather as between the claimants and all other parties who had provided a sample for the database. On this analysis, the claimants had been treated no differently, and the challenge on Article 14 failed. The Court of Appeal was at pains to point out that the purposes for retention were restricted to matters clearly in the public interest (prevention or detection of crime; investigation of an offence or the conduct of a prosecution) and the procedures for dealing with individuals were clear and reasonable. Finally, the discretion of the Chief Constable to exclude certain cases from the database in exceptional circumstances was held to be a proportionate and reasonable policy.

The subsequent consolidated appeal to the House of Lords was unsuccessful.[55a] Although Lord Steyn and Baroness Hale of Richmond were prepared to accept that the retention of samples in these instances did indeed engage Article 8(1), albeit modestly, the House of Lords was unanimous (5–0) in its rejection of the appellants' assertions that such an infringement of privacy was not a *reasonable and proportionate* crime control measure as within the scope of Article 8(2). The House reiterated the Court of Appeal's observation that the use of retained samples and profiles was strictly confined to the legitimate aims of the criminal justice system. Furthermore, Lord Steyn's discussion of *Attorney-General's Reference (No.3 of 1999)*[55b] stressed the considerable practical 'value of retained fingerprints and samples taken from suspects who were subsequently acquitted'.[55c] The appellants' Article 14 challenge to the PACE amendments was also dismissed, as the House of Lords approved the Court of Appeal's more restricted comparator group approach as representing the correct method for assessing discrimination in such cases. On the basis of this approach, no discrimination to the appellants had occurred. The House of Lords was explicit in its use of this consolidated appeal as a test case.[55d] As a result, the 2004 ruling would seem to settle decisively any legal uncertainties surrounding the compatibility of s 82 of the Police and Criminal Justice Act 2001 with Articles 8 and 14 of the Human Rights Act 1998.

Section 64(3) of PACE, as amended by s 57 of the CJOPA, is retained, meaning that if samples are taken from a person in connection with the investigation of an offence and that person is *not suspected of having committed the offence*, they must be destroyed as soon as they have fulfilled the purpose for which they were taken. This provision is subject to the newly-inserted ss 64(3AA), (3AB), (3AC) and (3AD). Under s 64(3AA), the sample is not required to be destroyed if it was taken for the purpose of the investigation of an offence of which a person has been convicted, and a sample was also taken from the convicted person of that investigation. Under s 64(3AB), subject to s 64(3AC), where a person is entitled to

---

55a *R v Chief Constable of South Yorkshire Police (Respondent) ex parte LS (by his mother and litigation friend JB)(FC)(Appellant); R v Chief Constable of South Yorkshire Police (Respondent) ex parte Marper (FC) (Appellant) (Consolidate Appeals)* [2004] UKHL 39. *On appeal from:* [2002] EWCA Civ 1275, [2002] 1 WLR 3223.

55b [2001] 2 AC 91

55c Lord Steyn at para 7.

55d Lord Steyn at para 10.

the destruction of any sample taken from him (or would be, but for s 3AA), then neither the sample nor any information derived from the sample shall be used in evidence against the person who is or who would be entitled to the destruction of the sample or for the purposes of the investigation of any offence, including using the sample or information derived from it to allow any check to be made against it under ss 63A(1) or (1C). Under s 64(3AC), where a person consents to the retention of his or her own sample, that sample need not be destroyed, and s 64(3AB) does not operate to restrict the use of the sample or any information derived from it. Under s 64(3AD), it is immaterial when such consent is given.

Section 82(6) further allows the police to retain and use samples that should have been destroyed under s 64 as it then was, but which have not in fact been destroyed, as well as any information derived from such samples. It should be noted that a recent internal government report suggested that approximately 80,000 samples had been illegally retained prior to the amendments introduced by the Criminal Justice and Police Act 2001.[56]

Northern Ireland

Time in the criminal process at which DNA sampling and testing may occur and powers to take and use samples

The relevant provisions governing the taking of samples and their use in Northern Ireland are contained in the Police and Criminal Evidence (Northern Ireland) Order 1989,[57] as amended, *inter alia,* by the Police (Amendment) (Northern Ireland) Order 1995,[58] Schedule 4 to the Criminal Procedure and Investigations Act 1996 and the Criminal Justice and Police Act 2001. To almost all extents and purposes, these provisions mirror those contained in PACE (as amended). The effect of the 1995 Order is to extend the amendments of the Criminal Justice and Public Order Act 1994 to Northern Ireland in respect of the taking of non-intimate samples and the establishment and maintenance of the national DNA database (see below). Schedule 4 to the 1996 Act amends Article 63A of the 1989 Order to incorporate the same provisions as s 64 of the 1996 Act provides for England and Wales (cross-checks and inter-jurisdictional provisions). The Criminal Justice and Police Act 2001 amends provisions relating to terrorism and the destruction of samples.

Authority to take samples from persons in police detention is contained in Articles 62 (intimate samples) and 63 (non-intimate samples) of the 1989 Order. The definitions of intimate and non-intimate samples are the same in England, Wales and Northern Ireland.[59] However, unlike England and Wales, Article 12(3) of the 1995 Order provides that 'where any power to take a sample is exercisable in relation to a person, the sample may be taken in a custodial establishment'.

---

56 Reported in *New Scientist*, 5 May 2001, 3, 10.
57 SI 1989/1341 (NI 12).
58 SI 1995/2993 (NI 17).
59 Article 53 of the 1989 Order, as amended by Article 8 of the 1995 Order.

Disparities between England and Wales and Northern Ireland

Currently, a deficiency that was present in PACE, but which was remedied by the Criminal Evidence (Amendment) Act 1997, remains in Northern Irish law. Under Article 63A of the 1989 Order (as inserted by the 1995 Order), a person can be required to attend at a police station to give a sample when he or she is neither in police detention nor in custody. One of the conditions for this is that the person has been charged with a recordable offence or informed that he or she will be reported for such an offence, and either he or she has not had a sample taken from him or her in the course of the investigation of the offence by the police or he or she has had a sample so taken from him or her but either it was not suitable for the same means of analysis, or, though so suitable, the sample proved insufficient.[60] A time limit is imposed on this power. As the Order currently stands, the person must be requested to attend within one month, beginning with the date of the charge. Importantly, nothing is said about the beginning of the time period if there is no charge but there is a case involving an individual who has been informed that he or she will be reported for an offence. A similar oversight existed in the English and Welsh legislation until it was remedied by s 4 of the Criminal Evidence (Amendment) Act 1997, which states that the time limit can also begin to run from the date when the person is informed that he/she will be reported for an offence. This Act does not, however, extend to Northern Ireland.

Another feature of the 1997 Act appears not, as yet, to have been extended to Northern Ireland. This concerns the position under s 63A of PACE, which now allows samples to be taken for DNA database purposes from persons convicted before the passing of the section (10 April 1995) if they have been convicted of a recordable offence and are still detained. Although the general thrust of these provisions – to allow the taking of samples – has been extended to Northern Ireland by Article 11 of the 1995 Order, samples can only be taken from persons convicted after the amendment came into force. This date is 29 July 1996, by virtue of the Police (Amendment) (1995 Order) (Commencement No 1) Order (Northern Ireland) 1996, R 1996 316 (c 19).

Use of DNA test results in the criminal process

So far only a few cases have involved debates and decisions on the use of DNA evidence in Northern Ireland.

In *R v Duffy*,[61] a defendant who had been convicted of murder and illegal possession of a firearm appealed against both conviction and sentence on the grounds that DNA evidence derived from buccal swabs taken from his mouth was illegally obtained under the 1989 Order and should have been excluded from the trial. Under Article 63 of the 1989 Order (as amended by the 1995 Order), consent to the taking of non-intimate samples is not necessary provided that: (a) the

---

60   The alternative grounds are that the person has been convicted of a recordable offence and either he or she has not had a sample taken from him/her since the conviction or he or she has had a sample taken (before or after his or her conviction) but either it was not suitable for the same means of analysis or, although so suitable, the sample proved insufficient.

61   Unreported, Court of Appeal (Criminal Division), 15 September 1997.

subject is in police detention or custody; (b) an officer of at least the rank of superintendent authorises a sample to be taken without consent; (c) the officer has reasonable grounds for suspecting the involvement of the subject in a recordable offence and that the sample will tend to confirm or disprove his/her involvement; (d) if written authorisation is not given, the oral consent should be recorded in writing as soon as is practicable; (e) where authorisation has been given, the subject should be informed of the giving of the authorisation and the grounds for giving it (including the nature of the offence which the subject is suspected of having committed); (f) the authorisation and the grounds must be recorded in writing as soon as is practicable after the sample has been taken; and (g) if the sample is taken from a person detained at a police station, the matters required by (f) must be recorded in the custody record. In essence, these provisions are the same as those contained in PACE. In *Duffy*, the accused refused to give written consent and refused to sign the refusal form. Oral authorisation to take mouth swabs was given, but no written record was made. In fact, of the above requirements, breaches occurred in respect of (e) to (g). On this basis, the validity of the evidence was challenged. The Court of Appeal held, however, that such procedural irregularities were not automatically fatal to the Crown case. It endorsed the view that such breaches 'could be categorised as technical breaches and not significant or substantial in the circumstances of the case'.

The court also considered whether the evidence should be excluded under Article 76 of the 1989 Order, which contains precisely the same provisions as s 78 of PACE (above). As in England and Wales, the court made it clear that breach of a provision of PACE in the course of obtaining evidence will not *ipso facto* require the judge to exercise his or her discretion to exclude that evidence. A balance should be struck in light of all the circumstances to determine the effect of the evidence on the overall fairness of the proceedings. Relevant to the court in the present case were the facts that there was no evidence of any trickery or bad faith on the part of the police, nor was the appellant misled in any way. Also, reasonable grounds for seeking a sample did exist and the appellant had given oral consent to the taking of the samples. On balance, the discretion to exclude was not exercised.

Additionally, the court considered the judgments under s 78 of PACE, which are discussed above; namely, *R v Cooke, R v Nathaniel* and *R v Keenan*, but rejected them as not being of 'material assistance'. It emphasised that in cases of discretion, decisions depend entirely on their own facts. In this respect they endorsed the view expressed in *R v Jelen and Katz*.[62]

The acceptability of using DNA evidence obtained from non-intimate samples for databases purposes was challenged in the case of *In the Matter of an Application by Michael McBride for Judicial Review* (Queen's Bench Division, 1 August 1997). On the facts of the case, the applicant had refused to open his mouth to allow buccal swabs in connection with a charge of grievous bodily harm. A hair sample was taken instead and without consent. The custody sergeant informed the subject that he had no discretion with regard to the taking of samples and that he was obliged to do so. The legal position in this respect does not bear this out and is the same as exists in England and Wales; namely, non-intimate samples *may* be taken

---

62 [1990] Cr App R 456.

from a person without the appropriate consent if he or she has been convicted of a recordable offence with a view to establishing and maintaining a database of DNA samples.[63] In practice, in Northern Ireland, the Chief Constable of the Royal Ulster Constabulary issued a Force Order on 1 September 1996 which embodied his policy on the taking of samples. This policy is that 'as a general rule', the power to take samples should only be used in specified categories of crime. The Force Order states in paragraph 2(i) that:

(1) While the law enables samples to be taken from offenders charged with, or informed that they will be reported for, all recordable offences, force policy is that samples will only be taken for the following categories:

(a) all sexual offences;

(b) all offences against the person;

(c) murder, attempted murder and manslaughter;

(d) offences of burglary, dwelling house only;

(e) in any instance where the offence does not fall within one of the above mentioned categories and it is the view of the investigating officer that a DNA sample should be obtained from the offender, such may be taken with the authorisation of an officer of inspector rank or above.

The basis of the applicant's case in *McBride* was to the effect that the Force Order fetters the discretion of police officers to judge cases on their merits, and that when the applicant was charged with a recordable offence within the prescribed categories he had no real discretion to decide whether or not he should have a non-intimate sample taken. As a result, a declaration was sought that the police acted unlawfully in taking the sample.

The court rejected this argument. It accepted that, as a general rule, a discretion should not be disabled by the adoption of a fixed rule that prevents the principals from admitting exceptions. However, when considering the purpose for which Article 63 was passed – to allow as complete a database as possible to be compiled – the court considered that 'it is difficult to see any ground on which an exception could be justified ... [t]o allow any such exceptions would undermine the effectiveness of the process provided for by the legislation'.

Article 5 of the Criminal Evidence (Northern Ireland) Order 1988[64] deals with the weight of a refusal to answer questions relating to unidentified samples found on a suspect or at the scene of a crime. It applies in circumstances where a person is arrested by a constable and there is:

(a) on his person, or in or on his clothing or footwear, or otherwise in his possession, or in any place in which he is at the time of his arrest, any object, substance or mark, and

(b) the constable reasonably believes that the presence of the object, substance or mark may be attributable to the participation of the person in the commission of an offence specified by the constable, and

(c) the constable informs the person arrested that he so believes and requests him to account for the presence of the object, substance or mark, and

(d) the person refuses.

63　Article 63(3B) of the 1989 Order, as amended; s 63(3B) of PACE, as amended.
64　SI 1988/1987 (NI 20).

In such cases, the court or jury can draw an adverse inference from the refusal or even treat it as corroboration of any evidence given against the accused in relation to which the failure or refusal is material. Thus, in cases where samples are removed from the accused or his clothing and he refuses to account for their presence, that refusal may corroborate any prejudicial findings revealed by DNA analysis.

Disclosure

As in England and Wales, evidence to be led against an accused must be revealed to the defence. The disclosure provisions discussed above under the Criminal Procedure and Investigations Act 1996 also apply to Northern Ireland.

In addition, under the Criminal Justice (Northern Ireland) Order 1996,[65] Article 52 provides that the rules of magistrates' courts may make, with respect to proceedings against any person for a prescribed offence or an offence of any prescribeable class, provision for requiring the prosecution to do such things as may be prescribed for the purpose of securing that the accused or a person representing him or her is furnished with, or can obtain, advance information concerning all, or any prescribed class of, facts and matters of which the prosecution proposes to adduce evidence. The court can adjourn proceedings if such rules have not been complied with, unless the conduct of the case for the accused will not be substantially prejudiced by non-compliance with the requirement. In any case, non-compliance is not a ground for appeal.

Special rules for specific groups

Terrorism

Mirror provisions to those outlined above in relation to England and Wales are provided for Northern Ireland under Schedule 8 to the Terrorism Act 2000.

Military personnel

The provisions of the Armed Forces Act 1996, discussed above in relation to England and Wales, also apply to Northern Ireland.

Destruction of samples

Section 83 of the Criminal Justice and Police Act 2001 provides for the amendment of Article 64 of the Police and Criminal Evidence (Northern Ireland) Order 1989, mirroring the amendments made to s 64 of PACE, removing obligations to destroy samples, except where, in certain circumstances, a sample has been provided voluntarily.

---

65   SI 1996/3160 (NI 24).

Scotland

Time in the criminal process at which DNA sampling and testing may occur and powers to take and use samples

Under Scots law it is important to distinguish between a variety of possible scenarios in the taking of samples for DNA testing, as well as the respective roles of statute and the common law.

The Criminal Procedure (Scotland) Act 1995 permits the taking of non-intimate samples from persons who have been arrested, are in custody or who have been detained for the purposes of investigation of crime under the Act. In addition, in defined circumstances, it permits the taking of non-intimate samples from someone already convicted of an offence. At common law, intimate samples can be taken from persons either before arrest or at any stage leading up to the commencement of trial, provided that a sheriff's warrant is obtained. Thus, as we can see, there is no necessarily relevant distinction as regards pre-arrest and post-arrest powers, or indeed the powers in respect of a charged and a non-charged person. Rather, powers to take samples depend on whether the sample to be taken is intimate or non-intimate in nature and, correspondingly, whether the power is grounded in statute or the common law. This leads us to consider several scenarios.

The taking of samples prior to arrest or detention

At common law, a sheriff can authorise the taking of samples for analysis even if the subject providing the samples is not suspected of a crime but is required to assist in the detection of crime. Thus, a warrant can be issued prior to arrest for the taking of samples.[66] As with all uses of warrants in this context, the question of whether or not a warrant will be granted is one of discretion for the sheriff, subject to the proviso that the warrant is sought in 'special circumstances'. In *Walker v Lees*,[67] a warrant was obtained to detain a person suspected of theft with a view to taking blood samples for analysis. It was objected that the sheriff had erred in the exercise of his discretion in allowing a warrant prior to arrest. The High Court of Justiciary held, however, that a warrant prior to arrest is possible provided 'special' circumstances exist, and that in balancing the public and private interests at stake, the public interest in justice weighs more heavily. This test is examined further below. It should be noted, however, that the court would not hear argument that it was in the suspect's interests to grant the warrant, in that it could help to eliminate him from suspicion. On this point the court said:

> we are inclined to think that the better view ... [is that] the liberty of the subject favours leaving it to the individual, unless he has been arrested, to decide for himself whether or not it would be to his advantage to submit to a procedure such as the giving of a blood sample.[68]

---

66   *HMA v Brodie* 1996 SCCR 862, and *Morris v MacNeill* 1991 SLT 607; 1991 SCCR 722.
67   1995 SLT 757; 1995 SCCR 445.
68   *Walker v Lees* 1995 SLT 757, 760.

This, of course, did not preclude the court sanctioning the grant of a warrant in the interests of justice.

In practice, a warrant to attend to give a sample will be drafted so as only to authorise the police to take a sample at a place and time to be agreed, and not so as to permit conveyance and detention at a police station.[69] Similarly, the warrant will ensure that the period of detention is minimal so as to impinge on the liberty of the subject as little as possible.

A warrant can be granted in such circumstances for both intimate and non-intimate samples. The only difference will be that the sheriff must consider the relative degree of bodily invasion required when balancing public and private interests.[70]

The taking of samples while detained or arrested under the 1995 Act

Section 14 of the Criminal Procedure (Scotland) Act 1995 gives a police constable the power to detain a person for up to six hours without arrest if there exist reasonable grounds for suspecting that the person has committed or is committing an offence punishable by imprisonment. During this period the police can carry out investigations into the offence and can decide whether criminal proceedings should be instigated against the person. Under s 14(7), where a person is so detained, a constable may (a) put questions to the person about the suspected offence without prejudice to any relevant rule of law as regards the admissibility of any answer given; (b) exercise the same powers of search as are available following arrest. Under s 14(8), reasonable force may be used to detain the person and to carry out powers of search. This clearly has implications for the obtaining of DNA samples. The arrest provisions are dealt with below. It should be noted that only one period of detention without arrest is permissible on the same or related grounds.[71] Presumably, if one such period has been lost in respect of a particular suspect and he or she is then released without samples having been taken, then the common law powers detailed above could be used to obtain samples prior to any later arrest. Arrest may be justified even though there is insufficient evidence to charge someone.[72]

Section 18 of the Criminal Procedure (Scotland) Act 1995 contains the current provisions governing the obtaining and use of prints, samples, etc, in criminal investigations. The section applies either when a person has been arrested, is in custody or detained under s 14(1). The powers conferred relate only to the taking of *non-intimate samples*.

The power to take samples is governed by s 18(6) and (7). A constable may, with the authority of an officer of a rank no lower than inspector, take from an arrested or detained person:

---

69 *Ibid; Smith v Cardle* 1993 SCCR 609.

70 *Walker v Lees* 1995 SLT 757.

71 Criminal Procedure (Scotland) Act 1995, s 14(3).

72 *Johnston v HMA* (1993) SCCR 693.

(a) from the hair of an external part of the body other than pubic hair, by means of cutting, combing or plucking, a sample of hair or other material;

(b) from a fingernail or toenail or from under such nail, a sample of nail or other material;

(c) from an external part of the body, by means of swabbing or rubbing, a sample of blood or other body fluid, of body tissue or of other material;

(d) from the inside of the mouth, by means of swabbing, a sample of saliva or other material.

This corresponds to the definition of non-intimate sample in England, Wales and Northern Ireland.[73] As in these jurisdictions, *reasonable force* may be used to take a non-intimate sample and consent is not necessary.[74] Samples can be obtained simply with the authority of a senior officer and without the need for a court order. In practice, in Scotland, samples are taken by police casualty surgeons. Among such professionals there is a reluctance to proceed, however, in the absence of consent from the suspect. In such cases a common law warrant is usually obtained by the procurator fiscal. Thus, we can see that the warrant can assist in supplementing the statutory powers.

It is important to bear in mind that the statutory powers are restricted to obtaining non-intimate samples. To obtain intimate samples, a warrant from a sheriff is required. This is obtained by the public prosecution service (the Crown Office) by the intermediary of a procurator fiscal (a public prosecution officer). The law pertaining to the retrieval of intimate samples is the common law, and is dealt with below. That said, s 18(8)(b) of the 1995 Act states that nothing in s 18 shall prejudice any power to take possession of evidence where there is imminent danger of its being lost or destroyed. The implication of this is that non-intimate *and* intimate samples may be justifiably obtained if a real danger of imminent loss were present. Clearly, however, the onus is thereafter on the police to show good cause for proceeding to take intimate samples without a warrant.

Currently there are few cases that test the limits of the provisions of the 1995 Act. One such case is *HMA v Shepherd*,[75] in which it was held that it is not inappropriate for sample evidence taken in respect of one crime to be used to prove guilt in another crime:

> The provisions of the 1995 Act, and in particular section 18 ... do not circumscribe the use to which the record of [samples] may be put in evidence if they have been obtained and are being retained in accordance with the provisions.[76]

In this case, the respondent was fully committed on a charge of assault and robbery but released on bail without the taking of fingerprint samples. Subsequently, he was arrested on a different charge of theft and fingerprinted. On being indicted for assault and robbery, the list of productions included the fingerprints taken following the arrest for theft. At first instance, an objection to

---

73 The non-Scottish definition also refers to footprints and body prints, but these are also governed by the Criminal Procedure (Scotland) Act 1995, s 18.

74 Criminal Procedure (Scotland) Act 1995, s 19B, introduced by s 48(7) of the Crime and Punishment (Scotland) Act 1997.

75 1997 SCCR 246.

76 *Ibid*, 251.

the admissibility of this evidence was upheld, but this was overruled on appeal. This decision must be read, however, in light of sub-sections (3), (4) and (5) of s 18. They provide that a duty to destroy evidence exists if a decision not to prosecute is taken, or if the proceedings end in something other than a conviction or a special order of expediency. In addition, although the information derived from a sample need not be destroyed if it can add to existing information already held by the police in relation to the person, it is specifically stated in sub-section (5) that information or samples so retained cannot be used in evidence against the person from whom the sample was taken, or for the purposes of the investigation of any offence. Thus, any *subsequent* samples that are taken from the person could not be used in evidence for prior crimes *if* a decision were taken not to prosecute, or if a prosecution was unsuccessful in respect of the crime for which the subsequent sample was taken. Given that DNA testing can be carried out on non-intimate samples, this is a point worth bearing in mind. It throws up problems similar to those dealt with by the English courts in *R v Cooke, R v Nathaniel and R v Attorney General's Reference (No 3 of 1999)* (as discussed above).

Section 19 of the 1995 Act deals with samples from persons once convicted. The section applies where a convicted person has either not had a sample taken from him/her since the conviction, or where a previously-obtained sample proved to be unsuitable for analysis. Subject to a time limit, the section permits a constable to take non-intimate samples on the same grounds as are laid down in s 18. A person not in custody can be required to attend at a police station.[77] Such a person must be given no less than seven days' notice.[78] Failure to attend can result in arrest without a warrant.[79] A person who is detained can be dealt with in the place where he or she is for the time being.[80] Any such samples must be taken within one month. When no sample has been taken since conviction, this time period begins to run at the date of conviction.[81] If a previously-obtained sample has proved to be unsuitable for analysis, the one-month period begins to run on the date on which a constable of the police force that instructed the analysis receives written intimation that the sample was unsuitable, or insufficient.[82] Note that a verbal communication to this effect would not, therefore, set the time period running.

The taking of samples under common law

Intimate samples are not defined by statute in Scotland, but clearly include blood and semen samples, pubic hair samples and those obtained by means of internal physical examinations, endoscopic or colonoscopic examinations. It is interesting to note that although the taking of a sample of saliva from the mouth is non-invasive under s 18(6)(d), at common law the obtaining of a dental impression has been declared to be invasive and would therefore require a warrant.[83]

---

77 Criminal Procedure (Scotland) Act 1995, s 19(3)(a).
78 *Ibid*, ss 19(5)(a) and (b).
79 *Ibid*, s 19(6).
80 *Ibid*, s 19(3)(b).
81 *Ibid*, s 19(4)(a).
82 *Ibid*, s 19(4)(b).
83 *Hay v HM Advocate* 1968 SLT 334.

We have already seen that intimate samples can be taken at common law under warrant, either prior to or upon arrest or detention. In fact, although there is a general rule that the powers of the police in relation to an accused are different before and after committal for trial,[84] this does not affect the taking of samples (for DNA testing or otherwise) that may be taken right up to the point where the trial begins. In *Frame v Houston*,[85] it was stated that:

> in our opinion ... since the service of the indictment does not irrevocably commit the Crown to go to trial, service of the indictment does not constitute the cut-off point beyond which the accused person cannot be forced to give evidence against himself ... in our view there is no bar to the competency of the granting of a warrant of this kind until the case comes to trial.[86]

When, then, does the trial begin? In *Williamson v Fraser*,[87] it was specifically stated that the cut-off point is the 'coming to trial', which for solemn cases is the swearing-in of the jury. The same test applies for summary proceedings, although the court gave no express indication of when a case 'comes to trial' on summary complaint. However, in s 268(5) of the 1995 Act, within the context of the admissibility of additional evidence, the expression 'the commencement of the trial' is defined as meaning (a) in proceedings on indictment, the time when the jury is sworn in; and (b) in summary proceedings, the time when the first witness for the prosecution is sworn. It would be very strange indeed if this did not represent the relevant time both under statute and at common law.

The sheriff's discretion

It has already been established that for the taking of samples that are not covered by the provisions of the 1995 Act, a sheriff's warrant is required. Before a sheriff can competently grant a warrant for the taking of such samples, he or she must be satisfied that:

(a) there are 'special' circumstances justifying the warrant; and

(b) the granting of the warrant will not disturb the delicate balance that is to be maintained between public interest in the prosecution of crime on the one hand and the interests of the accused on the other.[88]

Special circumstances

'Special' circumstances, *prima facie*, relate to the seriousness of the offence. Thus precedents exist for granting warrants to take samples in cases involving murder, rape and very serious assaults. In *Morris v MacNeill*, it was argued that the discretion to grant a warrant should be restricted to such crimes and not extended to theft by housebreaking, but this was rejected and the grant of a warrant upheld. A similar argument was rejected in *Walker v Lees*,[89] in which a sheriff's warrant

---

84 *Adair v McGarry* 1933 SLT 482; (1933) JC 72.
85 1992 SLT 205; 1991 SCCR 436.
86 *Frame v Houston* 1991 SCCR 436, 445. See also *Lees v Weston* 1989 SLT 446.
87 1995 SLT 777.
88 For this, see *Morris v MacNeill* 1991 SLT 607, 609.
89 1995 SLT 757; 1995 SCCR 445.

was held to have been validly granted in respect of aggravated theft (opening lockfast places). In this latter case, the court also took the opportunity to point out the fact that a sample from the complainer was necessary for a complete analysis and comparison of blood samples could also make the circumstances 'special'.[90] 'Special' circumstances can also exist if the Crown has problems obtaining evidence from other sources. Thus, in *Mellors v Normand*,[91] a warrant was granted because of the seriousness of the offence and because the victim had gone 'underground' for fear of repercussions.

It should be noted that there is no clear guidance available on which crimes are 'serious'. In *Mellors v Normand*,[92] the High Court of Justiciary expressed the view that it found it difficult to see how circumstances could ever be said to be sufficiently 'special' to justify a warrant when the crime charged was one suitable only for prosecution summarily (that is, without a jury). Nevertheless, the court went on to uphold a warrant that had been granted in respect of a 'serious' breach of the peace, a classic summary offence.

Balancing interests

In addition to deciding whether the circumstances are 'serious', a sheriff must apply a balancing test. As Lord Justice General Clyde said in the case of *Hay v HMA*:

> two conflicting considerations arise. On the one hand there is the need from the point of view of the public interest for promptitude and facility in the identification of accused persons and the discovery on their persons or on their premises of *indicia* either of guilt or innocence. On the other hand the liberty of the subject must be protected against any undue or unnecessary invasion of it.[93]

In balancing these interests, a number of factors are of relevance to the court. These include the nature of the invasion proposed, the degree of violation involved, the stage which the proceedings have reached, and whether there is a *prima facie* case to justify the grant of the warrant.[94] In particular, when dealing with intimate samples the private interests to be considered include the invasion of bodily integrity required to take a sample and the potential loss of liberty if an individual is required to attend at a police station to provide a sample.[95] The taking of a blood sample by a qualified doctor for the purposes of DNA analysis is, however, thought to involve only minimal invasion of bodily integrity.[96]

In order to satisfy the public interest in solving and prosecuting crime, it need only be shown that a blood sample is needed *either* to eliminate or implicate a suspect.[97] Indeed, it is not even necessary to have a sample of victim's blood or

---

90 See also *Curley v Fraser* 1997 SCCR 702, in which it was held permissible for a sheriff to grant a warrant for the taking of a second sample when a first sample provided inadequate results for analytical purposes.

91 1995 SCCR 313.

92 *Ibid.*

93 (1968) JC 80; 1968 SLT 334.

94 See, for example, *HMA v Milford* 1973 SLT 12.

95 *Walker v Lees* 1995 SLT 757; 1995 SCCR 445.

96 *Morris v MacNeill* 1991 SLT 607.

97 *Hughes v Normand* 1993 SCCR 69 and *Brodie v Normand* 1995 SLT 739; 1994 SCCR 924.

that of any other suspect to carry out a comparison. For example, in *Walker v Lees* (above), a warrant was authorised to take a sample of blood from a suspect simply to confirm whether spots of blood found on a bag in a damaged car had come from him. This has led one commentator to state that: '[w]e have probably now reached the stage at which the Crown will be entitled to obtain warrants of this kind in any case in which they can show that they have information which indicates that the samples sought will be useful evidence.'[98]

Limits

A warrant to take a sample for DNA testing will be refused if it is sought prematurely. Thus, in *Hughes v Normand*,[99] in a prosecution for assault, the Crown was in possession of an 'apparently blood stained' shirt, but had not analysed or grouped blood samples taken from victims. It was held that to seek a warrant at this stage to take a blood sample from the accused would not further the interests of justice, for it had not been established that a sample of blood was necessary for the prosecution of the crime. Subsequently, however, once the staining on the shirt was confirmed as blood that was not that of the victim, then a warrant was granted.[100]

In *KJG v Lees*,[101] it was argued that a complainer's suggested phobia of needles should prevent the granting of a warrant to take blood samples. He faced charges of rape and assault. On appeal, the High Court confirmed the sheriff's decision to grant a warrant and required merely that it be restricted to taking blood by finger pricks. The test that was applied was that outlined above; namely, that there were 'special' circumstances requiring the evidence – primarily because of the seriousness of the offences – and a need to balance the competing public and private interests. Thus, the possible phobia was weighed in the balance and had the effect of requiring a redrafting of the warrant. It was not, however, sufficiently weighty to defeat the interests of crime detection and prosecution.

It is at the moment unsettled whether a warrant is competent if it does not name a police surgeon or other qualified healthcare professional who is to take the sample.[102] While the normal practice is that a warrant to take samples should be intimated to the subject of the warrant, this is not necessary if the sheriff believes that to do so would defeat the purpose for which the warrant was granted. Thus, in *Mellors v Normand (No 2)*,[103] the fear that the complainer would make himself facially and bodily clean-shaven if he knew of the grant of a warrant to take hair samples was held to be a valid basis for non-intimation of the warrant. The police in this case had legitimate reasons to fear this outcome, given that the complainer had previously resisted attempts to take blood and saliva samples under warrant, risking a conviction for obstructing the ends of justice.[104]

---

98   G Gordon, 'Commentary on *Hughes v Normand*' 1993 SCCR 74.
99   (1992) SCCR 908.
100 *Hughes v Normand* 1993 SCCR 69.
101 1992 SCCR 252.
102 *Mellors v Normand* 1995 SCCR 313.
103 1996 SCCR 657.
104 See *Mellors v Normand* 1996 SCCR 500.

The authority of a warrant is to 'take' the sample required; this implies the legitimisation of reasonable force to obtain the sample even when faced with a refusal from the subject.

Refusal to comply with a properly constituted warrant would seem to result in a potential charge of attempting to defeat the ends of justice.[105] Whether or not such a crime is actually constituted by refusal to comply depends on all of the facts and circumstances of the case, but the court in that case was prepared to hold that 'it cannot be affirmed ... that what the complainer is alleged to have done at the material time could not constitute an attempt to defeat the ends of justice'.[106] In particular, the court rejected the argument that because samples could be taken with reasonable force, to refuse did not constitute a crime.

Precedents exist in Scots law that allow the admission of illegally obtained evidence. Of course, this power is used only rarely.[107] In *Lawrie v Muir*,[108] it was established that such evidence can be admitted only where to do so would not involve unfairness to the accused. In *Namyslak v HMA*,[109] the failure to arrest a suspect before fingerprinting him was not fatal to a subsequent charge of theft, because the accused had already been fingerprinted in relation to a prior charge of attempting to pervert the course of justice. The court exercised its discretion to admit irregularly obtained evidence and allowed the evidence. There are no cases dealing specifically with DNA evidence, but there is no reason to suspect that the courts would not deal with such cases in precisely the same way.

Transborder warrants

Under s 297 of the 1995 Act, it is now established that any warrant granted by a justice may be executed throughout Scotland without being backed or endorsed by any other justice, in the same way as it may be executed within the jurisdiction of the justice who granted it. Problems arise, however, in attempting to execute warrants outside Scotland. Warrants that are requested for execution in England and Wales must still be 'backed' or 'endorsed' in accordance with the Summary Jurisdiction (Process) Act 1881, c 24. The procedure requires that the Scottish warrant be docquetted in compliance with the Act and then presented to the appropriate magistrates' court having jurisdiction in England or Wales. Shiels opines that warrants granted in England and Wales under PACE (which clearly does not apply in Scotland) cannot be executed in Scotland. He states that the appropriate action is to apply directly to the Scottish court having jurisdiction for the warrant in question.[110]

Under s 8 of the Criminal Justice (International Co-operation) Act 1990, on application to the procurator fiscal, if it appears to a sheriff that (a) there are reasonable grounds to believe that an offence under the law of another country or

---

105 *Ibid*.

106 *Ibid*, 505.

107 See *Lawrie v Muir* (1950) JC 19 and *McGovern v HMA* (1950) JC 33. See generally, Sheldon (1996), Chapter 8.

108 *Lawrie v Muir* (1950) JC 19.

109 1994 SCCR 140.

110 R Sheils, 'Commentary on the Criminal Procedure (Scotland) Act 1995', Greens Current Law Statutes.

territory outside the UK has been committed, and (b) that the conduct constituting the offence would constitute an offence punishable by imprisonment if it had occurred in Scotland, then the sheriff shall have the power to grant a warrant authorising entry, search and seizure by any constable as he would have at common law in respect of any crime punishable at common law. A prerequisite to this is, however, that the authority of the Lord Advocate has been given after receiving a request from the overseas court or authority through the Secretary of State. If this provision is given wide enough interpretation, it could conceivably encompass a warrant to search and take samples. That said, the equivalent English provision under s 7 makes it clear that the power is available only in relation to property.

Use of DNA test results in the criminal process

For the purposes of any criminal proceedings (ie, solemn or summary) in Scotland, a report purporting to be signed by two authorised forensic scientists shall be sufficient evidence of any fact or conclusion as to facts contained in the report and of the authority of the signatories.[111] For the purposes of such evidence, a forensic scientist is authorised if the Secretary of State has so deigned it, or he is a constable or is employed by a police authority under s 9 of the Police (Scotland) Act 1967, possesses such qualifications and experience as the Secretary of State may for the purposes of these provisions prescribe, and is authorised for such purposes by the chief constable of the police force maintained for the police area of that authority. For these provisions to apply, a copy of the report must be served on the other party to the proceedings not less than 14 days before the trial.[112]

The provisions will be held not to apply if a challenge is lodged with the first party by the other party relating to the facts, conclusion or authority of the report. This must happen within seven days of the date of service of the copy of the report, or such later time as the court may in special circumstances allow. If this has happened and subsequent evidence in relation to the report is given by both of the forensic scientists purporting to have signed the report, then the evidence of these forensic scientists shall be sufficient evidence of any fact, or conclusion as to fact, contained in the report.[113]

It should be noted that these provisions simply state that the reports that satisfy the requirements are sufficient for the purposes of proving the facts, conclusion or authority of the report. This does not mean that the report and its contents cannot be challenged on grounds of credibility or unreliability.

At the time of lodging a forensic report as a production, the prosecutor may intimate to the accused that it is intended that only one of the forensic scientists, who shall be named, will be called to give evidence in respect of the report. Any objection must be lodged in writing not less than six days before the trial (or some later date if the court considers it appropriate), and this objection can require that both scientists attend at court. If no objection is timeously lodged, then the

---

111 Criminal Procedure (Scotland) Act 1995, s 280(4).
112 *Ibid*, s 280(6).
113 *Ibid*, s 280(8).

evidence of the single scientist is sufficient evidence of a fact or conclusion in the report and of the qualifications of the signatories.[114]

Pre-trial disclosure

Under s 68(2) of the 1995 Act, the accused is entitled to see the productions according to the existing law and practice in the office of the sheriff clerk of the district in which the court of the trial diet is situated or, where the trial diet is to be in the High Court in Edinburgh, in the Justiciary Office. Note, however, the right is only one to inspect 'productions'; ie, that which the Crown intends to lead in evidence in the trial. There is no obligation in law to reveal any tests results *per se* if the decision has been taken not to lead these in evidence. As Lord Cowie said in *Higgins v HMA*:

> There is no obligation on the Crown to provide any list of witnesses other than those which are attached on the indictment, and there is no obligation on the Crown to disclose any information in their possession which would tend to exculpate the accused.[115]

In practice, however, the Crown in Scotland takes a more equitable view than this. Indeed, in *HMA v Ward*,[116] the Crown expressly dissociated itself from the position expressed by Lord Cowie above. Nevertheless, the question of disclosure in legal terms remains that as expressed in *Higgins*, and the question of whether disclosure will be made in practical terms remains a matter of discretion for the prosecution.

During trial

No specific evidential rules exist in Scotland in respect of DNA evidence. No special standard of proof applies to DNA evidence in Scotland. It need only be noted that under s 276 of the 1995 Act, evidence as to the characteristics and composition of any biological material deriving from human beings or animals shall be admissible, notwithstanding that neither the material nor a sample of it is lodged as a production. A party wishing to lead such evidence shall, where neither the material nor the sample of it is lodged as a production, make the material or sample of it available for inspection by the other party, unless the material constitutes a hazard to health or has been destroyed in the process of analysis.

There is no evidence in Scotland of lawyers challenging DNA evidence *in se*. The majority of challenges relate to the validity of the warrants used to obtain the samples for DNA analysis. The law on this point is discussed above.

In the case of *Welsh v HMA*,[117] it was held that the courts will not lay down as a matter of law that a particular statistical probability has to be achieved before a jury can proceed on the basis of DNA evidence. The court stated that because DNA profiling depends largely on theory and statistics, it is for the jury to assess

---

114 *Ibid*, s 281.
115 1990 SCCR 268.
116 1993 SLT 1202.
117 1992 SLT 193.

the evidence and to determine whether they accept it as sufficient to warrant conviction. It must be presumed that the same will be true, that is, that DNA evidence is simply another factual matter to consider, when a judge sits alone in summary proceedings. In *Hynd v Ritchie*,[118] it was held that DNA evidence is comparable to fingerprint evidence, following *Welsh*, and that it is capable of providing a sufficiency of evidence for conviction when taken together with other circumstantial matters (in this case the presence of the same DNA evidence at two crime scenes).

Special rules for specific groups

In Scotland, the answer to this is straightforward. If samples can be taken from individuals for the purposes of crime detection and prosecution either before arrest, without arrest, after arrest and right up until the trial begins on the grant of a sheriff's warrant, and if that warrant can be granted at the discretion of a sheriff who will balance the public and private interests at stake, then any factor that might tip the balance a particular way – for example, that the sample must be taken from a minor or an *incapax* – will simply be weighed in the balance by the sheriff. Beyond this, no special rules or requirements have traditionally existed in Scotland. Now, under statute, the provisions of the Armed Forces Act 1996, discussed above in relation to England and Wales, also apply to Scotland.

Most recently, special provisions in relation to offenders convicted of violent or sexual offences have been introduced in Scotland (similar to those in England and Wales under the Criminal Evidence (Amendment) Act 1997) under the Crime and Punishment (Scotland) Act 1997. This has amended the Criminal Procedure (Scotland) Act 1995. Section 19A of the 1995 Act now provides that the police may obtain samples, prints, impressions or any other relevant physical data (such as a scan of the subject's skin) from persons convicted of specified sexual or violent crimes. The section contains a significant and definitive list of the offences covered, which includes rape, clandestine injury to women, assault with intent to rape or ravish, indecent assault, lewd, indecent and libidinous practice, sodomy, murder, culpable homicide, fire raising, assault, abduction and reckless conduct causing actual injury. A number of statutory offences are also covered. The powers may only be used if the person has already been convicted of a designated offence, and only if no relevant samples have previously been obtained, or where previously obtained samples, or the information derived from them, have been lost or destroyed. Similarly, the powers operate only if a sentence has been imposed – other means of disposal do not invoke the provisions (except with the disposal of mentally disordered offenders under Part VI of the 1995 Act). Crucial to the operation of these provisions is the date on which they came into force.[119] This was 17 November 1997. This date is important because the power to take samples only operates if: (a) the subject has been convicted on or after this date and is sentenced to imprisonment; (b) he or she was convicted before this date but was in prison on that date or still remains in prison; (c) he or she was convicted

---

118 2002 SCCR 755.
119 These have been brought into force by the Crime and Punishment (Scotland) Act 1997 (Commencement No 3) Order 1997, SI 1997/2694.

before this date and was in prison at any time in a five-year period prior to that date. In this latter example, a three-month time limit was imposed for the taking of samples. Note how this is a different approach to that adopted in England and Wales, where specific amendments to PACE were required by the Criminal Evidence (Amendment) Act 1997 to permit the operation of the sample-taking powers before 10 April 1995.

Reasonable force can be used on the authority of a police officer of a rank no lower than inspector to take samples. The power is to take non-intimate samples only (as defined above). As in England, Wales and Northern Ireland, these provisions assist greatly in the establishment and maintenance of a DNA database.

Under paragraph 20 of the Terrorism Act 2000, s 18 of the Criminal Procedure (Scotland) Act 1995 applies to a person detained under the Terrorism Act in Scotland, with the exception of the following modifications.

Sub-section (2) of s 18 is replaced with provisions providing that a constable may take from a detained person, or require a detained person to provide, relevant physical data only if he or she reasonably suspects that the person has been involved in an offence under s 40(1)(a) of the Terrorism Act, or he or she reasonably believes that the relevant physical data will tend to confirm or disprove his or her involvement, or it is necessary in order to assist in determining whether the person falls within s 40(1)(b) of the Terrorism Act.

Of further relevance is s 89 of the Anti-Terrorism, Crime and Security Act 2001 (UK), which amends the provisions of Schedule 8 to the Terrorism Act 2000 relating to the fingerprinting of terrorist suspects. Section 89(4) provides that physical data, including DNA, can now be used by police in Scotland for the prevention or detection of crime, the investigation of offences, and in conducting prosecutions. Unlike police in England, Wales and Northern Ireland, who already had this power by virtue of the Criminal Justice and Police Act 2001, police in Scotland could previously only retain physical data that was taken for terrorist investigations under the Terrorism Act 2000.

Destruction of samples

Under s 18(3) of the Criminal Procedure (Scotland) Act 1995, there is an obligation to destroy all samples and information derived from them as soon as possible following a decision not to institute criminal proceedings against an arrested or detained person. The same obligation extends to samples and information at the conclusion of criminal proceedings that have not resulted in a conviction or an order under s 246(3) of the 1995 Act, whereby a court involved in summary procedure releases an accused who has been found guilty on the grounds that in all circumstances it would be inexpedient to impose punishment.

The duty of destruction under s 18(3) does not apply in the following circumstances: (a) where the destruction of the sample or the information could have the effect of destroying any sample, or any information derived therefrom, lawfully held in relation to a person other than the person from whom the sample was taken; or (b) where the record, sample or information in question is of the same kind as a record, a sample or information lawfully held by or on behalf of any police force in relation to the person: s 18(4). However, no sample, or information derived from a sample, retained by virtue of sub-section (4) shall be used in evidence against the person from whom the sample was taken, or for the purposes of investigating any offence: s 18(5). Thus, where the same sample produces evidence against more than one accused, the sample need not be destroyed so long as criminal proceedings remain against any one of the accused, even if the other accused are released without further ado. Nonetheless, sub-section (b) permits information to be retained if it can be used to 'update' information already lawfully held on an individual.

It should be noted that the duty to destroy extends not simply to the samples themselves, but also to any information derived from them (unless the above exceptions apply). This must therefore include data contained in reports and other documentation. Arguably, anonymised data might not be included, but there is no express provision to this effect. Note, too, if the 1995 Act deals only with non-intimate samples, does this mean that the duty to destroy only extends to non-intimate samples? What about samples obtained under a warrant? Certainly, sub-section (3) clearly only applies to samples obtained under the Act. In practice, the guidance given under the Home Office Circular in connection with the national DNA database (see below) governs the use and storage of all kinds of sample, but it is not a legal instrument in the strict sense of the word.

In the recent White Paper on the criminal justice system, it has been recommended that Scotland should legislate to allow the retention of fingerprints and DNA samples given voluntarily, on the grounds that this would reduce the allocation of police resources in profiling the same individuals, and avoid the inconvenience to those individuals who are asked for repeated samples.[120] However, the Paper recommends against the retention of samples when an individual has progressed through the criminal justice system and is not found guilty of an offence. This is in contrast to the Criminal Justice and Police Act 2001 (UK), which allows the retention of samples even if there is no prosecution or the individual is acquitted.[121]

The Paper also recommends that the taking of a DNA sample by means of a mouth swab should not require the consent of an inspector, as does the taking of DNA samples via arguably more intrusive means, such as the sampling of bodily fluids and hair. The Paper proposes that because the taking of fingerprints does not require such authorisation, there is no basis for this requirement in relation to the taking of DNA samples by mouth swabs without the use of force.[122]

The Criminal Justice (Scotland) Bill 2002 follows each of these recommendations (see proposed ss 46 and 47) regarding the retention of DNA samples given voluntarily, and the taking of DNA samples via mouth swabs without the need for consent by an inspector. (Now see the Criminal Justice (Scotland) Act 2003 ss 55 and 56.)

---

120 Scottish Executive (2001), [68]–[70].
121 *Ibid*, [72]–[73].
122 *Ibid*, [71].

DNA collection, storage and access provisions

Databases

Since 1992, there has existed the National Crime Intelligence Service ('NCIS'), which has brought police forces from around the country together with Customs & Excise to collect, develop and analyse information in order to provide criminal intelligence that is more pro-active, organised and efficient. The Police Act 1997 puts the NCIS on a statutory basis and establishes the NCIS Service Authority, which has the remit of maintaining NCIS, ensuring its efficiency and effectiveness, and determining its objectives. The general functions of the Authority and NCIS itself include: the gathering, storing and analysis of criminal intelligence; and the provision of intelligence and support to the police forces of Great Britain, the Royal Ulster Constabulary, the National Crime Squad and other law enforcement agencies.

The Act also puts the Police Information Technology Organisation ('PITO'), established in April 1996, on a statutory basis. The Organisation has the responsibility of procuring information technology equipment and services for the police forces; developing, procuring and managing the delivery of national IT in support of the police; securing a co-ordinated approach to the development and delivery of IT services to the police forces of England and Wales; advising the Home Office on the use of powers to regulate police forces' exploitation of IT; and undertaking or commissioning research in relation to IT for police forces. This has clear implications for the establishment and maintenance of databases. Indeed, one of the existing projects of PITO prior to the 1997 Act was to work closely with the Forensic Science Service in Birmingham on the establishment and maintenance of the Home Office DNA database.[123]

The UK was the first country to establish a national DNA database for the purposes of criminal investigation and detection. In England and Wales, it was made possible by the provisions of the Criminal Justice and Public Order Act 1994, which gave powers to the police to take samples and retain information derived from them, even when the subject was not convicted of a crime based on evidence from the sample (see above). Similar provisions exist in Scotland under the Criminal Procedure (Scotland) Act 1995, and in Northern Ireland under the Police (Amendment) (Northern Ireland) Order 1995.

Most recently, s 64 of the Criminal Procedure and Investigations Act 1996 and s 81 of the Criminal Justice and Police Act 2001 inserted the following provision for 63A of PACE:

(1) Where a person has been arrested on suspicion of being involved in a recordable offence or has been charged with such an offence or has been informed that he will be reported for such an offence, fingerprints or samples or the information derived from samples taken under any power conferred by this Part of the Act from the person may be checked against:

---

123 The Forensic Science Service is based at Priory House, Gooch Street North, Birmingham B5 6QQ. It employs around 1,300 staff in laboratories across the country, and more than 800 of them are experienced forensic scientists. The services on offer are available to both prosecution and defence counsel. For more information see the website: www.fss.org.uk.

(a) other fingerprints or samples to which the person seeking to check has access and which are held by or on behalf of any one or more relevant law-enforcement authorities which are held in connection with or as a result of an investigation of an offence;

(b) information derived from other samples if the information is contained in records to which the person seeking to check has access and which are held as mentioned in paragraph (a) above.

(1A) In subsection (1) above 'relevant law-enforcement authority' means:

(a) a police force;

(b) the National Criminal Intelligence Service;

(c) the National Crime Squad;

(d) a public authority (not falling within paragraphs (a) to (c)) with functions in any part of the British Islands which consist of or include the investigation of crimes or the charging of offenders;

(e) any person with functions in any country or territory outside the United Kingdom which:

(i) correspond to those of a police force; or

(ii) otherwise consist of or include the investigation of conduct contrary to the law of that country or territory, or the apprehension of persons guilty of such conduct;

(f) any person with functions under any international agreement which consist of or include the investigation of conduct which is:

(i) unlawful under the law of one or more places;

(ii) prohibited by such an agreement; or

(ii) contrary to international law,

or the apprehension of persons guilty of such conduct.

(1B) The reference in subsection (1A) above to a police force is a reference to any of the following:

(a) any police force maintained under section 2 of the Police Act 1996 (police forces in England and Wales outside London);

(b) the Metropolitan Police Force;

(c) the City of London police force;

(d) any police force maintained under or by virtue of section 1 of the Police (Scotland) Act 1967 (c 77);

(e) the Police Service of Northern Ireland;

(f) the Police Office of Northern Ireland Reserve;

(g) the Ministry of Defence Police;

(h) the Royal Navy Regulating Branch;

(i) the Royal Military Police;

(j) the Royal Air Force Police;

(k) the Royal Marines Police;

(l) the British Transport Police;

(m) the States of Jersey Police Force;

(n) the salaried police force of the Island of Guernsey;

(o) the Isle of Man Constabulary.

(2) This section applies where a person:

    (a) is arrested on suspicion of being involved in a recordable offence,

    (b) is charged with a recordable offence, or

    (c) is informed that he will be reported for a recordable offence, after the day on which this Act is passed.

The aim of this section is to allow police to carry out cross-checks or 'speculative searches' of sample information, including, of course, DNA information held in databases by them or on their behalf. Although this was allowed under the 1994 amendments, importantly, the 1996 provisions allow such searches to be carried out using samples taken from persons who have not been charged with any offence or reported for a recordable offence, including where consent is given for a speculative search under s 63A(1C) of PACE, as amended by s 81 of the Criminal Justice and Police Act 2001. The section also allows the investigation of crime using fingerprints and samples to be done on a UK-wide basis. Samples can be cross-checked with samples taken as part of investigations anywhere in the UK, although for Jersey, Guernsey and the Isle of Man, the power to cross-check would seem to be limited to fingerprints, because the police there do not have the power to take samples. The section came into force on 4 July 1996.[124]

The reason for this amendment arises because PACE 1984 contained no provision for searching the fingerprints or samples of people who had not been arrested, convicted or cautioned. Moreover, there was no authority to cross-check information collected in the different jurisdictions within the UK.

The national database is maintained by the Forensic Science Service in Birmingham. The database began operating in England and Wales in April 1995. Scottish forces began submitting samples at the beginning of November 1996,[125] and the Royal Ulster Constabulary established its own database at the end of 1996/beginning of 1997. The latter is maintained by the Forensic Science Agency of Northern Ireland, which passes all DNA profiles to the national database as a matter of course. As a result, a single, consolidated UK-wide database has been created.

The legal foundation of the national database and guidance on its operational use are contained in the Home Office Circular HOC 16/1995: National DNA Database.[126] The circular sets out general conditions relating to the supply and use of DNA database services and describes the practical procedures relating to:

(a) the taking and submitting of samples;

(b) accessing the database; and

(c) security and data issues.

Samples, and the profiles derived from them, that have been taken from volunteers as part of a mass screening programme will not be the subject of speculative searches.

---

124 See Leng and Taylor (1996).

125 A Scottish DNA database has been operative in Dundee since 16 December 1996, but most information is processed via Birmingham.

126 As amended by HOC 47/1996, HOC 27/1997 and correspondence from the Home Office ref: PCP/95 14/5/54, 2 August 1995.

The following provisions are taken from the Home Office Circular. It should be noted that they contain directions not only on the database itself, but also about the tests to be done and accreditation of laboratories, the procedures to be employed in obtaining and storing samples, the rules on disclosure and the measures about security.

Paragraph 21 provides that the DNA database will be a national database, and will comprise details of individuals suspected, cautioned and convicted of a recordable offence. Together with the profile, it will include these details:

(i) the sample identification number;

(ii) the Phoenix Arrest/Summons Report Number (which provides a link to the Police National Computer Phoenix Criminal Record);

(iii) the subject's full name, sex, date of birth, ethnic appearance;

(iv) the force/station code;

(v) the name of the officer taking the sample.

The database will also hold DNA profiles derived from crime stains.

Paragraph 22: the DNA database will be a single, consolidated central database; it will not be partitioned by force, region or on any other such basis. This does not, however, preclude local searches being carried out. It is anticipated that, in time, the database will hold up to approximately five million records.

Paragraph 23: the DNA database is an intelligence database only. It is not intended that the results of any analysis carried out solely for the database, or that the fact that a match was found during a speculative search, will be used for prosecuting purposes. Casework and statements used for such purposes will be handled separately in the same manner as at present.

Paragraph 24: where a person is suspected of a particular crime and where a crime stain relating to that crime exists, a criminal justice sample should not be taken (a criminal justice sample is defined as a sample taken from a person for DNA purposes under the powers contained in ss 63(3A) and 63(3B) of PACE, usually in the form of two mouth swabs). Instead, samples should be taken and the analysis carried out in the same way as for casework. This is essential, since it may not be possible to obtain a further sample for prosecuting purposes. The results of the analysis will still be added to the database and will be used to check whether the suspect has been involved in any unsolved crimes that have a record on the database.

Paragraph 25: where no crime stain exists, the body sample will be taken and the analysis carried out as described in the rest of the circular. If a match is found as a result of a speculative search on the database, a further sample will be obtained and analysed to normal caseworking standards. This further sample can be taken under PACE because it will be taken as part of the investigation of a different offence (that relating to the unsolved crime stain).

Paragraph 26: initially, DNA profiles for the database will be obtained from the sample using a technique known as polymerase chain reaction ('PCR') to analyse short tandem repeats ('STR').

Paragraph 27: the results of the profiling processes will be stored electronically as a digital record in compliance with the Data Protection Act 1998.[127] These records will provide a high level of discrimination between profiled offenders. They will also provide information for investigating officers, such as potential links between individuals and crime scenes, which will directly contribute to investigations.

Paragraph 28: unlike the practice of fingerprints, if a convicted person's DNA profile is already on the DNA database, another DNA sample need not be taken for the database if that person is subsequently suspected of involvement in another crime. However, a further sample does not need to be taken if a prosecution is to follow and DNA evidence will be used, for the reasons set out in paragraphs 23–25 above.

Paragraph 29: the DNA database service can be considered as two distinct parts:

(1) the DNA database, which stores the data derived from DNA profiles and is where the searches are carried out; and

(2) profiling services, which take individual samples and analyse them to produce the DNA profiles.

Paragraph 30: the DNA database will be managed and run by a single custodian, chosen by agreement amongst chief officers and endorsed by the Home Office. This custodian will make available and run the computer system on which the database will be held. The initial custodian will be the Forensic Science Service.

Paragraph 31: the Forensic Science Service, as custodian of the DNA database, will provide and run a system for the database which:

(a) has a capacity that has been agreed with chief officers;

(b) conforms to the requirements of the National Strategy for Police Information Systems; and

(c) conforms with the requirements of the Data Protection Act 1984 (superseded by the DNA Protection Act 1998).

---

127 It should be noted that there is no specific right of privacy in the UK, either at common law or under statute. The Data Protection Act 1984 (superseded by the Data Protection Act 1998) was introduced to ensure the security of, and controlled access to, sensitive personal information held on computer. The Act sets up a Data Protection Register, administered by the Data Protection Commissioner, and data users must register their uses of the information in the public record. The subjects of that data can receive copies of the information held on them, subject to the payment of a fee and subject to certain exceptions. The address of the Office of the Data Protection Registrar is Wycliffe House, Water Lane, Wilmslow, Cheshire SK9 5AF. The workings of the Data Protection Office and more guidance on the Act can be found at the following website: www.open.gov.uk/dpr/dprhome.htm. It is also important to bear in mind that the Member States of the European Community were obliged to implement the provisions of the Directive Concerning the Protection of Individuals in Relation to the Processing of Personal Data (COM 90 314 final, SYN 287) by 24 October 1998. This Directive concerns all forms of personal information, however stored, and imposes similar control provisions on data users as already exist under the 1984 Act. Subject access rights also exist. For comment, see Hogg (1996).

Paragraph 32: in addition, the custodian will be expected to have British Standards Institution[128] ('BSI') registration and National Accreditation of Measurement and Sampling[129] ('NAMAS') accreditation.

Paragraph 33: if research leads to new methods of DNA profiling, it is essential that any investment in DNA profiles already stored on the DNA database is not lost. The custodian must therefore ensure that the DNA database system is capable of being adapted to new methods of DNA profiling (new profiles will have to be derived by re-analysing stored samples). Any such change will be the subject of a separate agreement between the custodian and individual police forces.

Paragraph 35: profiling may be carried out by the Forensic Science Service or by other organisations; this will be for the individual police force to decide. Whilst individual police forces are free to choose who provides their profiling services, it is essential that quality standards and compatibility with the central DNA database services are maintained. The Forensic Science Service, as custodian of the database, is responsible for ensuring compliance with set standards. These standards will be agreed with chief officers and are subject to continuing Home Office endorsement.

Paragraph 36: any organisation providing profiling services will use a standard protocol for DNA profiling to analyse specified regions of DNA, as agreed by chief officers and the Forensic Science Service and endorsed by the Home Office.

Paragraph 37: any profiling service must satisfy the Forensic Science Service, as database custodian, that they are competent and licensed to use the profiling technique agreed by chief officers and the Forensic Science Service and endorsed by the Home Office. In future, profiling services should have BSI registration and NAMAS accreditation.

Paragraph 38: any profiling service should adopt procedures and carry out an internal quality programme to the specification set by the Forensic Science Service, as custodian of the database, and endorsed by the Home Office. The Forensic Science Service will submit samples to all profiling services for repeat analysis at an agreed percentage of the total number of samples analysed. These samples will be re-coded so that they are identified as test samples, but in a way that does not allow the profiling organisation to know their previous identity. The results of the two analyses will then be compared. In the event of the failure of any quality assurance trial, the Forensic Science Service will not accept any further samples or the data derived from samples from that profiling service without re-inspection and revalidation. The Forensic Science Service will provide a written explanation to the DNA profiling service provider, to chief officers and to the Home Office.

---

128 The BSI is responsible for maintaining standards in consumer and commercial products. More information on its work can be found at its website: www.bsi.org.uk.
129 NAMAS is offered by the UK Accreditation Service (UKAS), which is run by the Department of Trade and Industry.

Profiling of criminal justice samples and analysis of crime stains

Paragraph 39: material for DNA profiling will come from either:

(i) criminal justice samples (from charged, reported or convicted persons);

(ii) casework samples (from suspects);

(iii)crime stains (via normal caseworking routes); or

(iv)samples for elimination purposes (ie, from victims, witnesses, etc).

The profiles derived from samples taken for elimination purposes will not be used in speculative searches, and will not be placed on the DNA intelligence database.

Paragraph 40: chief officers have agreed that all offenders committing recordable offences will be profiled, but that, in the first instance, the police should only obtain samples from offenders in the following categories:

(i) offences against the person;

(ii) sexual offences; and

(iii)burglaries.

This does not, however, preclude forces from obtaining criminal justice samples for other recordable offences for inclusion on the database, nor does it compel forces to take samples in all of the above categories, or in all cases in selected categories. All forces should have a clearly-stated policy on sampling. This policy should be notified to the Forensic Science Service (as database custodian) and any other organisations used for profiling services to ensure that sufficient infrastructure capacity is made available.

Paragraph 41: the demand on the database service may vary. For example, in time, sample numbers may fall due to recidivism. However, if other offender categories are included, this will negate the effect.

Paragraph 42: as with all forensic casework, the procedures for taking samples by the police, transferring them to the laboratory, all the internal handling processes used to profile them and the database handling procedures will conform to the rules of evidence. All procedures should be capable of withstanding examination, ensuring that evidence relating a named person to a crime stain is capable of total support. However, it is not intended (as stated in paragraph 23) that the database will be used for prosecution evidence. DNA evidence will come via normal caseworking routes.

Paragraph 43: training will be available from the Forensic Science Service to enable trainees to train others in the collection and submission of samples.

Sampling procedures

Paragraph 44: criminal justice samples will normally be collected in the form of two swabs taken from the mouth in accordance with PACE regulations (or in the case of Scotland, the Criminal Procedure (Scotland) Act 1995). This is the preferred option. As an alternative, they will be taken by plucking no fewer than 10 body hairs (not pubic hair) with the roots.

Paragraph 45: samples from victims, where required for elimination purposes, will be collected by normal caseworking methods. In future, all mass screenings analysed by the Forensic Science Service will be analysed at the DNA Database Unit in Birmingham. Mouth swabs and hair kits will be provided for this purpose.

Paragraph 46: the prescribed buccal comb swabs will be supplied as part of a sample collection kit by the Forensic Science Service or other approved profiling organisations, and must be handled and used in accordance with the instructions laid down in the kit. A sample consisting of two swabs per individual will be required. Normally, only one swab will be analysed to produce the DNA profile. However, analysis of the first swab will occasionally be unsuccessful, and the second swab will then be used to complete the analysis. Otherwise, it will be stored by the Forensic Science Service (or a sub-contractor chosen by the Service) until informed by the police that it is to be destroyed. Swabs will be destroyed when the corresponding record is removed from the database. Swabs will be stored in such a way as to ensure that they can, if required, be retained for the lifetime of the offender.

Paragraph 47: exceptionally, where a criminal justice sample forms part of the evidence, the stored sample should be accessible by the defence.

Paragraph 48: mouth swabs must not be taken within 20 minutes of the subject consuming food or drink.

Paragraph 49: samples should be sealed, packaged and labelled in the presence of the donor and sent to the profiler by one of the approved delivery arrangements. The following details should be provided on a form DNA–1:

(a) the subject's name, date of birth, sex and ethnic appearance;

(b) the sample type – mouth swab or hairs;

(c) the date that the sample was taken;

(d) the name, rank and number of the officer taking the sample;

(e) the sample identification number;

(f) the force/police code; and

(g) the Phoenix arrest/summons report number.

Where delivery is not possible within 48 hours, samples should be stored at –20°C (with the necessary identification information).

Profiling

Paragraph 50: the profiling agency will reject samples that do not arrive in a satisfactory condition, where they arrive without proper identification, or where continuity is in doubt.

Paragraph 51: the results of the profiling process will be sent for entry onto the database in a format agreed with the Forensic Science Service, compatible with the computer system and capable of quality assessment before addition to the database itself.

Addition to the database

Paragraph 52: profiles derived from criminal justice samples, casework samples and crime stains will be checked against the searchable profiles already held on the database. profiles from victims and witnesses will only be used for elimination purposes and will not be entered onto the database.

Paragraph 53: sample test results and reports will be confidential and will be available in a standard hard copy form agreed between the Forensic Science Service and chief officers. In the first instance, this will be by facsimile message.

Paragraph 54: samples that give a clear, unambiguous result and which are supported by the appropriate controls will be reported. Partial identification may, on some occasions, be reported for further investigation.

Paragraph 55: reports from criminal justice samples will fall into three groups:

(a) no matches found;

(b) a match found with a profile obtained from a person analysed previously, indicating whether a duplicate record or an alias;

(c) a match with an unsolved crime stain profile indicating a possible link between that individual and the crime.

Paragraph 56: likewise, reports from scene of crime stains will fall into three groups:

(a) no matches found;

(b a match found with a profile obtained from a person analysed previously, indicating a possible link between that individual and the crime;

(c) a match with another unsolved crime stain profile potentially linking the two unsolved crimes.

Paragraph 57: normally, only one profile will be retained on the database per subject. Where a profile is accepted as matching another profile already on the database and it is shown to be from the same person, the new profile will be retained on the database but flagged as a duplicate/alias.

Paragraph 58: it is intended that the Forensic Science Service will have direct access to relevant areas of the Phoenix database of criminal records,[130] and a user requirement is being produced by chief officers. Once links have been established and, provided that the identity of an offender can be verified, the Forensic Science Service will enter a marker on the offender's Phoenix record to denote that a sample has been profiled for DNA purposes, and will remove the marker when the sample is destroyed. Such a procedure will prevent the unnecessary re-sampling of recidivists.

Actions following matches on the database

Paragraph 59: there will be a nominated point in each force for receiving information from the database. Any identification found on the database will be sent to the nominated point. Where an identification is relevant to more than one force (for example, if it relates to offences in different force areas), the information

---

130 Phoenix is the computerised criminal justice record system that became operational for new convictions for reportable offences from May 1995. Eventually all offences will be recorded on Phoenix, accessible from around the country. Inquiries and the searching of criminal records will be undertaken by a new Criminal Records Agency that will have direct access to Phoenix and liaison powers with police forces throughout England, Wales and Northern Ireland. The equivalent body in Scotland is the Scottish Criminal Record Office.

will be sent to the nominated point in each force. For casework samples, the information will be passed in the normal way to the investigating officer submitting the case sample. Any identifications made on the database relating to other offences will be sent to the nominated point in each relevant force.

Data Protection Act

Paragraph 60: all results and administrative details will be stored electronically, and the operation of the database will be subject to the Data Protection Act 1984 (superseded by the Data Protection Act 1998).

Paragraph 61: the DNA database has been registered under the terms of the Data Protection Act by the Forensic Science Service, and all access to the DNA database will be via the Forensic Science Service for so long as it remains the database custodian. However, all police forces and other agencies with a statutory investigative role and who use the database will register their individual use of the data, and the purpose for this use, with the Data Protection Commissioner (see below).

Paragraph 62: the Forensic Science Service, as database custodian, will nominate a database system administrator who will maintain a list of authorised users with the Data Protection Commissioner, and also those persons with direct access to the database (ie, the operators).

Paragraph 63: data will be held on a password-protected system and the security will be layered so that the Data Protection Act requirements will be met.

Access will be to authorised users only. According to the status of the accessor, this will allow:

(i) the addition of individuals' profiles and the associated unique identifiers;

(ii) the addition of case stain profiles and the associated unique identifiers;

(iii) interrogation of the database.

Under s 29(1) of the Data Protection Act 1998, personal data (a category of data within which DNA profiles would fall) processed for the prevention or detection of crime, or the apprehension or prosecution of offenders, is exempt from s 7 of the Act, which regulates rights of access.

Data protection – access

Further to what is said above concerning access to the national DNA database, it is noteworthy that legal access can only be granted to those data users registered with the Data Protection Commissioner. The Forensic Science Service has four separate entries in the DP Register, one of which relates to the management of casework requiring DNA profiling (Registration No U0707089). Those who can be granted access to the database are:

• the data subjects themselves;

• legal representatives;

• other professional advisers;

• the Home Office;

- other central government, including Scottish, Welsh and Northern Ireland Offices;
- police forces;
- prosecuting authorities;
- other statutory law enforcement agencies or investigating bodies;
- the Metropolitan Police Forensic Science Laboratory;
- the Northern Ireland Forensic Science Laboratory;
- the Strathclyde Police Forensic Science Laboratory;
- the Lothian and Borders Police Forensic Science Laboratory;
- the Tayside Police Forensic Science Laboratory;
- the Grampian Police Forensic Science Laboratory;
- the courts;
- judges, magistrates;
- other organisations and individuals;
- the National Criminal Intelligence Service (NCIS).

For certain select purposes, access may be granted to additional bodies. For example, for the purposes of pure statistical and analytical research, access can be granted to the European DNA Profiling Group (EDNAP). For a copy of the full entries for the Forensic Science Service, see www.dpr.gov.uk.

Challenge and review

The National DNA Database was subject to review by the House of Lords Select Committee on Science and Technology, which recommended the establishment of an independent body to oversee the workings of the database 'to put beyond doubt that individuals' data are being properly used and protected'.[131] To date no such body exists.

The use of information on the database to cross-match genetic data has been challenged in the courts on occasion but with little success. In *R v Willoughby*,[132] an argument was put that the use of the database was a violation of ss 57(3A) and (3B) of the Criminal Justice and Public Order Act 1994, which required that information derived from samples that should otherwise have been destroyed could not be used 'for the purpose of any investigation of an offence'. It was argued that this meant any investigation, including the compilation of a resource such as the database to cross-match DNA results. However, the Court of Appeal held that 'investigation' related to the gathering of evidence and not its later interpretation. Moreover, the exercise of calculating statistical probabilities using the database was 'outside the investigatory process'.

---

131 House of Lords Select Committee on Science and Technology, *Human Genetic Databases: Challenges and Opportunities* (2001) HL 57), para 7.66.
132 [1996] EWCA Crim 1407.

More recently, the Court of Appeal confirmed in *R (S and Marper) v Chief Constable of South Yorkshire Police*[133] that the scale of the database and its consequent value was substantially increased by the availability of samples from individuals who had been investigated but never prosecuted or prosecuted but then acquitted, and that this was enough to justify the interference with the right to respect for private life protected under the Human Rights Act 1998 that was attendant on the collection of such samples.

The Proposed 'Universal DNA Database'

The high degree of objective certainty that DNA evidence can provide has meant that it has come to play an increasingly prominent role in the investigation of crime and the conduct of criminal prosecutions in the United Kingdom. Controversial recent proposals for a 'Universal DNA Database' would expand this role further still. The Universal Database, if established, will hold DNA samples from every one of the United Kingdom's 60 million citizens. Senior British police officers,[134] scientists[135] and judges[136] have advocated the Database as representing a highly effective, potentially even 'revolutionary', crime control resource. The Database would be in line with the above-described trends in the UK to expand police powers regarding the collection, retention and use of DNA evidence wherever this has been possible and practicable. However, the proposals have met with strong resistance from some quarters, notably the British human rights organisation Liberty, and it is therefore highly likely that the Universal Database would face legal challenges under Article 8 of the Human Rights Act 1998.

As we have seen, at the current time the boundaries of police powers are restricted at the point of being able to compel individuals to provide fingerprints or DNA where this is in connection with the investigation of a criminal offence.[137] The amendments to s 64 of the Police and Criminal Evidence Act 1984 (PACE) made by s 82 of the Police and Criminal Justice Act 2001 have further authorised the police to retain DNA samples even in instances where a defendant is subsequently acquitted or criminal charges are dropped.[138] However, the proposed Universal Database would necessitate a radical expansion of these current police powers, as the Database, by its very nature, would seem to

---

133 [2003] 1 All ER 148.

134 See 'British Police Propose Universal DNA Database', CNS News, September 9th 2003. *Available online* at: 1.2http://www.cnsnews.com/ForeignBureaus/archive/200309/FOR20030909e.html

135 *See* 'Scientist backs universal DNA bank', BBC News, 18 February 2001. Available online at http://news.bbc.co.uk/1/hi/uk/1177160.stm

136 *See* 'Judge calls for UK DNA database', BBC News, 24 November, 2004, Available online at http://news.bbc.co.uk/1/hi/uk/4038079.stm

137 Police and Criminal Evidence Act 1984, s 63, as amended.

138 Held as being compatible with the Human Rights Act 1998 by the House of Lords in *R v Chief Constable of South Yorkshire Police (Respondent) ex parte LS (by his mother and litigation friend JB)(FC)(Appellant); R v Chief Constable of South Yorkshire Police (Respondent) ex parte Marper (FC) (Appellant) (Consolidate Appeals)* [2004] UKHL 39. On appeal from: [2002] EWCA Civ 1275, [2002] 1 WLR 3223.

necessitate placing a legal obligation upon all British men, women and children to donate samples to the police (presumably involving sanctions for non-compliance), even though the vast majority of these citizens will have no criminal record, nor will they have ever been subject to criminal investigations. Compelling people not involved in specific criminal investigations to donate DNA samples would undoubtedly represent a breach of Article 8(1) of the Human Rights Act 1998, which guarantees the right to respect for private life. However, it remains to be seen whether British courts would be prepared to counter prevailing judicial trends and declare this violation as not being justified under Article 8(2) as a *reasonable and proportionate* crime control measure. The Database will not come to fruition for at least five to ten years. It seems that the next stage in its development will be to commission detailed research to examine, amongst other things, the likely costs for establishing such a resource. If and when it is established, the Universal Database would provide the British police with perhaps the most extensive powers of any jurisdiction in the world for the collection, retention and utilisation of DNA samples.

Law as stated current to May 2005.

References

Balding and Donnelly (1994) 'The prosecutor's fallacy and DNA evidence' Crim LR 711

Gordon, G (1993) 'Commentary on *Hughes v Normand*' SCCR 74

Grevling, K (1997) 'Fairness and the exclusion of evidence under section 78(1) of the Police and Criminal Evidence Act' 113 LQR 667

Hogg, MA (1996) 'Privacy and European Data Protection Rights' Scots Law Times 127

Leng, R and Taylor, R (1996) *Blackstone's Guide to the Criminal Procedure and Investigations Act 1996*, 117, London: Blackstone Press

Niblett, J (1997) *Disclosure in Criminal Proceedings*, London: Blackstone Press

Redmayne (1995) 'Doubts and burdens: DNA evidence, probability and the courts' Crim LR 464

Scottish Executive (2001) *Making Scotland Safer: Improving the Criminal Justice System*, Edinburgh: Scottish Executive

Seabrooke, S and Sprack, J (1996) *Criminal Evidence and Procedure: The Statutory Framework*, London: Blackstone Press

Sheils, R 'Commentary on the Criminal Procedure (Scotland) Act 1995', Greens Current Law Statutes

Sheldon, D (1996) *Evidence: Cases and Materials*, Edinburgh: W. Green/Sweet & Maxwell

Zander, M (1995) *The Police and Criminal Evidence Act 1984* (3rd edn), London: Sweet & Maxwell

INDEX